MAR 2 8 2017

P9-BZH-633

ALSO BY HELENE COOPER

The House at Sugar Beach

MADAME PRESIDENT

The Extraordinary Journey of
ELLEN JOHNSON SIRLEAF

———

HELENE COOPER

Simon & Schuster

New York   London   Toronto   Sydney   New Delhi

Simon & Schuster
1230 Avenue of the Americas
New York, NY 10020

Copyright © 2017 by Helene Cooper

First Simon & Schuster hardcover edition March 2017

SIMON & SCHUSTER and colophon are
registered trademarks of Simon & Schuster, Inc.

For information about special discounts for bulk purchases,
please contact Simon & Schuster Special Sales at
1-866-506-1949 or business@simonandschuster.com.

The Simon & Schuster Speakers Bureau can bring authors
to your live event. For more information or to book an event,
contact the Simon & Schuster Speakers Bureau at
1-866-248-3049 or visit our website at www.simonspeakers.com.

Interior design by Devan Norman

Manufactured in the United States of America

1   3   5   7   9   10   8   6   4   2

Library of Congress Cataloging-in-Publication Data

Names: Cooper, Helene, author.
Title: Madame President : the extraordinary journey of Ellen Johnson Sirleaf /
Helene Cooper.
Description: New York : Simon & Schuster, 2017.
Identifiers: LCCN 2016042087| ISBN 9781451697353 (hardcover) | ISBN
9781451697360 (pbk.)
Subjects: LCSH: Johnson-Sirleaf, Ellen, 1938– | Women
presidents—Liberia—Biography. | Presidents—Liberia—Biography. |
Liberia—Politics and government—1980– | Liberia—Biography.
Classification: LCC DT636.53.J64 C66 2017 | DDC 966.62031092—dc23 LC
record available at https://lccn.loc.gov/2016042087

ISBN 978-1-4516-9735-3
ISBN 978-1-4516-9737-7 (ebook)

To Nyenpu, in memoriam

Contents

Contents

Author's Note

I have always been a daughter of two countries, in large part because without America, my adopted country, my native country of Liberia would not exist.

On February 6, 1820, eighty-eight American blacks and freed slaves and three white men boarded the ship *Elizabeth* in New York Harbor, their destination West Africa. The white men were agents of the American Colonization Society, sent to acquire land that American blacks would be encouraged to settle in America's sole effort at colonization. Eventually, these men and women ended up in what would become Liberia.

One of them was my great-great-great-great grandfather, Elijah Johnson.

Many of Liberia's twenty-eight tribes, belonging to sixteen ethnic-linguistic groups and led by the Dey tribe, fought the new colonists. They lost, and the American settlers asserted their control over the country, establishing in Liberia an antebellum way of life similar to that in the American South from which they had fled, except that in Liberia, the American blacks were the rulers and the native Liberians became the ruled.

On July 26, 1847, Liberia declared its independence from America. For almost a century after that, Liberia, along with Ethiopia, could proudly claim that it was one of only two African countries not ruled by whites.

But descendants of the freed American slaves who ruled Liberia behaved, in many ways, like the white colonists who ruled other African countries, setting up a two-tiered system with two very distinct classes. On April 12, 1980, a military coup led by men from the Krahn, Gio, and Vai ethnic groups left Liberia's rulers dead or on the run.

Nine years after that coup, on December 24, 1989, a civil war erupted. It was a war that introduced the world to the child soldiers of West Africa, as young children were drafted to fight. More than 200,000 people died in

Liberia and neighboring Sierra Leone and Ivory Coast. Thousands of women and girls were raped.

In August 2003, the Civil War in Liberia finally ended. But there was no electricity or running water. Schools that had been shuttered for years stayed closed. The capital city of Monrovia had no infrastructure. Social norms had disintegrated. An entire generation had seen nothing but war.

My immediate family had fled Liberia in 1980 after the first military coup, and I had lived in the United States since then, becoming a naturalized American citizen and journalist writing about the world—except Liberia. In September 2003, I finally returned home to Liberia, where I found a shell of the country I had fled twenty-three years before, and a sister, Eunice, whom I had not seen in two decades.

When I returned to the United States, I went back to my daily job as a reporter, covering the presidency of George W. Bush and following his secretary of state, Condoleezza Rice, to Jerusalem, Hanoi, and points between. When Barack Obama was elected America's first black president, I was proud to be one of four *New York Times* reporters assigned to cover his first term. I traveled the world aboard *Air Force One*, writing for the most influential of newspapers about the presidency of Barack Obama.

But while I was writing about the seizure that was taking place on the American political landscape, the women in my home country were staging their own power play, one just as dramatic as the toppling of the racial barrier to the U.S. presidency that I was chronicling.

On October 11, 2005, Liberians went to the polls to choose the man who would take on the task of resuscitating the country. Voter turnout was 75 percent of 1.35 million registered voters.

On November 23, 2005, after a runoff, the National Electoral Commission declared the winner of Liberia's elections. Not a man. A woman.

Her name: Ellen Johnson Sirleaf.

Somehow, while I wasn't paying attention, the market women of Liberia, along with thousands of other Liberian women, had allied themselves with Ellen Johnson Sirleaf, a Harvard-educated global bureaucrat, to upend centuries of male political dominance in one of Africa's most devastated places. The women in my native country had managed something that still eluded their female counterparts in my adopted country.

Then, those women had simply returned to their tables and stalls and oranges and kola nuts and gone about their business making market, except that now they were a force in politics.

After spending four years writing about a historic presidency in my adopted country of America, it was enough.

It was time to look at my other president, and her historic presidency, an ocean away, in my native-born country of Liberia. It was time to look at Ellen Johnson Sirleaf.

Chapter 1

THE PROPHECY

Monrovia, 1938

In Liberia, a woman's place is in the market, the church, the kitchen, or the bed. But not for one little girl.

One little girl, delivered in the back bedroom of her family's house on Benson Street in Monrovia on October 29, 1938, was, her relatives believed, destined for great things. After all, the Old Man, one of the many prophets who wandered through Monrovia spreading their wisdom, predicted it when he showed up at Carney and Martha Johnson's half-concrete house days after the birth of baby Ellen—nicknamed Red Pumpkin because she was "red like one pumpkin"—to have a look at the baby. "This child will be great," he said, after peering into the crib. "This child is going to lead."

Actually, that is not what he said—no Liberian talks like that. Decades later, when Ellen Johnson Sirleaf wrote her own autobiography, she titled it *This Child Will Be Great*, referencing the Old Man's prophecy.

She was anglicizing it, assuming an international audience wouldn't understand Liberian English, which can be perfectly transparent one moment and perfectly impenetrable the next. It is not pidgin, the West African English that evolved from England's colonial efforts at communicating with Africans. But there is pidgin in Liberian English. Nor is it Creole (see above; insert French). But there is Creole in Liberian English as well.

Instead, Liberian English is a wonderful hodgepodge of all of the above, an international language that borrows freely from British phrasings and American slang, with the added seasoning of the American South, courtesy of the freed American slaves who settled the country, the twenty-eight different ethnic groups who met the slaves when they arrived, and the African parables that are part of daily life.

In Liberia, people talk in continuous parable. Most of the time it makes sense.

"Crab baby die, crab don't cry, da big-eye bumpy here crying?" (Translation: Why is Marcia more upset about Jan's ugly afro than Jan is?)

"Fanti man won't say his fish rotten." (Do you seriously expect a Chelsea fan to admit they are an awful football club?)

"Me and monkey ain't make no palaver." (Why would I turn my nose up at eating the nice monkey meat you put in that palm butter? I've got nothing against monkeys.)

"Ehn you know book?" (You're the one with the Ph.D. You figure it out.)

"I going walkabout." (I'm going out to visit people, probably a secret boyfriend, and it's none of your business who, so leave me alone.)

"Monkey work, Baboon draws." (I do the work, you relax and enjoy yourself.)

"Ma, de pekin wa' na easy oh." (This child will be great.)

Armed with that prophecy, which her family repeated to her throughout her childhood, Ellen set out to create what would become an extraordinary life. Because before she even uttered her first word, certain things had already been put in place that determined she would be no ordinary Liberian woman.

For this, blame America.

In the early nineteenth century, America found itself with a growing class of freed blacks, many of them the children of slaves who had somehow found themselves freed, for reasons ranging from happenstance to, in many cases, interracial rape. White slave owners had impregnated their slaves, who then had mixed-raced children whose skin color was a daily reminder of the hypocrisy that infused antebellum life. Many of these mixed-race children were eventually freed.

The rising number of freed blacks worried the white slave owners, who believed they served as a beacon to enslaved blacks who might rebel and seek their own freedom. And so began the "back to Africa" movement, centered around the thought that the best way to prevent slave rebellions was to send free blacks back to Africa.

In 1820 the first of many shiploads of mixed-race freed slaves and blacks headed to West Africa. Mulatto, Quadroon, Quintoon, Octaroon—

these new colonists were, for the most part, lighter-skinned than the native Liberian population; they could read and write; and they were ostentatiously Christian. The colonists were met by locals who suspected—rightly—that their land and way of life (many of them still actively engaged in the slave trade themselves) were under threat. This was not as morally complicated as it sounds. The Europeans did have to purchase their human cargo from someone, and that someone was usually Africans who had caught and enslaved other Africans. So, many locals in Liberia were worried that this practice would be stopped by the newly arrived former slaves.

And thus was born Liberia, a country of almost impossible social, religious, and political complexity.

The American Colonization Society, a group made up of an unholy combination of white antislavery Quakers and evangelicals and slave owners who wanted to rid their South of freed blacks, purchased land from the native Africans. The Society did this at gunpoint and named the new country Liberia. The freed slaves who colonized Liberia were now the ruling class, and the native Africans largely became the laborers, household help, and underclass.

Liberia is three thousand miles from the Congo, but the black American settlers became known derisively as "Congo people" because native Liberians associated the Congo River with the slave trade. The Congo people controlled the government and owned most of the land. They quickly outlawed the slave trade that had provided income to many of the native Liberians, whom the Congo people referred to insultingly as "country people."

To the American colonists, the "country people" were an unvariegated mass, with their elaborate beaded jewelry, Fanti clothing, and incomprehensible language. But these were complicated people, from twenty-eight different ethnic groups, with individual beliefs, practices, and centuries-old enmities. The Kru were fishermen who hated slavery. The Krahn brokered deals in slave markets. The Gio came from a line of Sudanese warriors who never ran away from a fight. No one is sure why, but the Gio and Krahn seemed to hate each other.

After several bloody battles in the initial years after their arrival, the American colonists eventually imposed themselves on Liberia's Gio,

Krahn, Bassa, and Kru. What developed next was a symbiotic relationship, particularly in matters of faith. From the Congo people, native Liberians took Christianity. But not the more refined European version. Liberians seized on the robust Christianity of gospel hymns, prayers, and beliefs that the Congo people had brought with them from the land of slavery. The suffering of Jesus Christ and the enslavement of the ancient Jews were things American slaves had intuitively understood. The delivery of his people by Moses, the selling into slavery of Joseph by his brothers, the throwing of Daniel into a lion's den captured the imagination of the slaves in America.

The Christianity they took with them to Africa was altered dramatically by the native Liberians, who added their own religious interpretations and traditions, including exuberant beating of drums, dancing, singing, and speaking in tongues, creating the background music that the country sways to today.

So when baby Ellen was born, it was to two deeply divided societies that were linked by religion. Yet she, like few others, would not need religion to straddle both groups.

On the outside, Ellen looked like a Congo baby, but she did not have a single drop of Congo blood. She was a native Liberian, a point that would become hugely significant in the coming decades, when the Congo people were finally brought low. Her father's father was a Gola chief named Jahmale. He had eight wives ensconced in the picturesque village of Julejuah, in Bomi County. He and one wife did what so many Liberians do routinely: they sent one of their sons—Ellen's father, Karnley—to Monrovia to become a ward of a Congo family. There Karnley could go to school and acquire the refinement that, in early twentieth-century Liberia, was becoming acknowledged as necessary to make something of yourself. Karnley's name was Westernized to Carney Johnson, beginning the slow Congoization of the family.

Ellen's mother's mother was a Kru market woman from Greenville, Sinoe County, named Juah Sarwee, who fell for a white man, a German trader named Heinz Kreuger, who was living in Liberia. The two married in 1913 and had a daughter, Martha.

During World War I, Liberia, eager to show the United States its loyalty, declared war on Germany and expelled all Germans, including Heinz. He left his family behind and was never heard from again. But thanks to Heinz Kreuger and Juah Sarwee, Ellen's mother, Martha, would go through life with what was then the ultimate symbol of beauty and status in a country with so many hang-ups about race: long hair and light skin. She could almost pass for white. The Congo families soon started offering to take her into their homes—common practice in Liberia, where better-off families often took in poorer children who served as playmates (and sometimes servants) for the children of the house in exchange for room, board, and schooling. Eventually Juah Sarwee, who was poor, illiterate, and abandoned by the white man she had married, agreed to give her daughter away.

The first Congo family Martha lived with made her sleep on the kitchen table, or sometimes under it with the family animals. Early twentieth-century Liberian society might accept that fate for a native, dark-skinned child, but Monrovia wouldn't tolerate such treatment of a light-skinned half-white girl. So another Congo couple, Cecilia and Charles Dunbar, stepped in to right the wrong.

Martha took the Dunbar name, went to the best schools in Liberia, then headed abroad for a year to acquire even more refinement. She came back and was in the yard of the Dunbar house when Ellen's father, now Carney Johnson, spotted her.

"Oh," he said, taking in the hair, figure, and flushed high-yellow skin. "Oh. I like you."

Martha and Carney's four children—first Charles, then Jennie, Ellen, and Carney—would grow up with the gift of camouflage in a fractured country. Among the Congo people they could easily fit in, yet their Gola roots also gave them an entrée, should they ever want to use it, into native Liberian culture. Ellen, the third child, in particular had the ability to use the gift with which she was born.

She looked Congo, and like most Congo people, she spoke two languages: English and Liberian English. She certainly lived Congo: she went to school with the Congo kids and lived in a real cement house on Benson Street with a big yard surrounded by coconut trees and filled with fruit and flower bushes. Her older sister even went to school in England, a prized status that was the height of Congoness. By local standards, the family was upper middle class, thanks to Martha's light skin, but especially to Carney's profession as a lawyer. He was eventually elected to the Liberian House of Representatives, the first native Liberian to do so.

Ellen was four years old when William V. S. Tubman was elected president in 1943. Luckily for their family, the president appeared to like her father. Tubman would often dispatch Johnson abroad to represent the country, and when Johnson returned from such trips, the president sometimes visited the family home with his entourage, an event that certainly enhanced their standing in society but led to mayhem in the kitchen as servants and helpers cooked palm butter, jollof rice—the proper Liberian jollof rice, with chicken and ham hock and beef in it—and fufu for the head of state. Naturally Ellen and her siblings were banished from the living room, but Ellen always hid around the corner to listen.

Ellen was firmly in the ruling Congo class, except when she didn't want to be. She attended the College of West Africa, an elite high school. During vacations, she and her sister and brothers went to Julejuah, the village in Bomi County where their father was born. Julejuah was twenty miles from Monrovia, but the road ended well before the village, so their car could take them only to that point. Men carried Ellen and her siblings in hammocks the rest of the way.

Once in Julejuah, Ellen and the boys—Jennie turned her nose up at such tomboyish behavior—climbed trees, swam in the river, hitched rides in the canoe that ferried people from one bank to the other, and sat under a tree out of the hot sun with their grandmother eyeing the birds that approached the growing rice. Recognizing that Jennie was their father's favorite, Ellen and her brothers sent her to canoodle sweets and favors from him. They learned a smattering of Gola words, the language of their ancestors. Those few phrases would one day save Ellen's life.

Throughout Ellen's growing-up years, her family reminded her, often with irony, that she was a pekin who wa' na easy oh, destined for greatness. Often they brought it up when she did something that didn't seem so great. Like, for instance, the day she fell into the latrine.

The family house on Benson Street was luxurious by the standards of 1950s Liberia: a two-story concrete structure with a big yard. But it didn't have an indoor bathroom; an outdoor latrine of rough plank boards over a deep hole was the family toilet. Once, when she was small, Ellen fell in. She hollered and carried on until a passing neighbor pulled her out and helped her mother wash her off.

The family invoked the prophecy when Ellen made her first public speech, at the age of eight. Or, at least, she tried to, spending the whole afternoon the day before her much anticipated Sunday recitation sitting under a guava tree memorizing her lines. Alas, when she was called before the congregation at church the next morning, she froze, looking at her mother's agonized face, standing there for minute after unbearable minute. Finally, the congregation started clapping in sympathy, and Ellen, tears running down her face, returned to her seat in disgrace.

They should definitely have invoked the prophecy when, at the age of seventeen, Ellen became a bride.

It was 1956, and the once-prosperous family had had a change of fortune. Carney Johnson had suffered a stroke that paralyzed his right side. "I have been witched," he informed his family. "Someone has put juju on me." In Liberia it is still common for people to reach for ominous explanations for otherwise scientifically explicable phenomena. His wife also eschewed the scientific for the less tangible. "Pray for healing and for the forgiveness of your sins," Martha advised her husband.

Carney's speech and movement were compromised by the stroke, and with that, his hopes of becoming the first native Liberian speaker of the House died. His past closeness to the ruling class wasn't enough to insulate his family from the results of his vanished income. Martha quickly turned to the Liberian woman's standard for survival, marketing, and began making baked goods to sell. She also took over the all-encompassing care and feeding of her now-homebound husband, rising early to bathe, dress, and feed him before helping him to the chair on the porch where he spent his days staring out at the street.

At sixteen Ellen was nearing the end of high school, hoping that she would follow her sister and go abroad to college. Most of her friends were going to America or Europe to acquire finishing, including her best friend,

Clavenda Bright. But Carney's stroke destroyed those hopes. The money Martha was making selling bread out of the house was not going to get Ellen a ticket on an ocean liner anywhere, let alone school tuition.

Over the warnings of her sister, Ellen chose the next best option: marriage to the handsome James "Doc" Sirleaf, who had just returned from the famous Tuskegee Institute in Alabama. Doc was twenty-four, Ellen seventeen.

To this naïve girl, Doc was suave and sophisticated, with the ramrod bearing that Tuskegee encouraged. He was a "been-to," a badge of honor in Liberia, designating that you have been to America or Europe and therefore are sophisticated and cultured.

After their first date, at the movies, Doc began pursuing Ellen, escorting her to school dances and assuring her wary parents that his intentions were honorable. Neither Ellen nor Doc let on to her parents that Doc had already seduced the teenager, a huge potential scandal in pious 1950s Congo society. Just months after they began dating, the two were married, in 1956, at the Presbyterian Church on Broad Street. The bride and bridesmaids were so young the Liberian press dubbed the affair a "Tom Thumb wedding."

The two headed to Bong County for their honeymoon, where the eagle-eyed matriarchs of Doc's family showed up the morning after the wedding to inspect the sheets for signs that Ellen had been a pure bride. Hearing them outside the couple's bedroom, Ellen fought to stifle her snickering as her new husband used a razor on his wrist to produce the necessary spots of blood, in their very first "us vs. them" moment as husband and wife.

The couple moved in with Doc's mother, Ma Callie, in her house on Carey Street, across from Central Bank. Ten months after the wedding, on January 11, 1957, Ellen and Doc had the first of their four boys, whom they named James E. Sirleaf after his father. They called him Jes, and he slept between them on the bed downstairs at Ma Callie's house because they didn't have a crib.

Ma Callie did have a houseboy and a cook, though, so Ellen helped out with the dishes but didn't have to cook. A young girl, Korlu Besyah, who lived upstairs with Ma Callie, helped Ellen with her baby. She needed all the help she could get, because a few weeks after having Jes she was pregnant again.

Eleven months later, in December 1957, the couple's second son, Charles, was born. Two children in one year, and Ellen just nineteen. They could no longer live in Ma Callie's house. Doc got a job at the Ministry of Agriculture, Ellen got a job as an assistant to the accountant at a garage, and the family moved into their first own home together, near Booker Washington Institute in Kakata, just outside Monrovia but, at an hour's distance by car, an eternity away from Ellen's family.

Because Doc had his Tuskegee degree and Ellen had graduated from high school—and both came from families that were acceptable to the upper Congo society—they were considered upper class in a country where people were either poor or rich, with nothing in between. Although they saw themselves as young and struggling, in the eyes of most Liberians, the family was blessed with money and privilege. So many people aspired to government jobs in Liberia, in part because they were viewed as the fastest route to power and the easiest way to guarantee a steady paycheck. Of course, getting those jobs was a matter of who you knew. Ellen and Doc knew the right people.

But already the bloom was off the relationship. One day she borrowed her husband's car to run errands. Far from home, the car broke down, and Ellen hitched a ride home to get help from Doc. Except help wasn't offered.

"You better go bring my car," Doc said.

Stunned, Ellen went back out into the street. Why was he acting that way? Was he just trying to show that he was a traditional African man, keeping a firm hand on his wife?

She hitched a ride to the garage where she worked and persuaded a mechanic friend there to go with her to Doc's car and fix it, allowing her, hours later, to do what her husband had demanded: bring his car home. She learned a lesson that day: when push came to shove, she could not count on her husband; she could only count on herself.

The children kept coming. By the time the third son, Robert, arrived in 1960, the family had moved back to Monrovia. A year after Rob came Adamah, born in 1961.

At the age of twenty-two, Ellen had four sons, all under the age of five. She piled the children into her Volkswagen Beetle every day to do the running around that characterizes daily life in Monrovia: going to church, taking the children to see their grandmothers, getting gas slips from Doc so she could fill the tank.

Her best friend, Clavenda, just back from America, where she had gone to college, visited Ellen, marveling over her four boys. There was Adamah, cooing in his crib; Rob, toddling into the furniture; and Charles and Jes running around outside. Clavenda said all the right things, but when she left the house, Ellen was convinced she had seen pity in her eyes.

Watching her drive away, Ellen saw her own life; it seemed stationary, filled with the endless drudgery that was the fate of so many women in Africa. The tending and feeding of men and children, the day-to-day struggle to put food on the table and to find tuition and school fees, all under the hot equatorial sun, knowing that when you are finally boxed up and buried, the only thing that will mark your time on this earth will be the children you leave behind.

Surely there was more for her than this? After all, she was bound for greatness.

When her husband applied for a scholarship to pursue a master's degree in agriculture at the University of Wisconsin, Ellen drove to the Liberian Department of Education and made her own application for a scholarship, to study business at nearby Madison Business College. She hadn't thought it through completely—what she would do with her boys if she got the scholarship, how she would feel separating from them to go to America. She would figure that out later. She just needed to do something to change the trajectory she was on.

Doc and Ellen knew people in the government, and that was how people got government scholarships: they lobbied the people they knew. In 1962 they both got their scholarships. And suddenly Ellen was faced with a seminal choice: Children or career?

She could stay in Liberia while Doc went to America, take care of the boys—packing them into her tiny Volkswagen, going to the farm or village on weekends, taking them to church on Sundays, and working at the garage. She would have her children and would be the maternal presence they needed. She would be a good wife.

But that would be all. With a high school diploma, that would be all.

Or, at the ripe age of twenty-two, she could miss out on the childhood of her four sons. She would not be there when Adamah, the youngest, took his first steps, or when Rob lost his first tooth. But she could shoot for the moon. Ellen chose the moon.

That is not to say that leaving her four young boys was easy—it was, in fact, a gut-wrenching decision that would forever create a hairline fracture in the relationship with her youngest son, Adamah. Neither of them knew it at the time, but this was to be the first of many separations, and Adamah would face a childhood filled with aunts, uncles, and in-laws, but no mother. Years later, when Ellen was reminiscing with Adamah about something that happened when he was a child, he stopped, looked at her, and said, "But Mom, you can't remember. You weren't there."

There is no way to stop how much it hurts to leave your children behind. Even in the Western world, with its day care centers and family work leave, women routinely must make the choice of children or career. In some ways, that choice was easier for Ellen to make because she was in Liberia, where the extended family will step in to raise the children. It is normal for Liberians to take their children to their grandparents—grandmothers, to be more accurate—and ask them to care for their children for a year, or two years, or ten years, while the parents go to school.

So Ellen and Doc left two boys with his mother, Ma Callie, and two with her mother, Martha. Doc went to America first, and Ellen followed him a few weeks later, driving an hour from Monrovia to Robertsfield Airport. It was her first time on an airplane, and she was torn between grief at leaving her boys, terror of what was ahead, and exhilaration that she was launching her life.

Her friend Clavenda had warned her that in America, all the buildings are tall and everything feels closed in around you, not like empty Liberia. Not to mention it is so cold you can see your breath in front of you.

"I gwen to America," she thought to herself excitedly as the plane taxied down Robertsfield's only runway. She had sharply veered off the path her life was on, had taken control. Hadn't the Old Man said she wa'na no easy pekin?

Ellen arrived in Madison, Wisconsin, in the fall of 1962: driven, impatient, and fully aware that this was her main chance.

But she had decided that she would stay only two years, long enough to get her associate's degree; she didn't have time to waste, she was already twenty-two, and she didn't want to be away from her boys for the four years it would take to get a bachelor's. She would study and work. That was it.

She got a job sweeping floors and waiting on customers in the Formica booths at Rennebohm Drug Store, famous for grilled Danishes, Bucky burgers, and phosphate drinks. To a Liberian, the food was revolting. But no matter. She was on a mission. When she wasn't at work, she was either in class or sequestered in the tiny apartment off campus that she and Doc had rented, buried in books.

Unfortunately, all that studying didn't go over well with her husband, who wanted more of her attention when the two of them, now alone for the first time in their lives, were at home. Doc had always had a jealous streak. A few years earlier, at a party in Liberia, he had gotten so annoyed when Ellen casually danced with another young man that he left, went home, put on his full military uniform, and returned to the dance to intimidate his competition. Now his competition was his wife's job, schoolbooks, and studies, and he didn't like it.

One evening, Ellen was sweeping the floor at Rennebohm's while the laughing students drank coffee and ate ice cream when the door burst open and Doc stormed inside. He strode up to his wife, ripped the broom from her hands, and yelled, "You should be home!" Horrified, Ellen watched as he threw the broom across the floor. Desperate to end the scene, she left with him.

The next day she went back to the drugstore, her stomach in a knot. Her supervisor, an older white woman, laid it on the line: "You have to tell your husband he can't come here ever again."

Of course she wasn't about to tell Doc that, but Ellen nodded anyway. Things quieted down at home, but Doc continued to complain that she was not giving him enough attention and was spending all of her time studying.

One day a few months later, Ellen went out to dinner with friends and stayed out late. It was cold and snowing when she got home that night, and her fingers felt frozen as she opened the door.

A furious husband waited for her. Trying to forestall what she saw was coming, Ellen went into the bathroom and turned on the hot water to fill the bathtub. "It's so cold outside!" she called out. "I need to get warmed up."

She was sitting in the bathtub when Doc came in and struck her on the side of her head with the butt of the gun he often carried. Stunned, she crumpled to the side of the tub, her arms over her head as she braced for the next blow. This wasn't the first time he had hit her; their fights had increasingly been punctuated by slaps. But this was the first time he had used a weapon.

The second blow didn't come; Doc left the bathroom.

Ellen didn't cry.

After a year, Doc finished his degree and returned to Liberia, and Ellen suddenly found herself alone for the first time in her life.

Blessedly alone.

She moved to a smaller apartment, a one-room studio. Finally she could study as much as she wanted without a man standing over her demanding his corned beef and rice. She didn't take holidays or vacations; instead she used that time to study. She was on track, if she kept up the pace, to finish her degree in one more year.

There were no letters from her boys; the oldest, Jes, was just learning to write. No telephone calls; the boys' grandmothers didn't have telephones. Occasionally there were letters from her mother. "Adamah is walking," one said. "Don't worry, the children alright," said another.

Ellen constantly found herself thinking about her youngest, Adamah. He was walking, but he hadn't been baptized yet. In Liberia, baptizing your children is socially and religiously mandatory. People don't mess around with that—especially not the Congo people. Almost every Congo Liberian has godparents, sometimes nine or ten of them, who have stood in church during the baptism and promised to be there for the child. But Adamah didn't have any godparents yet. Ellen made a note to herself to make sure she and Doc got him baptized as soon as she got home.

In the summer of 1964 Ellen received her associate's degree in accounting. It was Freedom Summer in the United States, the year after the death of John F. Kennedy, and efforts were under way in Mississippi to register as many blacks to vote as possible. White segregationists were hurling Molotov cocktails at volunteers, and the national news media, after decades of ignoring it, were finally paying attention to the persecution of blacks in the South.

But Ellen's cause was elsewhere. There were four young boys in Liberia she had not seen in two years. As soon as she got her degree, she was on the first flight home.

Adamah was now three, Rob four, Charles was six, and Jes was seven. The three older boys ran up to her and hugged her, but Adamah held back. Ellen reminded herself again to see about getting him baptized as soon as possible.

Now that she was back, the strains in her marriage that had begun in Madison got worse. Doc stopped going to church with her; planning for a baptism seemed discordant; they were barely speaking.

In fact nothing was the same anymore. Armed with her new degree, Ellen wasn't about to be a stay-at-home Liberian wife. So when Doc resumed his old job at the Ministry of Agriculture, Ellen got a job as the head of the Debt Service Division at the Treasury Department—a huge job for a young woman in Liberia in the 1960s. She would focus on domestic debt and debt relief—skills that she would put to huge effect some forty years later, when, as the new president, she was confronted with the mountain of debt Liberia had amassed during the war years.

Her husband watched sullenly, but Ellen loved every minute of her new job. She brought her work home, and at night, after the family went to bed, she crept down to the dining-room table with her adding machine and her books. Inevitably that led to more problems with Doc. One night when her husband found her out of bed, he followed her to the dining room and beat her over her papers.

Over the months, the abuse escalated. During one fight, Doc grabbed her by the throat and started to strangle her, leaving a mark that would remain for decades.

In Monrovia in the 1960s, people didn't talk about domestic abuse, and women certainly didn't file charges. If a woman was smacked by her husband, her best recourse was a strong father or brother who would go and beat some sense into the man. Ellen didn't have that; Carney Johnson had died in 1957, and her brothers were away at school. The closest she had to a male protector was her sister's husband, Estrada "Jeff" Bernard. But Doc had already threatened to kill Jeff, a friend of his, because one night he brought Jeff to the house when the both of them were drunk and Ellen greeted them at the door in her baby-doll nightgown. Doc, who could be garrulous and friendly one minute and homicidal the next, had taken it as a personal affront that his brother-in-law saw his wife scantily attired and chased Jeff out of the house and down the street with his gun.

She would handle Doc herself, she thought.

Then, in 1965, at a party, Ellen met Chris Maxwell.

A budding corporate attorney who palled around with Steve Tolbert, the brother of Vice President William R. Tolbert, Chris Maxwell was charming and flirtatious and sophisticated. Liberian men love titles, especially "Honorable," which they bestow on any Congo man for anything. They granted Maxwell the title "Counselor" since he had a law degree. Counselor Maxwell.

At the party, Counselor Maxwell walked up to Ellen. Five-foot-three and around 125 pounds despite the four boys she had carried, Ellen turned heads all around Monrovia. She had Bette Davis eyes—sharp, clear, a little bit buggy—and a head full of curly reddish-brown hair. In Liberian parlance, she was "fierce." But Counselor Maxwell seemed fascinated by Ellen's intellect as much as her looks.

The relationship developed quickly. One minute she was going to social events wondering if he would be there to liven up a dull evening, and the next minute he was showing up at her office and inviting her to lunch. Then to his house, on the evenings that Doc was out of town, to "watch television." They talked for hours on those nights, sitting in Maxwell's living room.

It didn't take Maxwell long to make his move, and soon they were intimate. Ellen was euphoric and scared at the same time. She knew that Doc was having affairs, but that didn't matter; if he found out about Chris Maxwell, he would blow up. But she didn't end the affair.

With household labor so cheap in Liberia, she now had a cook and a houseboy and a yard boy and all the staff that Congo Liberians couldn't manage to live without, so there was always someone at home to watch the boys. Adamah was spending much of his time with his uncle, Doc's brother, Varsay Sirleaf, up country. This was the way of extended family life in Liberia.

One night Ellen and Maxwell received a telephone call that Doc had come home and been alerted that his wife's car was parked at Maxwell's house. He was on his way to confront the lovers.

As Ellen sat, frozen, Maxwell went outside and moved Ellen's car down the road, slightly away from his house. When he returned, he went into his bedroom and got out a gun.

"Wha' you doing?" Ellen cried, shocked into speech.

Doc arrived, pulling his car into the yard. "Where's my wife?" he yelled. "I came for my wife."

Before Maxwell could point his gun, Ellen darted out of the house to her husband, who demanded, "Get in the car."

What happened on that drive home was not something she would talk about often in the years that followed—in fact, fifty years would pass before she talked about it in any depth. "He hit me again and again," she said, a weary smile on her face.

What did you do?

"I just bent my head, tried to cover it. Until we got home."

Did he keep hitting you after getting home?

She chuckled. "No, he stopped when we got home. I guess he had already hit me enough times."

From the vantage point of Liberian society, the Sirleafs looked like so many other young upper-class Liberian families. Their marriage looked solid. Four beautiful boys. Two ambitious, working parents. A sprawling extended family, ready to step in to help.

But the reality was a brutalized wife pretending to bend to the will of an abusive husband, who was becoming angrier and angrier all the time. Ellen stopped seeing Maxwell for a time, then started up again. He had become her solace.

One night Doc came home after drinking but didn't get out of the car for two hours, beset by demons. Ellen stood at the window, watching him. Would he hit her again? Maybe. Maybe not. Maybe he would just toy with her this time, like when he put the gun to her head and said, "Move, and I'll blow your head off."

Clarity would come soon.

Ellen arrived home late one night to find Doc, drunk and angry, waiting for her with his gun out. He pointed it at her.

Just as Ellen was bracing herself for another fight, she noticed a movement to the side. To her horror, she saw their eight-year-old son, Charles, watching from the doorway. The boy ran into the room with a can of mosquito repellent and began spraying his father's face. "Stop!" Charles screamed.

He couldn't reach Doc's eyes, but something about the desperation Charles felt must have touched his father's soul, because Doc put the gun down and stared at his son in shock.

Doc had finally pushed his wife to her limit—her son had seen her about to be shot by his father. After two years away in the United States, she had rebuilt her life with her sons, and now her husband was shaming her in front of them. Furious, Ellen stalked out of the room. The next morning she told Doc she had had enough. She was leaving him.

"You can leave," he said. "But I'm going to take our children."

She walked out anyway. She wasn't stupid; she knew how her society worked. In Liberia, the disposition of the children after a divorce is never simple. The default position, especially in the 1960s, was that the father got to keep the children. After all, the man was head of the household. It is still true that in the immediate aftermath of many divorces, Liberian men often make a big show of taking their children. But inevitably the children end up being sent to their father's mother to be raised, or to another relative, or to boarding school. If the father gets remarried, the children might stay and live with him and his new wife. The "I'm keeping the children" pledge is often just for show.

Clavenda went with Ellen to the courthouse for the divorce hearing, standing nervously next to her friend, with $100 in her pocket to pay the lawyer. The two were terrified that Doc would make an appearance and end the proceedings. Whether fair or not, they knew that if he showed up and said "Dis my wife, she jes lyin'," the judge—the male judge—would send Ellen home with Doc and tell her to work out her differences with her husband as a good wife should. He would say, "Y'all go fix your palaver."

The minutes ticked by, and Doc did not walk through the door. The judge called the case, and Ellen and Clavenda nervously looked behind them at the door, still convinced that at any second Doc, in full military uniform, would come storming in.

"Look, you better hurry up and finish or people wi' not pay you," Clavenda told the lawyer nervously.

Doc never did show up to contest the divorce. When it was over, he sent the two oldest boys up country to boarding school. The two youngest, Rob and Adamah, would stay with him. But that didn't last long. Adamah soon went to live with Doc's brother, Varsay, a medical doctor, in Yekepa, Nimba County. Eventually, after Doc remarried, Adamah returned to live with his father and his new wife. Rob, meanwhile, refused to stay with either Varsay or his father. He wanted to be with his mother. He cried and begged and fought so fiercely that finally a fed-up Doc dropped him and his bags on his pleased ex-wife's front step. "Here's your son," he said. "Take him."

Ellen was thrilled to have at least one son back. She was trying to get closer to Adamah too, but that was proving a harder task. She blamed herself for that. Decades later, after that relationship had long been repaired, she would still be blaming herself for what she called that initial "hairline fracture" that occurred when she allowed herself to be separated from her youngest son. "You know," she said, "Adamah has never been baptized."

Women carry so much internal baggage. First democratically elected woman president, Nobel Peace Prize winner, global female icon, in the middle of battling an Ebola epidemic ravaging her country, and Ellen Johnson Sirleaf had fixated, again, on her failure to baptize one of her sons half a century ago.

"He has no godparents, Adamah. Not one."

Chapter 2

Big Mouth

Monrovia, 1969

Doc Sirleaf was fuming in the waiting room at the Treasury Department again. A frightened junior official had ushered him into the room when he showed up demanding to see his ex-wife. Several times now in the years since the divorce, Doc had strode into Treasury asking for Ellen.

This visit was going to turn out the same as all the others. Doc sat in the waiting room and waited. And waited. Until, angry, he stomped out of the building.

His ex-wife never came out of her office to see him. It was too soon. If she saw him, she reasoned, there would be a fight. And she had had enough fights.

For the first time in her life, Ellen felt free. At thirty years old and sharp-eyed, she was coming into her own.

It had taken some time to reconstruct her personal life. Even in 1969, four years after she left Doc, she still sometimes felt like she was walking around Monrovia with a scarlet *D* embroidered on her dress. Whenever she had to fill out a form that asked for her marital status, she hesitated, wondering if she would be marked as a failure.

She was still using Doc's name, finding herself unable to drop it. The name kept her connected to her boys, she felt. It showed that the five of them were still tied to each other.

In the months after she left Doc, she had moved in with her mother. Martha Johnson was supportive of her younger daughter. The physical scars, apart from the one on Ellen's neck, had healed, but the emotional scars were still there, and Martha was using the Liberian woman's go-to method for helping one's child: prayer. She prayed for her daughter morning and night, that she would heal from her bruising marriage, that she would escape the buzz saw of Monrovia gossip.

But Monrovia society was moving on too. In the late 1960s, divorce was becoming increasingly common. Of course, it was usually followed by second, third, and fourth marriages, and there Ellen was deviating from the norm. She had no intention of tying herself to a man again.

Eventually Ellen moved out of her mother's house and into her own, and slowly she began acquiring the confidence that came from making her own living, collecting her own paycheck, and answering to herself.

She had only one son, Rob, living with her full time; Adamah was still in Yekepa with Doc's brother, and Jes and Charles were still at their mission boarding school up country. But even as her personal life was still fragile, Ellen's professional life was flourishing. Freed from the control of an abusive husband, she was outgrowing her position at Treasury.

She had a comprehensive view of the economy of Liberia, and she enjoyed trying to tease out the numeric answers to the small questions of interest rates and financing that came across her desk. But the pekin who wa' na easy was not satisfied. She had already started questioning the absurdity of the two-tiered structure of which she had become a part. The Congo elites had embraced her—she was, after all, light-skinned and beautiful and had a white grandfather—but she had not forgotten her Gola roots and moved easily in and out of the different strata of Liberia's classes, even as she grew uncomfortable at the contradictions.

Enter Gustav Papanek, a boy-wonder economist, visiting Liberia for the first time. Papanek was head of the Harvard Institute for International Development and had spent much of his time traveling the world, from Pakistan to Iran, giving economic advice to struggling developing countries who needed it. Arriving in Monrovia in 1969, Papanek saw on the surface a bustling, vibrant small town. At fewer than 100,000 people, it was a town of church women in wide-brim hats; of Fanti cloth head-ties on the market women who sold kola nuts by the side of Old Road; of single-breasted tuxedo jackets worn by the men in charge, who sipped Chivas Regal as they preened in plastic chairs at the Executive Pavilion.

But for all of its Western aspirations, Liberia in 1969 was an economic mess. During the 1940s, while Ellen was growing up in the family house on Benson Street, and the 1950s, when she was attending high school, the country had registered staggeringly high economic growth; from 1954 to 1960, thanks to a rubber boom led by the Firestone Rubber Plantation in Harbel and the rapid exploitation of the country's iron ore deposits, growth in production and income had shot to 10 percent. Only Japan performed better during that same period.

Unfortunately those numbers masked a chronic and familiar narrative: the rich were getting steadily richer, and the poor were stuck. This was all quite evident to Papanek. Most of the growth was generated by a handful of foreign firms, like Firestone, that focused on exporting raw materials without building or developing the factories and manufacturing plants that would allow Liberian workers to join the industrial revolution. So all that export profit fled the country along with the iron ore and rubber. In 1951 Firestone Liberia reported profits that were three times the total income of the Liberian Treasury.

President Tubman, the strongman at the helm of the country, paid lip service to improving the country's dismal literacy rate and building primary and secondary schools. But he didn't take the simple steps that were standard for countries trying to develop: there was no talk of diversifying the economy. Most of Liberia's available jobs were low-paid service positions: houseboys and cooks and drivers in the homes of wealthy foreigners or Congo families, rubber tappers on Firestone's numerous plantations, messengers and hustlers whose daily bread depended on whatever they picked up on the recently paved Tubman Boulevard or the dusty side streets of the capital. Or, in the case of the women, making markets on the side of the road—one of the only real entrepreneurial activities in the country.

The hospitals that were built served the foreigners and the Congo people. The native Liberians still made do with home remedies when they got sick, or went to local healers. Tubman touted a new Unification Policy that he said would open the way for native Liberians to get on a professional ladder that largely consisted of landing a job with a government ministry. But the vast majority of high-ranking government bureaucrats were still chosen from the ranks of Congo society.

By 1969 the economy was unraveling. Expecting a boom in iron ore and rubber prices that never materialized, the government had borrowed more than $125 million to build grand new government ministries and public buildings, including $6 million to build the Executive Mansion, where Tubman would reside.

The poor were the first to feel the impact of new "austerity measures" that Tubman put in place to deal with the debt problem. To limit political dissent, he bought off the men who served as paramount chiefs of Liberia's many ethnic groups up country. It was a system of political largesse that Tubman had raised to an art form: the chiefs took the money—or the bags of rice, fish, or palm oil—that Tubman "donated" to them, and they, in turn, doled out smaller quantities, much smaller quantities, of the same to their villagers.

Tubman, an autocratic leader and a member of the True Whig Party of Congo people—the only political party ever to rule Liberia—ran the country as if it were a village and he was its chief. He held visiting hours at the eight-story Executive Mansion, which came complete with an atomic-bomb shelter, on the off chance that a global nuclear power decided to obliterate Monrovia. Everyone, from senior members of his cabinet to the market woman begging on behalf of her chicken-thief son, waited in the cabinet meeting room for an audience with the big man.

The morning after he arrived in Monrovia, Papanek joined the line. He wanted to discuss with the president an economic conference Harvard was holding in Liberia. As he waited, Papanek noticed something strange about a large painting on the wall of the waiting room. In dramatic colors, it depicted the original settlement of Liberia by the freed American slaves. There was the ship, the *Elizabeth*, that sailed from New York to West Africa in 1820. There was the palm tree depicting the African shore. And there were the people, the native Liberians and the American blacks. But the freed American slaves were so light-skinned they looked white. They wore Western garb, beaver hats, and appeared, by Western norms, civilized. The native Liberians, meanwhile, were half naked, wearing animal skins and carrying spears.

Papanek stared at the painting in disbelief. When he finally met Tubman, he did not mention it. But he never forgot it.

Originally Papanek had wanted a mix of local officials and Western economists to speak at his conference. But one of the first things he real-ized upon arriving in Monrovia was that most of the men running the government, having gotten their jobs because of who they knew and not what they could actually do, didn't know how an economy actually func-tioned. Most of them seemed to see the government as a bank from which they could withdraw cash for their personal needs.

Nevertheless he asked and President Tubman granted him permis-sion to take his pick of panelists from the Treasury Department. There he met a slew of bombastic men who strained to show him how well the economy was doing under their guidance. There was also one woman, who didn't.

Ellen was eager to talk about the contradictions she found so vexing in Liberia's economic structure, surprising Papanek with an independent and critical analysis of her country's dilemmas. Her business degree, combined with the fact that unlike most of her Congo colleagues she had native Liberian family members, including those in her father's village who were struggling to make a living, meant she saw things her colleagues missed. Looking at the bright woman before him, Papanek decided he had the perfect midlevel official to speak at his conference, and he invited her on the spot.

Ellen accepted Papanek's invitation—why not? The country was standing on the wrong foot and wobbling, she thought. Someone needed to stand up and say something. Why shouldn't that someone be her? She banged out a three-page speech on her manual Underwood typewriter.

Traditionally, talks by government officials in Liberia were long, rambling, polysyllabic-word-filled homages to biblical passages, the splendor of this great land of liberty, and the wise counsel of the country's rulers. Ellen too was learning how to throw around big words. The differ-ence was that the word she used wasn't one anyone in Liberia had ever invoked when standing before a microphone: *kleptocracy*.

Standing at the lectern to give her speech, Ellen opened with a techno-cratic dissertation on the country's economic stagnation. Then she suggested that one reason for that stagnation was because government officials were stealing money from the public till. Perhaps, she suggested, the decline in revenue had something to do with kleptocracy.

It was the first time Papanek had ever heard the word. He wasn't sure she hadn't made it up.

Ellen made sure her audience knew what she meant, defining *kleptocracy* as "abuses of meager public funds such as payroll padding and outright stealing of public monies." When clerks at the Temple of Justice refused to put the court case of a wife seeking to divorce her husband on the docket until they were given a bribe, that was kleptocracy. When workers at the Ministry of Education added a little something to the fee high school students had to pay to take their national exams, that was kleptocracy. When immigration officers at Robertsfield Airport greeted arriving Pan Am passengers with a grin and an outstretched palm before stamping their passports, that was kleptocracy.

Heart racing, she ended her speech. A stunned audience stared back at her. She was shaking when she walked off the stage to a quiet room.

Afterward people milled outside, glancing at her furtively. Papanek too kept looking at her; he couldn't believe what she had just done. He finally pulled her aside. "I wonder if it would not be a good idea to leave Liberia for a while," he said, adding, "As soon as possible."

Papanek said he would arrange a fellowship for Ellen at Harvard, where she could study economics more formally. By also enrolling for one summer at the Economics Institute in Boulder, Colorado, she could skip the bachelor's degree and go straight to a master's degree in public administration from Harvard.

But she would have to leave her boys again.

It was an easier decision this time. Jes and Charles were settled at boarding school and Adamah in Yekepa. Ellen decided to take nine-year-old Rob with her to America, where he would live with American friends in South Dakota. She didn't know if this next separation would be worth the sacrifice, but she had chosen her road seven years before, when she left her boys to go to Madison. She wasn't going to veer off that course, even if it meant more years of distance from them.

When she arrived in Cambridge in 1969, Ellen collided with the American civil rights movement. Martin Luther King Jr. had been killed the year before, and black students at Harvard had demanded the creation of an

Afro-American Studies Department. All around her there was talk of equal rights and demands to correct centuries of injustice.

Buried in the library stacks to study Liberian and West African history, Ellen was struck by the parallels between the treatment of blacks in America and the treatment of native Liberians back home. This was not the history presented at her elite high school in Monrovia, which taught of black American settlers who brought civilization and God to a heathen population. Now Ellen was learning that the settler-African relations in Liberia were vastly more complex than the simple narrative of Christianity's triumph over paganism that she had been taught.

Here is what she hadn't been taught about Liberia's history: that the native village and tribal kings who had sold their land—for the equivalent of $300—to the freed slaves and the white agents from the American Colonization Society did so at gunpoint; that even so, those kings didn't realize they were selling their land forever but thought the black colonists were coming to assimilate into their culture and village structures.

At Harvard, Ellen was moved by the anger and euphoria of black Americans as they resisted the white aristocracy. But at the same time, she battled a disconnect in her own psyche: How could she identify with the civil rights movement under way on her radicalized Harvard campus but also identify with the Congo aristocracy back home?

She wrote a paper seeking to come to grips with that disconnect. Liberia, she reflected, had received a golden opportunity to show the world that black people could govern themselves, that a black-led government could spread the wealth of its country and not hoard it. But Liberians had squandered that opportunity. The result was a two-tiered society in which the rich lived lives of oblivious comfort and the vast majority lived on scraps.

Looking at the landscape around her at Harvard, with all of its social turmoil, Ellen felt certain she was looking at the edge of a tidal wave that was bound to cross the Atlantic and engulf her country. Change had come to America; it would come to Liberia.

She was on track for an A in every course except econometrics, a concept she could barely understand—something to do with mathematical models describing economic relationships. She pored through the textbook, with its formulas and graphs and curves, and got more frustrated. Finally, at the end of the semester, worried that she would fail, she called her professor. "Look, I am an A student in every other course," she announced baldly. "If you fail me in econometrics, you know you're going to ruin my transcript." She got a B.

It was 1971. She had her master's degree in public administration, and from Harvard, no less. She was ready to go home.

Ellen's sister, Jennie, visiting the States, suggested they return to Liberia by sea instead of by air, aboard a Farrell Lines ocean steamer. For reasons completely bewildering to Ellen, her sister had developed a love for sea voyages and preferred them to flying. So for two weeks, buffeted by the winds and ocean currents, the two sisters, along with Jennie's teenage son, Jeff Jr., shared a claustrophobic cabin with two bunk beds and chugged toward the port at Bushrod Island, Monrovia. Rob, meanwhile, was still in school in South Dakota.

On the first day on board, Ellen stood on the deck watching the New York skyline recede in the distance, listening to her sister carping at her for taking out another cigarette, which she was preparing to light. She had started smoking during her marriage, then accelerated to a pack-a-day habit at Harvard. Jennie, a nurse, was having none of it. "You need to stop!" she yelled at her sister.

Ignoring her, Ellen lit up.

"Smoking is terrible for you."

Ellen inhaled and exhaled appreciatively, savoring the taste.

"I taking it from you."

Another inhale, another exhale. Then, "Okay. This will be the last cigarette I ever smoke." She took her time with it. When all that was left was the smoldering butt between her fingers, she stubbed it out, never to light up again.

A few nights later, on July 23, the sisters and Jeff Jr. were in the dining room having their evening meal when they noticed one of the stewards looking at them. He raised his hand as though holding a knife and swept it across his throat.

Confused, the sisters stared at him. Eventually, he came over to their table and bent low to whisper, "I'm sorry. Your president has died in London."

It's always surprising to people when their long-term autocrat dies, but this time the surprise was tempered by the fact that one of Liberia's most famous Holy Ghost women had warned against this very thing.

See what happens when you don't listen to Holy Ghost women?

The whole country was populated by fiercely religious women who wore white and preached the scriptures on the radio. They fasted and prayed and prophesied. One of the most well known, Wilhelmina Bryant-Dukuly, was relatively new to Holy Ghosting, having only recently repented from a life of sin running a nightclub called The Liberian Jungle on Bushrod Island. Wilhelmina became Mother Dukuly after the Lord Jesus saved the life of her ailing husband, Joseph, and she founded the Faith Healing Temple of Jesus. In recent years she had taken to the airwaves, where she displayed an uncanny talent for prophecy.

One particular prophecy stood out: Mother Dukuly said that President Tubman shouldn't allow a knife of any sort to touch his body while on his medical checkup in London. Alas, upon advice from those foreign doctors of the need for surgery for his prostate cancer, the president yielded. Now he was dead at seventy-five.

He had presided over the country for twenty-seven years, pledging to elevate the lives of ordinary Liberians while doing little to actually make that happen. He relied, rather, on his system of payments to the paramount chiefs to keep their flocks under control, while seeing to it that his own private coffers—and those of the Congo elite—continued to swell.

The Liberian Constitution directs that if the president dies, the vice president finishes out his term. So there would be no election, no challenge to the True Whig Party rule, no questioning of the continued domination of the Congo aristocracy in Liberian power. When the period of public mourning was over, along with the nights of wake-keeping and hymns and wailing in the streets, the man known as "Willy Tolbert"—Tubman's vice president, William R. Tolbert—took up residence in the presidential quarters at the Mansion. It would be the last peaceful transfer of power in the country for more than three decades.

William R. Tolbert Jr. was one of twenty children borne by multiple women to William Sr., a legislator and the son of a freed American slave from

South Carolina. He had spent twenty years in the purgatory that is the vice-presidency before becoming president. A largely unassuming bureau-crat, Tolbert was overshadowed by Tubman's charismatic secretary of state, Joseph Rudolph Grimes. In fact so confident was Grimes that he was the real heir-apparent to Tubman that upon receiving the telegram on July 23 that Tubman had died, Grimes argued that Tolbert, who was out of town on his farm in Bellefanai, wouldn't reach Monrovia within the constitu-tionally prescribed twenty-four hours to take the oath of office and there-fore couldn't succeed Tubman.

Tolbert roared into town in a borrowed Volkswagen—his own car had broken down—with hours to spare, and, still clad in a dust-covered, short-sleeve, open-neck cotton suit, he was sworn in as Liberia's nineteenth pres-ident. The suit became known as the "swearing-in" suit; Tolbert, wanting to separate himself from Tubman's grand tuxedo ways, started wearing swearing-in suits every day and ordered his cabinet ministers to do the same so they would be viewed as men of the people.

He began his term in a blaze of progressiveness that quickly agitated the ruling class. He went to one of Monrovia's worst slums and handed out $50 notes to the families that lived there. "I identify myself with you," he said. "If you are poor, I identify myself with your poverty, and together we should work to better our conditions." He stopped the bribes to the para-mount chiefs that Tubman had instituted, announcing it was time for Liberians to start pulling themselves up by their bootstraps. He adopted the language of pan-Africanism and said it was time for Liberia to stop acting like a ward of America, which treated the tiny country as an unwanted stepchild. He opened up diplomatic relations with the Soviet Union and allowed it to build an embassy in Monrovia. He said Liberians weren't reaping the benefits of all the foreign investment in the country and started renegotiating previous deals that gave tax breaks to foreign companies. He coined new catchphrases aimed at wooing native Liberians—"Total Involvement for Higher Heights" and "from mat to mattresses"—to show he planned to run an inclusive government. He even changed the designations of the government departments to make them sound less American and more African. The Treasury Department, for example, became the Ministry of Finance.

When the ocean steamer finally arrived at the port on Bushrod Island, Ellen walked off to find a job offer waiting for her at the Ministry of Finance, where Tolbert's brother Stephen had been appointed minister. She would be deputy minister of finance in charge of fiscal and banking policy. Ellen's social consciousness, awakened in America, would make this new job an uncomfortable one. But Tolbert had promised progressive policies. She would help the president, she decided, to work for change from within.

President Tolbert certainly began his tenure saying all the right things about opening up the government. He talked of a new Liberia as no longer the domain of the few wealthy Congo elite. But he had installed one brother as the minister of finance. Another brother was president pro tempore of the Senate; a cousin was mayor of Monrovia; another cousin, assistant minister of finance.

In any case the entrenched old guard was going to allow Tolbert to reform only so much. Liberia high society openly mocked the swearing-in suits he wore. One of the more anthropologically interesting things about Congo society was the degree to which the children of freed slaves had adopted the manners and sartorial affectations of southern slave owners. They too wore top hats and tails to formal occasions and discouraged their native Liberian servants from entering the house through the front door. By the time Tolbert came to power, those affectations had started to drop away, but not fast enough; wearing a swearing-in suit still raised eyebrows in many swank living rooms, even as Tolbert advised his cabinet to adopt the habit. And within his government, hard-liners fought his attempts to open up the economy.

At the Ministry of Finance, Ellen had an increasingly familiar relationship with the most powerful men running Liberia. Besides Stephen Tolbert, she was now on a first-name basis with Rochefort Weeks, the minister of foreign affairs, and later his successor, Cecil Dennis. Her "kleptocracy" speech now forgotten, she attended the high-level meetings of the officials deciding the economic future of Liberia. And it didn't take long for the newly minted Harvard grad to realize that she didn't like what she was seeing.

For one thing, more and more people were leaving the countryside for the urban areas—Monrovia, Sanniquellie, Buchanan—creating job short-ages in those cities. The reason they were leaving could be attributed to economic policy: the government held down prices paid to farmers to subsidize the food bill of the privileged classes living in Monrovia along with their poor native neighbors. But Monrovia and the other cities couldn't handle the influx, and the repressed prices led to a vicious cycle, as more farmers abandoned the land for urban life, a social dislocation that led to more crime, more slums, and overall demoralization of the poor.

Real estate taxes were collected from businesses, but also from the poor, in the form of an odious "hut tax." While the Congo elites figured out ways to dodge the tax man, poor people who lived in mud huts up country remained the prey of government tax collectors.

In November 1972, a year into her new job, Ellen was invited by her high school alma mater, the College of West Africa, to deliver the commencement address. Once again, she unloaded on the powers that employed her. Approaching the podium, she saw the panoply of young faces looking back at her. This was an elite school—one of the best in Liberia. But the student body was not limited to the privileged. In another sign of anemic progress under Tolbert to expand opportunity, some native students were now part of the senior class. These students would be enrolling in the University of Liberia, which was already becoming a seedbed of political activism.

Behind Ellen sat the members of the old guard Congo aristocracy, wearing academic robes. These were some of the most conservative and prominent members of society.

Everyone knew what was meant to happen at graduation ceremonies in Liberia: praises should be heaped on the institution, fine opportunities promised the graduates if they only reached out and grabbed them. For a deputy minister of finance, the task seemed straightforward. Just stick to the script.

"It's time," she announced instead, "to stand up and speak the truth about who we are as a country."

Like the United States, she said, Liberia had failed to extend its founding principles of freedom and liberty to all her citizens. The very symbols of the country—its seal, which depicted that ship headed to the shore and the words "The love of liberty brought us here"—was a symbol of exclusion of native Liberians. While neither she nor the students could change history, they could certainly try to change the future. She told them to read the Liberian Constitution and think about how all its high-minded talk had been "ruthlessly prostrated."

On the podium Ellen battled mounting feelings of anger and frustration. There was so much potential before her, but the old guard sitting behind her would stamp it out. And that widening economic gulf would breed more tension, until things exploded. She could see what was coming; the students before her could see what was coming. Why couldn't the old guard?

"Perhaps," she ended, "you, like I, may conclude that those who now make empty, sanctimonious claims about rights are worthy of only our deep contempt."

Behind her the elite sat in silence, their stares hot on her back.

By the end of the day, Ellen's speech was banned. A Monrovia newspaper printed it anyway.

When Ellen arrived at the Finance Ministry the next morning, she was summoned by the furious minister. He read passages of the speech aloud to her, becoming more and more angry as he read. "You don't say things that will put the public against the government!" he yelled. "We not gonna tolerate that!"

Dismissing her from his office, he went to a cabinet meeting with the president to discuss how she should be punished. The men at the table were furious, using words like "saboteur" and "treason." A couple called for Ellen to be summarily fired, and one hard-liner suggested prison.

In the end, Ellen wasn't fired; Steve Tolbert spoke up for her at the cabinet meeting. But she soon found herself sidelined at work. Underlings who used to ask her approval for projects were suddenly going to other midlevel deputies instead. Bit by bit, her duties were given to others. Soon word spread that she was an outsider at the Ministry of Finance, so much so that critics of the government, from both inside and out, people who would never have approached her if she were in good favor, started coming to her office to complain about government policies and corruption.

Her position was now too precarious for her to say much to her superiors; she felt she was living on sufferance and one wrong step would mean her ouster.

Finally, four months into her professional exile, Ellen had had enough. She telephoned a World Bank official whom she had worked with. "I think I'm in trouble here," she said.

The World Bank and the International Monetary Fund were two global institutions set up in 1944 at the famous meeting in Bretton Woods, New Hampshire, to launch the rebuilding of Europe after World War II. The Bank was now the preeminent global organization for development assistance for middle- and low-income countries. It specialized in giving loans and offering training in both the private and the public sector, and it employed a global army of bureaucrats, who learned and then preached the Bank's preferred prescriptions for economic growth, from structural adjustment to loosening up trade barriers and cracking down on corruption. With its focus on looking for ways to help countries lift themselves up, the Bank was the perfect spot for a midlevel finance bureaucrat who had found herself in trouble for taking her own government to task for squandering its resources.

It was the spring of 1973, the end of the dry season. The country's glorious but fleeting mango season—"plums," Liberians call them—was in full swing, and the fruit was piled high on the tables of the market women's stalls all along the sides of the road. These intensely sweet, juicy mangoes that grew on trees all around Monrovia and were even more plentiful up country heralded the new rains.

Looking to the World Bank as an exit from the frustrating Finance Ministry, Ellen was, again, of two minds. She didn't want to leave Liberia. The country was a mess, true, but it was *her* mess. They didn't have plum season in America. Or Club Beer, or fufu and soup. Or singsong Liberian English.

What was she doing? The country was sweet—at least for the Congo people, and she might as well be Congo. She could see Chris Maxwell whenever she wanted. She had arrived, after many years, at a place where she didn't hide in her office from her ex-husband and could even hold a civil conversation with him. She could go to parties in the evenings and hold court while during the day she held a job most women couldn't even dream of, even if she had just been marginalized in that job. Her boys were teenagers and doing well with her extended family; sometimes they stayed with her, and she could see them when she wanted.

She could enjoy the sweet Liberian food her country excelled at. The jollof rice cooked the way it was supposed to be cooked, with all manner of meat in it. The cassava and smoked fish gravy, the bitterleaf and fufu. She could go to Caesar's Beach on Saturdays and sit under the palaver huts sipping Club Beer and arguing with Jennie's husband and his friends about politics. Palaver huts were the Liberian equivalent of back patios in the West: circular huts with thatched roofs where people received visitors, enjoyed Club Beer, or just hung out. The name originated in the old days because that was where village chiefs met with quarreling subjects to judge their palavers. Now in modern 1973, they were just social gathering spots outside. For Ellen, the Caesar's Beach palaver huts could serve perfectly as the place to make nice with all those men she worked with and maybe they would stop being so angry about her speech. Why couldn't she just enjoy her life instead of trying so hard to change it?

But even as those thoughts went through her mind, Ellen was handing in her resignation to the Ministry of Finance and filling out the application her friend had sent her, to be a loan officer with the World Bank. She had decided, almost unconsciously, that the status quo was not going to be enough.

When he heard she had resigned, Steve Tolbert showed up at her house and barged into her bathroom, where she was combing her hair. "What's this 'bout you leaving the ministry?" he demanded.

Ellen told him about her new job.

"I could easily stop you by telling them you have misused your official position for personal gain," he replied. Government officials weren't supposed to use their overseas connections to get a job.

Ellen stared back at her boss. Now he was trying to stop her from leaving? She thought he would be glad to see her go.

After a brief face-off, Tolbert relaxed. Before Ellen left, he even threw her a big going-away party.

So Ellen left Liberia, again. At first it felt like she was fleeing. She had her mom and her son Rob with her. Jes, Charles, and Adamah were a different story; she was now more used to being without them than being with them, although it still hurt every time she said goodbye.

Looking out the window as her plane took off from Robertsfield Airport, she reassured herself that this was a strategic retreat, not a surrender. She would be coming back.

With her mother and Rob, Ellen arrived in Washington, DC, in 1973, moved into a suburban home in Alexandria, Virginia, and began her assault on the global financial system.

The Organization of African Unity had been haranguing the World Bank about hiring more Africans; the Bank was exerting enormous financial power in Africa, and OAU officials there wanted to make sure Bank officials understood their needs. So when Ellen walked into World Bank headquarters at 1818 H Street as their newest loan officer to Barbados, she suspected there were probably people there who would look at her as a token.

Let them. She was not going to worry about it. There was too much to do, a new job to learn. She spent evenings stuffing her head with the language of international economics, making phrases like *structural adjustment* part of her vocabulary. During the day, she found herself on the phone lecturing officials in Barbados about fiscal responsibility.

More significant, she began to build her international contacts with the Western lenders who controlled the purse strings for developing countries dependent on their aid. This was a network of high-level people she would call on again and again in the years to come.

Within months of her arrival, the World Bank promoted her to loan officer to Brazil. A giant jump, that, from tiny Barbados to raucous Brazil. One of her first assignments was to oversee a Bank nutrition project in the country. A colleague said aloud, right in front of her, that it was too big a project for Ellen; if she went before the board to present it and got tough questions, she wouldn't be able to handle it.

Hearing this, the head of the division, Alan Berg, responded, "Give her a break." But privately he pulled her aside to say "Listen, I'm taking a big risk with you."

Ellen spent her nights preparing for the board presentation, and when the time finally came, she answered their questions so well that Berg bought her flowers. He would go on to a storied career in global nutrition, and as early as 1974, Ellen was building a professional relationship with him.

These would be peaceful years in Washington, full of cocktail parties at World Bank headquarters, long meetings about structural reform in Brazil, and arcane arguments in smoke-filled hallways about whether the Bank was just a front for American business.

The Bank promoted her again, to loan officer for Kenya, Tanzania, and Uganda. Thus she found herself traveling the world. The World Bank had stamped its imprimatur on her, a sheen of global sophistication. She had learned how to say "Thank you" in Portuguese and had acquired a working knowledge of candomblé, the animist religion acquired by Brazilian descendants of African slaves. Now, in her trips to East Africa, she learned how to use her Liberian background to establish a rapport with finance officials there, how to roll her eyes conspiratorially at the demands of the West.

Two years into her World Bank stint, on April 29, 1975, a twin-engine Cessna took off from Greenville, Sino County, Liberia, and ran into trouble. Minutes later, it crashed into the Atlantic Ocean. On board were six people, including Stephen Tolbert, Ellen's former boss.

The new minister of finance, a reformist member of the Congo aristocracy, James T. Phillips, was quick to get on the phone to the ministry's prodigal daughter in Washington, asking her to come home.

Ellen wanted to go home; as much as she loved the global development bank scene, she was homesick for Liberia. She missed her sons; Charles and Jes, seventeen and sixteen, would soon be graduating from high school; Adamah was now a teenager. And she missed Chris Maxwell. It was as if she had put her personal life on hold during those two years; now she wanted it back. But she was also worried; she knew that at some point she would anger the Liberian government again. What would happen the next time she got marginalized at work for speaking her mind?

So she convinced her bosses at the World Bank to detail her to Liberia. She would return home as a Bank official, but working at Liberia's Ministry of Finance. It was a distinction the government of Liberia was happy to accept. Whatever ill feelings she had created with her graduation speech had dissipated.

She didn't know it at the time, but she would be in Liberia for the two events that would change the country forever.

Chapter 3

BULLSHIT

Monrovia, 1979

Like people all over the world, Liberians have their big dates. The most famous, for years, was July 26, Liberian Independence Day, a time to extract money and gifts from your well-off friends and relatives. It was far more rare to hear someone say "Happy 26" than to hear someone say "Where my 26?"

There's also Decoration Day, a day to put flowers on graves, and Armed Forces Day, when soldiers march at the army barracks at Barclay Training Center. But aside from knowing the former is in March and the latter in February, most Liberians couldn't tell you the date of those holidays.

In 1979, April 14 would become just as famous, but for very different reasons.

Early in 1979, President Tolbert set in motion the events that would lead to the explosion of April 14 by doing something unthinkable, incomprehensible, almost apocalyptic. He messed with people's rice.

At least once a day Liberians eat rice. Monday to Friday they eat rice with palm oil in a stew cooked with either cassava leaves, potato greens, or bitter leaf. On Saturday, they eat fufu—a fermented cassava dumpling—with pepper soup filled with fish heads and goat meat and crawfish and chicken and beef, but on Saturday night they will be back to eating their tried-and-true jollof rice. On Sunday—because for some reason Liberians don't eat palm oil on the weekend—they eat rice at lunch in stews of pumpkin or cabbage or collard greens, with beef, chicken, and smoked or dried fish for those who can afford meat, and salt and pepper sauce for those who can't.

But rice is the staple. Rice is what you give a village family if you are visiting and want to bring a present. It's what every Liberian kitchen will have, first and foremost, before bread, before milk, before eggs.

In 1979, when President Tolbert announced a 50 percent increase in the price of rice, Ellen was busy at the Ministry of Finance, buried under invoices from contractors who were working on the upcoming Organization for African Unity summit in Monrovia.

Now forty-one, Ellen was wearing her hair curly and wild—not quite the Angela Davis afro she had sported a few years earlier, but a modified, medium-length, looser style that somehow managed to look both coiffed and insouciant at the same time. She had recently taken to accenting her outfits with jaunty scarves around her neck, presenting the image of a confident woman who knew she looked good but didn't actually care. She was exactly the kind of woman Liberian men found irresistible, and they were chasing after her like ants after sugar. In a tactile society such as Liberia's, where it is impossible to walk down Broad Street without having to stop, kiss, and chat with a universe of people, Ellen charged purposefully around town.

She was still in a romantic relationship with Chris Maxwell and often spent the night with him, although they had their own homes. Maxwell had proposed to her, and she had thought about it, but she had seen his lightning-quick temper. One afternoon, he got so mad when his cook burned the rice that he threw the hot pot at him. It was at that moment Ellen knew she would not be marrying anyone ever again.

Nevertheless she was enjoying her life, though she sensed with each passing day that the government for which she worked was growing more out of touch with the people it led.

In 1979, at the same time Tolbert was trying to raise the price of rice, Monrovia was busily preparing for the biggest party the country had ever seen: the 1979 meeting of the Organization of African Unity. Liberia held the presidency of the OAU, the umbrella organization of African countries (except apartheid South Africa). When it was first founded in 1963, the organization was dedicated to opposing colonialism and white minority rule; it also viewed itself as an avenue for emerging African countries, most of them freshly independent after centuries of European colonization, to try to have a united voice on the world stage.

The OAU proclaimed the usual lofty principles about development and betterment, but it was in fact a dictators' club. The main concern of this all-male club was not universal health care but the prevention of coups.

It was in the middle of preparations for the summit that President Tolbert announced a 50 percent increase in the price of rice. His stated rationale was that if he increased the price of imported rice, then Liberians would be forced to grow their own rice and would learn self-sufficiency.

But the average monthly income of Liberians living in the city was around $80. No one had ever bothered to calculate the income of Liberians living up country, it was so little. The increase would raise the price of a bag of rice to $30. Stories surfaced that years earlier Tolbert's sprawling family had planted thousands of acres of rice on their private farms, and the price increase would undoubtedly result in increased demand for Tolbert family rice.

Amid the growing furor among native Liberians over the planned price increase, the clueless, cash-strapped Tolbert government embarked on a spending spree to spruce up Monrovia for the upcoming OAU meeting. Giant posters of each OAU head of state lined Tubman Boulevard, although six of the posters were blank because those countries were in the middle of a coup or a revolution and functionally leaderless. Liberia purchased forty motorcycles to escort the visiting African heads of state; within three days, half of them had been wrecked by their drivers. At Ellen's desk at the Ministry of Finance, invoice after invoice came in from both local and foreign contractors for OAU-related projects. Many looked fraudulent; all boasted exorbitant price tags that the government was going further into debt to pay. There was the more than $35 million to build Hotel Africa, the instant white elephant resort that would house the delegations. Each head of state got his own villa. There was the brand-new terminal at Robertsfield Airport and street lights to line the sixty-kilometer road from Robertsfield into the city. There were the seven cars provided for each of the fifty-three delegations attending the summit. There was the ocean liner the government rented to house some of the delegates, complete with floating casino. The final tally would end up at $101 million— one-third of the annual Liberian budget.

Early in the year, an invoice landed on Ellen's desk atop a pile of bills from foreign vendors for services rendered. A British contractor had written directly to President Tolbert to complain that the company hadn't been paid for work it had performed to help Monrovia prepare for the summit. Ellen hadn't signed off on the bill because she thought it was padded. The fact that, instead of revising the numbers downward, the contractor had complained to the president himself was the last straw. She hunted in her desk drawer for a rubber stamp she had bought on a lark from Spencer Gifts, the sophomoric souvenir shop that was ubiquitous in American shopping malls in the 1970s and 1980s. Smirking to herself, she stamped the invoice "Bullshit" and sent it back to the contractor.

A few days later, she was summoned by Finance Minister J. T. Phillips. "You can't use that in this place!" he told her, confiscating her stamp.

But the sentiment reflected the fury of native Liberians. Here they were, being told the price of their daily staple was increasing to an unbearable 40 percent of their monthly income, a rise that would literally take rice off most family tables. And the government was spending money on OAU amenities and gift bags for bloated delegations?

On Saturday morning, April 14, 1979, encouraged by the political movement of students and professors at the University of Liberia and by the Progressive Alliance of Liberia, the first party in a hundred years to oppose the ruling True Whig Party, thousands of people showed up for a protest march. They began assembling in front of PAL headquarters, near the Ministry of Finance, at dawn, although the march wasn't scheduled to start until 3 p.m.—a march Tolbert had preemptively declared illegal.

Ellen lived in an apartment building across the street. Padding over to her window early that morning, she saw the young people gathering. A large banner hung across the street. "Our eyes are open," it said. "The time of the people has come."

Nothing like this had ever happened in politically somnolent Liberia. By midmorning, two thousand people had gathered; by late morning, there were ten thousand. When the march began they moved en masse to the Executive Mansion. Peering out the window at the burgeoning crowd, Ellen felt a mounting sense of trepidation. Something was coming; she could feel it. Everyone in Monrovia, really, could feel it.

Tolbert had deployed police and soldiers along the main route of the march and placed army tanks at the intersections. The soldiers didn't fire on the unarmed protestors. But the Monrovia police did. They quickly dispensed with the tear gas they were supposed to be using and started firing bullets indiscriminately into the crowd. People screamed and ran in every direction to escape. The planned demonstration quickly degenerated into a full-fledged riot. By the end of the day, more than fifty protestors were dead; hundreds more were injured. Uncontrolled looting continued over the next two days.

Ellen spent those two days in her apartment, telephoning family members and friends to learn if they were safe. Because she lived close to the epicenter of the riots, her phone was constantly ringing with people checking on her. She didn't go outside; this was not a time to show that red-pumpkin complexion out on the streets of Monrovia.

Tolbert was hysterical; he called a number of the leaders of the protests to the Mansion on that first afternoon and screamed at them, calling them "ungrateful," "agitants" undeserving of all the benevolence with which he had treated them. He ordered his justice minister, Joseph Chesson, to arrest the ringleaders, which included Chesson's own adopted son, Chea Cheapoo. As Chesson's henchmen were making the arrests, Tolbert called for reinforcements from neighboring Guinea. The Guinean president, Sékou Touré, sent MiG fighter planes to make low passes over Monrovia, terrifying the city.

But Tolbert also found himself on the defensive. The police killing of unarmed protesters drained him of whatever moral authority he might have possessed. Speaking to the *New York Times* a month later, he tried to explain away the killings. "When they did not check the demonstration by using tear gas then the next thought was to fire in the air," he said. "That made no effect. Not until they were very near the Mansion with whatever plans they had in mind to do, then someone got injured from the security side."

In the days after the rice riots, the recriminations fell. Tolbert called the leaders of the demonstration "wicked, evil and satanic" and charged fourteen with treason. He shut down the University of Liberia. But, bowing to the furor in the streets, he also appointed thirty-one people to a commission to investigate the rice riots and make recommendations to prevent further unrest. Needing to calm the masses, he put Ellen on the committee, the Commission on National Reconstruction; since she did not shy away from criticism, her presence would give the panel legitimacy.

Ellen had plenty to say during the commission's meetings. The country needed to look into increases in the minimum wage; there were people working seven days a week as household help for elite Congo families and receiving only $25 to $30 a month. Society, she argued, had been radicalized—the riots had proven that. The people would no longer be passive before such a huge gap between rich and poor.

Two months later, in June, the commission issued its recommendations: amnesty for the leaders of the rice riots, who were in jail awaiting treason trials; a code of conduct for all public officials and for the government to tackle corruption and conflicts of interest in a real way; and investigations of possible corruption by the ministries of justice, agriculture, defense—and finance. Ellen was, in essence, calling for the investigation of her own boss.

In a fourth recommendation that would be seen as ironic decades later, when Ellen herself came under similar criticism, the commission pointedly called on Tolbert to consider how widespread nepotism in the power structure affected the image of the government, where so many of his relatives controlled high-profile, monopolistic business ventures.

Tolbert made a belated effort to address some of the causes of the riots. He quietly rescinded his order raising the price of rice. He gave a speech acknowledging that the people needed more schools, roads, and hospitals and said he was working hard to improve the standard of living of all Liberians. And because it would be unseemly to have all those protestors locked up in jail during the OAU summit, Tolbert struck a deal with Gabriel Baccus Matthews, who, as head of the new dissident party, PAL, represented the rice protestors. In return, Matthews wrote a groveling letter of apology from his prison cell, promising to refrain from public acts against the government.

Tolbert "extended the hand of forgiveness" by declaring a general amnesty. Then he released the rice riot detainees. Just a few months later—conveniently after the OAU meeting—the truce was over. Matthews registered PAL as a political opposition party, renamed it the Progressive People's Party, and held a rally calling for Tolbert's ouster. The president responded by banning the PPP and rounding up thirty-eight political dissidents, including Matthews, whom he charged with sedition.

Tolbert made one more move to stem the furor in the streets: he fired his finance minister, James T. Phillips, Ellen's boss.

Ellen had just arrived home after a trip to the United States. Still wearing her travel clothes, she stopped by her office at the Finance Ministry to pick up some work. The phone rang; Reginald Townsend, one of Tolbert's aides, was on the line. "The president say you ma' come to the Mansion," Townsend told her. "He wan' see you right now."

Ellen looked down at her clothing. "But I in jeans, oh," she replied. In Liberia, women did not wear trousers, let alone jeans, to the Executive Mansion.

There was some murmuring across the line, then Townsend came back on. "The president say he'n't ask you wha' you wearing. Come."

Fifteen minutes later, a jeans-clad Ellen was sitting across from President Tolbert. "I'm making you minister of finance," he said.

And so it was that on April 12, 1980—the second new date to become famous on the Liberian calendar—Ellen Johnson Sirleaf was the country's finance minister.

Early that morning, native enlisted soldiers, led by twenty-eight-year-old Master Sergeant Samuel Kanyon Doe, twenty-five-year-old Sergeant Thomas Quiwonkpa, and twenty-nine-year-old Corporal Harrison Pennue, stormed the Executive Mansion. Tolbert had just returned from a reception for religious and diplomatic guests in downtown Monrovia to his private quarters on the top floor of the Israeli-built Mansion overlooking the Atlantic Ocean. His room had a security elevator that was capable of delivering him deep into the basement, where a tunnel could shoot him out to the nearby beach and, presumably, to safety, if ever that was needed. But the elevator was not working.

Just after one in the morning, with the help of a few turncoats in Tolbert's presidential guard, Doe, Quiwonkpa, and Pennue scaled the Mansion's iron gate with eighteen other noncommissioned officers of the Liberian Army. They quickly killed the security detail. During the firefight, a stray bullet severed the telephone line between the Mansion and Barclay

Training Center, the army barracks known as BTC, a shot that would prevent Tolbert from summoning help.

Not that help would necessarily have been quick to come. Many of the Executive Mansion guards were collaborators, and others in the army who were supposed to be guarding the Mansion knew Quiwonkpa, Doe, and Pennue and had no problem with what they were doing.

In less than an hour, the soldiers had reached the top floor of the Mansion. But the presidential private quarters were surrounded by heavily fortified locked doors and bulletproof glass. The soldiers couldn't get in.

They knocked on the outside door. "Mother, Mother, open the door," they said, when First Lady Victoria Tolbert demanded to know who they were. "We just want talk to you, Mother. We will not hurt you." When she didn't open the door, the men went back downstairs and obtained a key to the private quarters from the Executive Mansion guard. President Tolbert, who had been hiding in an even more secure section of the private quarters, was crossing the hallway trying to get to his wife and children when six soldiers burst through the door.

The soldiers fired three bullets into Tolbert. Pennue fired the second shot into Tolbert's head. Then he took out a knife and ritually gouged out Tolbert's right eye and disemboweled him. They arrested Mrs. Tolbert and the children.

Quiwonkpa had done most of the planning of the attack, but he was an army man filled with ambivalence about whether the military should actually run the government. So he agreed that his friend Doe would go on the radio to make the announcement that Liberia was now under new management. All government officials, Doe declared, must immediately report to the army barracks.

The minister of finance was spending the night with her boyfriend, Chris Maxwell, when the coup took place. She was asleep when Maxwell touched her on the shoulder. "They're shooting," he said.

The telephone started ringing with panicked friends and relatives on the line. "They're shooting around the Mansion." Nobody had ever heard of Samuel Kanyon Doe before, much less Thomas Quiwonkpa or Harrison Pennue. They certainly weren't part of the well-known group of political "agitants" who had been giving Tolbert so much grief. But now the disembodied voice on the ELBC radio station was repeating, over and over, "The People's Redemption Council na take over the government to end all this corruption. Master Sergeant Samuel Kanyon Doe is in charge. All government ministers are to report to BTC."

The Holy Ghost women, who often dominate broadcasts with long sermons, hymns, and prayers, had disappeared from the airwaves. No more singsong chants about the power and love of Jesus Christ or calls to fast for days on end. They had all been swept away, replaced by patriotic music and the broadcast announcing the military coup.

The radio broadcasts continued into the morning, interspersed with the Liberian national anthem. Then, around midafternoon, someone inserted a new twist: the calypso antidictator ode by Manhattan Transfer that suddenly seemed ominous: "Wanted Dead or Alive."

After that, the PRC broadcast came back on: "The People's Redemption Council na take over the government to end all this corruption. Master Sergeant Samuel Kanyon Doe is in charge. All government ministers are to report to BTC."

The disembodied voice then read the names of the government ministers ordered to report in. Cecil Dennis, minister of foreign affairs; Frank Tolbert, the president's brother and president pro tem of the Senate; Joseph Chesson, minister of justice; James T. Phillips, former minister of finance. Surprisingly, the current finance minister's name was not included in that list. Instead the name of Ellen Johnson Sirleaf was heard in a separate broadcast, alongside that of Charles Green, governor of the Central Bank. Those two were ordered to report to the Executive Mansion, not BTC.

Heart racing, Ellen looked at Maxwell. "I not going," she said. "Not without protection."

Indeed for a light-skinned Congo-in-everything-but-name government minister to step out in Monrovia that Saturday morning would be suicide. In the streets, native Liberians had poured out in jubilation, singing, dancing, and cheering the demise of their president. Soldiers drunk on cane juice and newfound power swaggered from house to house, confiscating cars and trucks to take them on raids to collect government ministers and sundry Congo people. Now was the time to gang-rape

Congo women, to brutalize the young daughters of the old power structure, to shoot their sons while swigging from bottles of Club Beer.

In the streets of Monrovia, native Liberians were yelling a new chant: "Who born soldier? Country woman! Who born minister? Congo woman!"

If Ellen went out, no one was going to ask her if her father was actually a Gola man or check whether her mother's fair complexion actually came from her German father and not some white American slave owner in the not-too-distant past. At that point, she had no way of knowing whether anyone remembered her kleptocracy speech from 1969, or the 1972 speech at the College of West Africa that almost got her fired, or that she had helped write the scathing rice riots panel report just the year before.

She telephoned Charles Green, the Central Bank governor who was also being summoned. "What are you going to do?" she asked.

"We have to go to the Mansion," Green said. "They want us to open the bank and give them money."

Ellen balked. "Charley, you see the color of my skin? I will never reach! At least you part, you can reach." She asked him to give a message to the PRC. "Tell them I will come, but they gotta send for me. I need protection."

Hours passed, and no one came. The patriotic broadcasts on the radio continued; so did the announcement ordering Ellen Johnson Sirleaf to report in.

From the moment Maxwell had awoken her that morning, Ellen's mind had been racing around two central questions. The first was simple: Had she criticized the government enough from within to buy herself an exemption from the witch hunt that was under way? The second question was more fundamental to who she was, but mattered only if the answer to the first question was yes: Whose side would she choose?

The broadcast continued. "Ellen Johnson Sirleaf, minister of finance, report to the Executive Mansion." Finally, Maxwell turned to her and suggested he take her in his pickup truck. With trepidation, the two set out.

The streets were filled with celebrating people. "Who born soldier? Country woman! Who born rogue? Congo woman!"

The two arrived at the Mansion without incident. At the gate, soldiers surrounded Maxwell's pickup. There was a rustle through the air. "De finance minister now come." Soldiers opened the gate and pointed down the driveway, toward the yard. Slowly Maxwell drove on.

Neither Maxwell nor Ellen said a word to each other. He had driven her to an uncertain fate, delivering her safely to the mansion. But now it was every man for himself. He would not be sticking around to witness the afternoon's events personally. One soldier opened the door, and Ellen hopped out and began walking toward her fate. She never looked behind her. Maxwell turned his pickup around and drove home.

The yard was filled with wild-eyed soldiers; they strutted around, glittering with excitement, surrounded by the usual hangers-on: young men clapping them on the back in congratulations.

Sitting to one side, heads down and guarded by gun-wielding soldiers, was a far more somber group: some of Ellen's colleagues from the Tolbert cabinet.

Charles Green had apparently already opened up the Central Bank vaults to the soldiers, so it was unclear what Ellen was now expected to do.

Liberia's new leader, Samuel Doe, sat on a chair in the middle of the palaver hut outside. In his hands he held a copy of the annual budget. He wore army fatigues and had a baby face. On his head was a petite fatigue cowboy hat whose strap was around his chin, and he wore a pair of dark aviator sunglasses.

He glanced up at Ellen as she was escorted into the palaver hut. "Do you know this budget?" he asked.

Less than twelve hours earlier, this man and his comrades had ripped the guts out of her boss, President Tolbert.

"Of course," she replied. "That's my work."

"Explain it to him," Doe said, gesturing to one of the soldiers.

For the next two hours, Ellen sat in the palaver hut explaining the Liberian budget to Doe's appointed budget man. She wasn't sure he understood, but she plowed on anyway. At one point one of the soldiers told her that how well she performed would determine whether she was sent home or to jail when she was done. She tried not to look at her colleagues as they were interrogated and beaten, although she could hear their cries.

Finally Doe looked at her. "Okay," he said. "Let her go home."

She stood up to leave, but when she got to the entryway of the palaver hut, Doe called out, "Stop."

Ellen froze.

"Send some people with her. To take her home safe."

A couple of soldiers accompanied her. But before taking her home, they took her to the morgue. "We carrying you to see something," one told her, before marching her into the room. The remains of Liberia's twentieth president, gutted, lay on the table.

The message was clear.

Afterward the soldiers took her back to Maxwell's house, parking in the front yard. They stayed all afternoon, and they stayed into the night. Ellen kept going out to them, trying to make a connection, anything so they would not want to kill her if orders came.

"How y'all doing?" she asked the first time.

Then, "Y'all want something to eat?"

Then, "Can I get y'all anything? Some rice? Some bread?"

"Anything to drink?"

Finally one of the soldiers turned to her. "Go to sleep, woman. The man ain't send us here to kill you."

Two days after the coup, Doe went on ELTV to address the nation. He wore his green army fatigues, his cap, and his sunglasses and had a grenade dangling from his pocket. He was "prepared to let the past go quickly into history." Gone forever were the days of "'who you know' and 'Do you know who I am?'" Now was the time for the country to enter the days of "what can you do."

But three days later, the military trials of Ellen's former colleagues in the Tolbert cabinet began.

For Ellen, the days took on a hallucinatory quality. Her entire family was in disarray; her brother Carney had been arrested and was being held at BTC, leaving her mother distraught. Her sister had been brutalized by soldiers who were looking for her husband, Jeff Bernard, who, as Tolbert's minister of labor, youth and sports, had been at a football game in Ghana with the Liberian national team the night of the coup. If he had been in Monrovia that night, he would surely be locked up with the rest of the

Tolbert cabinet; no one was sure at this point whether the soldiers wouldn't try to lock up his wife and sons.

Ellen's own sons were away at college in the United States and telephoning daily—when they could get through—with the same questions: "How they treating you? When you leaving?"

Each morning, Doe's soldiers put Ellen in the car and escorted her from Maxwell's house to the Executive Mansion. There was a mandatory dusk-to-dawn curfew in place, but even during the day there were fewer people out in the streets, and certainly almost no Congo people. The elites who hadn't been arrested were hiding at home, huddled in living rooms watching the television news or making calls trying to find out what had happened to family members.

Once Ellen arrived at the Mansion, the routine was the same: she went through Liberia's financial documents, budget, and outstanding loan agreements for the new government. The questions mostly revolved around how the Doe people could get their hands on as much money as possible. But they also needed a crash course in the balance of payments for running a country—even one that was looking increasingly like the stereotypical banana republic.

Everywhere there were soldiers, riding around in the confiscated vehicles of former government ministers. They rumbled into private yards, quickly separating the men from the women. The men were hauled off to the army barracks. The women were raped—some of them in front of their children.

Suddenly there were checkpoints on Tubman Boulevard, where soldiers drunk on newfound power and cane juice extorted money from drivers and passengers. This was a time for score-settling. Ellen's brother Carney had been taken to BTC with the Tolbert cabinet ministers not because he was a minister as well but because a few months before, when he was in the legislature, Carney had laughed at Chea Cheapoo—now Doe's minister of justice—when he lost his legislative seat. So Cheapoo was out for blood.

Carney wasn't the only person to feel Cheapoo's wrath. Joseph Chesson, Tolbert's minister of justice, who had had his adopted son arrested during the April 14 rice riots, was now imprisoned at BTC with the rest of

Tolbert's cabinet, awaiting their fate. The fortunes of the Congo father and the native son were now completely flipped.

Other members of the Congo elite found themselves in similar straits, as all the high-handed behavior of the past came back to haunt them. Congo people furiously described their kind acts toward native Liberians, hoping such remembrances would save them now.

One morning when Ellen arrived at the Mansion, Doe met her outside. He was wearing his aviator sunglasses. Striding to the car, he gestured to her. "Come," he said, taking the wheel of the car.

The two drove to BTC, with Doe smugly looking around at his new subjects. The car stopped in the yard. The place was its usual dusty frenzy of activity. There were soldiers milling around and there were men lining up under guard as the soldiers heckled them. The prisoners wore no shoes and were in various states of undress, some of them wearing only trousers. They were brutally familiar. Her colleagues from the Tolbert government. There was Varney Dempster, the former chief of police. There was her brother Carney.

Of all her siblings, Ellen was closest to her sister, Jennie. But she had grown up with Carney, had played with him on the family farm in Julejuah. He was her family; he had been around all her life. Now he was imprisoned at BTC by the man with whom she was arriving in a car.

Her face blank, Ellen slowly got out of the car with Doe. If ever she looked like Judas, it was this moment, as her former colleagues stared at her.

She looked at her brother. He looked back at her.

Then he winked.

She felt a small release of the tension.

Doe strutted around a while, talking to his soldiers and jeering at the prisoners, as Ellen stood by silently. Finally he told her to get back in the car and they drove out of BTC.

Ellen was quiet for a few minutes, then she could hold it in no longer. "Why you got my brother on that line? He ain't do nothing wrong."

Doe replied, "I don't know myself." Not long after that, Carney was released.

"They will kill those people?" Throughout Congo Monrovia, that question dominated the conversation.

The military trials of Ellen's colleagues had begun, with highlights broadcast every night on ELTV. The accused were all well-known, familiar men: Chesson; Dennis; Clarence Parker, the husband of Ellen's best friend, Clavenda; James T. Phillips, Ellen's former boss. There were thirteen in all. These were not the men Ellen had seen that day Doe took her to BTC, when her brother winked at her from the prison line. The thirteen facing the military tribunal were much more powerful and influential figures from the Tolbert cabinet.

The trials were in a second-floor conference room with bare cement walls. The accused men, most of them shirtless, wore trousers or, in some cases, only their underpants. They sat before a five-member military tribunal.

On the beach outside, four telephone poles had been erected.

There were no details of specific charges—the thirteen men were simply accused of treason, "rampant corruption," and "gross violation of human rights."

Dennis, the tall and strikingly handsome former minister of foreign affairs, had gone to the American Embassy and asked for political asylum. He was turned down. He had then driven to BTC and turned himself in. Now he stood before the tribunal, wearing jeans but no shirt. He told the men that he had seen a lot of problems with the old guard system and that he had urged the hard-liners in the government to liberalize.

Most of the other men on trial delivered a similar statement. They said the system they had been a part of—that they had established—was unfair. They pleaded not guilty. Frank Stewart, the former budget director, his hair flaked with sawdust, tried to tell a story of himself as a young man, making only $250 a month, using small loans to build his house as he struggled up the ladder of success. But the tribunal was far more interested in how many houses he had managed to build. "Four houses," one officer repeated when Stewart told them. "Mr. Stewart got four houses."

Tuesday, April 22, 1980, dawned hazy, hot, and humid. Monrovia was nearing the end of the dry season, and the rains that would saturate the earth for the next seven months were on the horizon. The new minister of information, Gabriel Nimely, called a press conference at the Executive Mansion. "Gentlemen of the press," he announced, "you are all invited to some executions at Barclay Training Center."

Asked who would be executed, he replied, "Enemies of the people."

At BTC, hundreds of people stood or danced on the beach near the four execution poles. Then two large mechanical hole diggers and five additional poles were brought to the site.

Now there were nine execution poles.

In Liberia in 1980, women were to be raped, not killed. So many of Ellen's female friends and relatives were sexually assaulted. Daughters were gang-raped on the beach by drunken soldiers; sisters were assaulted with gun butts; wives were forcibly violated in front of their husbands. The way to best a woman, in those days, was to demean her, not to kill her.

So on April 22, 1980, when Tolbert's condemned cabinet were packed into a white Volkswagen bus and driven to the beach, Ellen Johnson Sirleaf was not among them. The female minister of finance would spend that afternoon in her mother's house, uneasily watching the steadily darkening sky as heavy clouds moved in.

Inside the bus, the thirteen men huddled and watched the execution poles go up. Close to one hundred drunken soldiers clapped each other on the back and waved their machine guns toward the bus. A crowd jostled around the bus and yelled at the thirteen inside. They pounded on the windows and kicked at the doors.

Then the soldiers opened the door of the bus and pulled out nine men, including Phillips and Dennis. They marched them to the poles and tied each to one, their backs facing the ocean, using a single long green rope. From inside the bus, the remaining four men watched.

Soldiers milled around the execution posts jeering at the men, who were tied by their waist. It took half an hour for their commander to get them to move back far enough to make room for the firing squad.

Two of the men fainted before shots were fired. Two of them, Dennis and Reginald Townsend, the Tolbert aide who the year before had told Ellen to come to the Mansion in her jeans so Tolbert could appoint her minister of finance, stared defiantly at the soldiers.

The order was given, and a volley of shots rang out. The condemned men, save one, had collapsed onto their poles, dead or dying.

Dennis was still standing, looking at the soldiers.

Finally, one soldier walked up to him and shot him in the face.

The crowd cheered and the soldiers dragged the bodies from the poles, then returned to the bus and collected the remaining four. Shots rang out again.

The soldiers then sprayed all thirteen bodies with automatic fire, emptying, and then replacing, their ammunition clips.

That night, Liberians, including Ellen, watched the executions on the television news.

Chapter 4

IDIOTS

Monrovia, May 1980

Two weeks after her colleagues and friends were executed on the beach, Ellen reported to the Mansion—as she did every morning—for her daily question-and-answer session with the man who had murdered them. She was no longer under escort by Doe's soldiers but was again moving around town with her own car and driver.

The execution of the thirteen men had ignited international protest and seemed to have sated the quest for vengeance among Doe's soldiers. Congo people were lining up at the Interior Ministry to get exit passes, a bureaucratic innovation of the new regime, to leave the country. Many of Ellen's friends and family were fleeing, including her sister, Jennie, whose husband would have been killed with the thirteen if he hadn't been in Ghana with the national football team at the time of the coup. Jennie smuggled her boys out of the country and then left as well. She advised her sister to do the same.

But Ellen wasn't ready to give up on Liberia. Doe seemed to feel that he had spilled enough blood for the moment. Now, Ellen thought, perhaps he would focus on providing opportunities for native Liberians that they had not previously had. Appearing at the Mansion for her session with Doe, she told herself that she could do more to help the new government from the inside than if she ran back to her World Bank cocoon in America.

Usually Doe focused his questions on the budget, looking for hidden money. Which countries were the most forthcoming with aid? How much could the Maritime Office transfer to the government every month? But this morning he had a new question for Ellen: "You will be my next president of the Liberian Bank for Development and Investment?"

Ellen accepted. Every moment of her life after the coup was exceedingly strange; this moment was only slightly stranger. With studied casual-ness, she mentioned to Doe that, technically, she was still a World Bank employee. What she didn't say was that at any moment she could ask the World Bank to recall her to Washington. It was a lifeline she kept hidden, even as she set about in her new role as president of the Development Bank. She was soon preparing for a trip to Washington to plead for more money for her new boss.

It was June 1980, two months since the coup, when Ellen arrived in Washington with Togba-Nah Tipoteh, the new minister of planning and economic affairs, on the government's first official trip overseas. The aim was to secure emergency aid while trying to convince all the usual donors that although Doe's collaborators had disemboweled the president, murdered much of the presidential guard, and executed the cabinet, this was no reason to abandon the country. The presence of Ellen, the former minister of finance and a favorite of the international finance community, was supposed to provide the new government with the patina of respectability.

Ellen certainly knew she was being used, and she was conflicted about her new role. Many of her old colleagues in the Tolbert regime—the ones who weren't executed—considered her an opportunist. From the outside, she certainly looked like one of those people who put power above loyalty or morality. Yes, she had heckled and criticized the previous government, but still she had been a beneficiary of its decisions, and members of her family had suffered at the hands of the new government. What was Ellen doing working for these people? It wasn't as if her new colleagues in the Doe regime were welcoming her with open arms. Most of them didn't trust her.

It was a very thin rope to walk, yet she was determined to tiptoe out onto it. She was convinced that Liberia would collapse if the new regime didn't get certain things right. Let people talk; they were going to talk about her anyway. Maybe, she thought, she could help steer the Doe group onto the right track. And then, when Doe turned over the government to civilian rule—as she was convinced he would do eventually—maybe the country could finally find some equilibrium in the relationship between country people and Congo people.

In those initial months after the coup, another thought began to creep up on her. Ellen had begun to see herself as presidential material. It was still a zygote of a thought, not fully formed or explored. But she was already sure she could do a better job than the men who had governed Liberia into the ground.

Ellen set up many of the meetings in the United States, including one with Citibank, which for years had served as Liberia's main institutional financial supporter. Jack Clark, a vice president of Citibank and a friend of Ellen's, hosted one meeting in his office in New York. Walking in flanked by Tipoteh and other officials, she took immediate control of the meeting, beginning her pitch with a plea to stabilize the country's teetering economy. Yes, there had been a coup, but the new government would honor existing debt obligations. The country's economy, she argued, was strong enough, thanks to all that rubber and iron ore. None of this was actually true, but Ellen asserted as much anyway, believing that the alternative—complete economic abandonment of Liberia by the outside world—would be catastrophic.

The meeting went fine until she let Tipoteh talk.

The new minister of planning launched into a strident verbal assault on the old Liberian guard, apparently oblivious to the fact that many of the people his government had taken pride in executing had been close friends of the people from whom he was now seeking money.

As Ellen felt some of the eyes in the room turn to her, her blood started to boil. She knew the coup would probably have been accepted if the executions of the thirteen hadn't taken place. The international finance community might have been able to look the other way at the killing of Tolbert, which occurred during the throes of the coup. But the executions on the beach, days after Tolbert's killing, by a squadron of drunken, jeering soldiers, which news cameras and journalists had been invited to record for posterity, had made Liberia an international symbol of barbarity.

Ellen grew increasingly uncomfortable as Tipoteh spoke, until, unable to sit still any longer, she got up and stalked out of the meeting.

It was her first openly subversive act in the Doe regime. Her old feistiness, so boldly displayed during her rise up the ladder in the Tolbert years, was starting to resurface. But this was a new era, and at no time in the two months since taking power had Doe shown himself to be open to criticism.

Ellen's mini-rebellion drew no response this time. A few months later, back in Liberia, she tried it again.

It was November 1980, seven months after the coup. On the streets of Monrovia and in the villages up country, the euphoria with which many people greeted the demise of Tolbert and the Congo elites had already given way to the reality of lives increasingly dominated by a cadre of uneducated teenagers. Doe's soldiers were extorting money from people, moving into the unoccupied homes of the former cabinet, and intimidating foreign businesspeople, which had the effect of driving away the very people who were providing what few jobs were to be had in Liberia.

Doe himself may not have intended this; in fact, his commanding general of the armed forces, Thomas Quiwonkpa, publicly issued order after order taking soldiers to task for "unrevolutionary" behavior. He and Doe tried to at least appear to be addressing the problem. They publicly executed three soldiers for looting and had the government sentence eight others who molested Liberians to the dreaded Belle Yalla prison up country. But they could go only so far before alienating the soldiers who supported them. Beyond that, the ranks of the People's Redemption Council was increasingly made up solely of members of Doe's Krahn tribe—demonstrating the same kind of favoritism the Congo elites had shown. To many Liberians, it seemed the Congo elites were simply replaced by Krahn elites.

Doe was quickly acquiring a taste for power. Liberians revere their cars as status symbols, and Doe had given his wife, Nancy, the Mercedes of the former first lady Victoria Tolbert and ordered police escorts for her trips to the supermarket. He moved into the Executive Mansion, although it was not known whether he took over the same bedroom where he, Pennue, and Quiwonkpa had assassinated his predecessor. He lost the gauntness and high cheekbones he had sported as a low-paid army master sergeant and acquired the paunch that Africans the continent over associate with wealth.

To fund his new lifestyle and that of the PRC's new cadre of high officials, the Doe government began to use the treasury as a personal bank account. In this they were helped by the United States, which, in a cold war effort to keep Liberia and its maritime access to the West African coast away from any Soviet infringement, started propping up the Doe regime through grants and loans. Liberia would not go the route of other socialist-leaning African countries because the United States would not allow that to happen. If it meant doubling American aid to Doe's regime, so be it. The loans, unfortunately, didn't come with any good-governance criteria, so Doe and Company were able to fund their new lifestyle without having to account for anything.

Ellen's old persona—mostly suppressed for seven months—reemerged suddenly at a graduation ceremony in November at Booker Washington Institute in Kakata. She wrapped her criticism of the government she served in a complex parable about a farmer and a rat trap.

Once upon a time, there wa' one farmer, Ellen told the crowd, adopting the patois that she could turn on and off at will. The rat wa' stealing the farmer rice, evry day the rat was stealing the rice. So one day, the farmer set trap for the rat. But the rat wa' clever, itn't fall in no trap. Instead, the farmer wife step in the trap by mistake and hurt her foot. The foot started to get rotten, and the farmer had to kill his chicken for soup to try help hi' wife. The woman drank the soup but she died anyway. Now the farmer had to kill hi' cow to make feast for the woman funeral.

The moral of the story, incomprehensible to foreigners but totally clear to Liberians, was that going after your enemies can rebound against you. It was not lost on Doe's henchmen when they got word of Ellen's little parable at Booker Washington. Within days, Thomas Weh-Syen, Doe's second-in-command, showed that he too could speak Liberian English, spreading the word that he was "setting for Ellen."

Weh-Syen was one of the original plotters of the April coup; he was with Doe that night at the Executive Mansion. Now vice chairman of the People's Redemption Council, he was a specialist in threats. Just a few days before, he had told the national football team that if they lost to Gambia, they would all be jailed. (The team held Gambia to a goalless tie, and Weh-Syen spared them because they had played well.)

"He setting for you," one of Ellen's colleagues warned. This new government was not going to tolerate the same "ashtray" (rubbish, or nonsense) Ellen had pulled when she worked for Tolbert.

Heart pounding, Ellen picked up the phone and placed a call to her old bosses at the World Bank in Washington. "I need you to recall me," she said bluntly. Within days, Doe received a letter from the World Bank asking that Ellen be released back to the Bank. Doe agreed; he needed the Bank too much for development money to tangle with them over someone he wasn't sure he still wanted in his government anyway.

It was December 1980, eight months after the coup. Like so many Congo people, Ellen was leaving Liberia. She was leaving her mother. She was leaving Chris Maxwell. She had wanted to be one of the ones who stayed, who showed she was willing to stay and fight for her country. But she was scared. The place felt too uncertain, and her life increasingly felt like the property of madmen. Sitting on the plane as it taxied down the runway at Robertsfield, she felt both relief and a sense of failure—relief that she could stop looking over her shoulder, relief that she would soon see Jennie and her boys again. But failure loomed as well. For the first time, she was leaving Liberia with no idea when or if she would be coming back.

For the next four years, until 1985, Ellen lived wrapped in the embrace of her second family—the family of international financiers, World Bank bureaucrats and Citibank professionals who spent their days at debt relief conferences in Geneva and São Paolo and Addis Ababa and their evenings in smoke-filled restaurants eating moules-frites. It was a world in which she thrived, this quick-witted female from Liberia of all places. There were few women around the conference table talking about structural adjustment and rural development. Ellen was both a novelty and a prized asset.

In 1982, after only a year at the World Bank, she accepted a job with Citibank, which appointed her the first African woman to hold the title of vice president. She was sent to Nairobi and put in charge of scouting investment opportunities across Africa.

Her boys were grown now and either finishing college—medical school for Adamah, she noted proudly—or starting their own lives in the United States. She had already been back to Liberia once to visit her mother and to see Maxwell, and during that visit, she had paid a courtesy call on Doe, who had seemed pleased to see her.

For a development banker, the Citibank Nairobi posting was plush. Ellen got a beautiful home in Muthaiga, the Nairobi equivalent of Beverly

Hills, a car and driver, a cook, and a maid. Nairobi in the early 1980s was vibrant, a combination of British colonial charm and brash pan-Africanism. It was a flight hub for all of Africa and a gateway to the tourist world of tented safari camps and luxurious adventure travel.

The corporate culture at Citibank was daunting; every month Ellen had to write a report showing what she had accomplished to justify her salary. But she was meeting everyone who mattered in the African and global development scene. She became good friends with Yoweri Museveni, who would rule Uganda for almost three decades after leading the rebellion that toppled Apollo Milton Opeto Obote. She met finance ministers in Rwanda and Ethiopia, central bank presidents from Zambia and Zimbabwe, presidents and future presidents throughout eastern, central, and southern Africa.

Perhaps even more important, she got to know the Citibank hierarchy. And through them and her World Bank contacts, she became part of the global financial hierarchy, moving seamlessly in and out of the Bretton Woods circle of international development, monetary policy, and trade, despite coming from a country where few people had ever even heard of Bretton Woods.

Certainly Liberia's rulers had never heard of Bretton Woods. Basic training teaches men where to punch for maximum damage, how to hit the deck the second they hear incoming fire, what to wear when trying to blend into the background, and how to intimidate a foe—or a misbehaving populace. Militaries, with the possible exception of the Romans, do not teach their men how to govern.

Liberia's military government was far more military than government. Machine guns and rifles were now part of daily life for most Liberians. The ordinary citizen driving from Congo Town to Mamba Point in the evening went through several checkpoints. But the soldiers with their guns weren't positioned just at hastily constructed road barriers: they showed up in the markets to harass the women selling kola nuts; they posted themselves outside movie theaters to shake down members of the audience; they popped up at gas stations to make sure they got a cut of pump proceeds.

And of course, now that the military suddenly had cars and drivers and the trappings of power, they weren't very interested in turning control over to civilians anytime soon. So General Doe (he had promoted himself from master sergeant) tried his hand at governing. At first he didn't take on the title of president, and he sprinkled his speeches with talk of his planned "return to the barracks." But he called himself the head of state, and it would be four more years before he set elections for a new president.

In the meantime, he got to work trying to collect revenue from a tax base where the vast majority didn't have income to tax. Doe ordered his new finance minister to print up more money. When the new Liberian dollar arrived on the scene, it featured Doe's face. The currency, which had been pegged to the U.S. dollar since 1847, took a nosedive, dipping from 1–1 to 25–1. The country stopped paying its international postal dues, so Liberians stopped using the mail. When they wanted to send mail, they found people who were traveling out of the country to hand-carry their letters.

Meanwhile Chairman Doe began developing a prescient paranoia that the people around him were out to get him. Remember, Thomas Weh-Syen, who had chased Ellen out of town after her Booker Washington speech, was among a small cadre of the original coup plotters who came to question Doe's wholesale denunciation of the Soviet Union in exchange for American dollars; in particular, Weh-Syen was angry that Doe had shuttered the Libyan diplomatic mission after the United States told him to do so and had ordered the reduction of the Soviet Embassy staff to six from sixteen. He voiced his criticism to the press, complaining that Liberia was assuming an "errand boy" status toward the United States. Doe's answer was to accuse Weh-Syen of plotting a coup against him.

On a Sunday night in August 1981, the twenty-nine-year-old Weh-Syen was returning from an all-day football match in Bassa when he was arrested by some of his own army security forces. By then the second most powerful man in the country, he was hauled back to Monrovia to stand before a military tribunal, accused of plotting to kill Doe.

The usual booing, jeering Greek chorus assembled to watch the proceedings; Doe went on the radio and announced that the plotters, led by "my dear friend, Thomas Weh-Syen," wanted him dead. Weh-Syen wept and professed his innocence: "If I die, I will die for nothing. I will never kill Doe."

Doe chose not to promise the same restraint. After two days of what everyone in Monrovia had assumed were pretrial hearings, Weh-Syen and four others were executed at midnight by firing squad.

The next year, Doe arrested, and then released, several university students who he said were disobeying a ban on political activities.

Still, the outside world was becoming adjusted to Doe and his peculiarities; after all, Africa was populated by strongmen who locked up political enemies. He received an honorary doctorate from the University of Seoul and, thus anointed, started referring to himself as Dr. Doe. He continued following the American cold war line, and aid from the United States continued to flow, far surpassing the amount sent to Liberia during the Tolbert years. But the economy struggled as the most educated Liberians continued to flee.

While away on a foreign mission, Tipoteh resigned his post as minister of planning and economic affairs in what was viewed widely as a defection. The foreign minister, Gabriel Baccus Matthews, had a falling-out with Doe and was fired. But those schisms could not rival the divorce of Doe and Thomas Quiwonkpa, the army chief, a split that would engulf the nation and bring Ellen closer to death than she had ever come.

Thomas Quiwonkpa was just twenty-five when he joined Doe and his other brothers-in-arms to storm the Executive Mansion the night of April 12. A Gio soldier of humble origin, suddenly Quiwonkpa was a general and head of the five-thousand-man Liberian Army. Within two months of the coup, the *Los Angeles Times* had flown a reporter to Liberia to write a story about a day in the life of "the man to see in Liberia."

"After any revolution," the *Times* reported, "there is always a new man to see, and three months after the coup that ended the life and the government of President William R. Tolbert Jr., the word is out that Quiwonkpa can provide a job, correct injustice, get a prisoner out of jail."

The Liberian press quickly fell in love with Quiwonkpa; he was the one who was tasked with the difficult job of trying to rein in the worst abuses of the military and instill some kind of discipline among the soldiers roaming the streets. He was behind the quick executions of several soldiers who were convicted of looting. He coordinated joint training exercises with American Green Berets who were there to train the Liberian military.

Quiwonkpa soon became the most high-profile member of Doe's inner circle, and the most beloved. While Doe was cruising Monrovia in his new Mercedes and living the high life in the Mansion, Quiwonkpa was still living in the soldiers' barracks, driving his own Jeep, and generally making himself more popular around the country. Within months, Quiwonkpa had acquired the moniker "Samuel Doe's conscience."

In November 1983, Doe had had enough of the competition. He concocted charges to have Quiwonkpa detained, but the chiefs and elders in Nimba County, where Quiwonkpa was from, joined the enlisted soldiers in pressuring Doe to let Quiwonkpa leave the country.

That same year, Ellen made another of her periodic visits to Liberia. These visits were injections of home right when she was the most homesick. She saw her mother and reunited with Maxwell. Their relationship was no longer as intense as it once had been, and they both saw other people, but Ellen still spent time with him whenever she went home.

Landing at Robertsfield, she was immediately hit by the noise and smell of Liberia—the scent of coal fires and smoked fish, which Liberians love so much they use it as seasoning for their food. And the language, the musical, fabulously oxymoronic patter of Liberian English: "I coming go" (I am about to leave your presence) and "I going come" (I am about to leave your presence but will return). Here was a chance to stuff herself with some good Liberian food, to stock up on beat-up pepper, which she had gotten into the habit of carrying around with her to bank meetings in America and Kenya, surreptitiously sprinkling the fiery stuff on the bland rubber chicken breasts before slipping the Ziploc bag back into her purse.

She was always thrilled to be back in Liberia.

She was also appalled at what she saw. It was as if time had stopped. There was no new development, no progress. The road from Robertsfield into Monrovia had so many potholes, the drive that used to take forty-five minutes now stretched to an hour and fifteen minutes. The checkpoints established by Doe's soldiers didn't help; at each one, the soldiers demanded money to let the car through. Liberia had become a police state where the police—in this case the soldiers—expected ordinary citizens to pay them personally for the privilege of going about their business.

A few days after arriving, she went to the Executive Mansion to pay the requisite respects to the man she knew she must address as Dr. Doe. One of the first things she noticed was that he was no longer wearing army fatigues or a uniform but was now in a three-piece suit. He had also gotten fat.

Doe was welcoming and asked Ellen how her mother was doing. Her mom had never met Doe, but he had been telling people that he hadn't had Ellen executed during the coup because her mother had been nice to him in the past and given him a drink of water. Ellen had no clue why he believed this story.

The meeting seemed to go well. "Next time you go to America, I want you bring me something," Doe told Ellen. "I want those trousers that got pockets them in the front and in the back." He patted his thighs and butt. He also asked for "that medicine you put in the glass that says 'Voo!'"

Ellen grinned and agreed to bring him a pair of cargo pants and some Alka-Seltzer the next time she came through town.

But things went sour when she dared to mention that Liberia wasn't looking too good these days. Soldiers were harassing citizens and market women; the checkpoints were a constant hindrance to movement. "You made promises to the Liberian people that you need to keep," she ventured.

Doe looked her in the eye. "I didn't promise them shit."

The next year, 1984, Doe declared he was ready to return the country to civilian rule. Political parties could now legally register with the Board of Elections, and promptly almost a dozen popped up. A new National Constitution Commission drafted a new constitution that set thirty-five as the minimum age to be president—a requirement that would appear to take Doe out of the running for several years.

Except that it didn't. Doe closed the gap by adding two years to his age. He established a Special Elections Commission to run the election and appointed his friends as members. And in case he hadn't made his intentions clear, he formally announced that he would run for the presidency.

Early in the summer of 1985, Ellen told her Citibank bosses that she needed a vacation. But instead of relaxing on a beach she flew to Monrovia and helped found the Liberian Action Party, which would organize a ticket to run against Doe in the upcoming elections. At the top of the ticket would be Jackson F. Doe, a popular politician, not related to Samuel Doe. The vice presidential nominee would be Ellen.

It was a daring and, from Citibank's perspective, completely unsanctioned thing to do; as a member of a private financial firm involved in global financing, she was not supposed to get involved in politics. But Ellen wasn't going to let Citibank policy stand in her way. She told herself that when her bosses found out—as she knew they eventually would—she would just quit. She'd have to quit anyway if she won, right?

Besides, she had a fallback plan.

From Monrovia she flew to the United States, to Hartford, Connecticut. Citibank thought she was still on vacation, but on July 25 she stepped through the doors of the red brick building at 11 Charter Oak Avenue that housed the Equator Bank headquarters. Ellen had met the chief executive of the bank during her Ministry of Finance days. Niles Helmboldt had founded the bank in 1974 to fund projects in Africa and had stayed on after selling it to HSBC in 1981. He had had his eye on Ellen for a while, and she had agreed, finally, to join Equator as a sort of rainmaker.

On the morning of July 25, there was excitement in the air; everyone at Equator Bank was whispering about how Helmboldt had just pilfered Ellen Johnson Sirleaf from Citibank's Nairobi office.

Ellen hadn't told Citibank yet. And she hadn't told Equator about her newly formed Liberian Action Party. Decades later, it remained unclear just how long she thought she could keep both of those financial institutions in the dark, or even why she did. When asked, she said she doesn't remember what she was thinking.

In any event, Ellen strode out of the elevator at Equator Bank, walking straight past Steve Cashin, a young bank associate, who, years later, remembered how she sailed past him, full of purpose. She paid no attention to the buzzing around her, just headed straight into the small boardroom to sit down with Cashin and a few other Equator suits to talk about the network that Helmboldt had hired her to build, full of Africa types who could provide financial consulting services to Equator's corporate finance group.

Ellen rattled off a list of people she thought could be helpful to Equator. There was S. Byron Tarr, Doe's former minister of planning—Ellen had recommended him for the job to Doe himself during one of her visits to the Liberian strongman—who, after the requisite falling-out with Doe, was now the secretary general of Ellen's new party. There was Yoweri Museveni, the new president of Uganda. There was Abdul Faragi, the fixer in Tanzania who could help Equator serve as the middleman for the German company that was trying to convert a payment from the Tanzanian government for aerial photos into U.S. dollars from Tanzanian shillings. Ellen and Faragi's proposal: buy Tanzanian cashew nuts and export them to the United States.

Equator needed locals on the ground in Africa who could help its emerging financial platform across the continent, as it provided short-term bridging loans and structured financial packages for businesses. Ellen, who had spent the previous four years at the World Bank and Citibank fattening up her Rolodex, knew a lot of locals.

At the end of the meeting, Ellen glided out of the Equator Bank office and headed to the airport. She was going to catch a flight to Nairobi to pack her things, she told her new colleagues, after two brief pit stops, in Philadelphia and Monrovia.

Of course she wasn't being honest with either Citibank or Equator.

It was July 25, the day before Liberian Independence Day—"26"—when Ellen alighted in Philadelphia and headed to a meeting of the Union of Liberian Associations in the Americas, where she would be giving the keynote speech.

In what should have come as no surprise to anyone who knew her, she spent her speech criticizing the Doe government. She took Doe himself to task for putting more time and money into building government ministries than into developing any kind of entrepreneurial structure that could build up a middle class. She called on Liberians to look into investing in the country themselves instead of leaving all of it to the growing number of foreign-owned businesses that—with the exception of the Liberian market women—ran the mercantile show in the country and then sent the profits they made back to Lebanon or Cyprus or America.

"I look at this cross-section of Liberians in this room today," Ellen said, addressing an audience that included people close to General George Toe Washington, the Liberian ambassador to the United States, whose name, unsurprisingly, drew attention in America. "I look beyond this room to several cities in several countries. I look at the many walking the streets of Monrovia or sitting quietly in an unbusy office and then I look at the many idiots in whose hands our nation's fate and progress have been placed, and I simply shake at the unnecessary and tremendous cost which we pay under the disguise of righting the wrongs of the past."

Ellen felt in the grip of a political fever she was sure was sweeping across Liberia. During her three weeks in the country forming the Liberian Action Party, she had felt a sense of destiny. Monrovia had seemed tense with almost the same kind of tension that had gripped the country in the weeks before the 1979 rice riots that marked the beginning of the end of the Tolbert regime. Everyone—at least in the growing circle of political dissidents Ellen now called friends—was talking about the looming elections and that it was finally time for Liberians to take their political destiny into their own hands and vote for sweeping change—a change not delivered by the barrel of a gun but through the ballot box.

Now was the time, she thought, to harness the country's civic awareness and deliver a rousing speech that would galvanize people to vote for change. "A government is not legitimate merely because it exists," she said. "It must belong to the people, respond to the people, acquiesce to the wishes of the people. Any government which refuses to be and to do these things must be removed by the people."

When she was done, she stepped back from the podium to cheers from the audience of Liberian expats. She did not notice that a few people were not clapping.

That same night, she left for Monrovia. She would check on her mother and the progress toward the elections that were scheduled for the end of the year, before she headed back to Nairobi to pack her things and tell her Citibank bosses she was quitting.

The summons to appear at the Mansion came a few days after her arrival; the soldiers who came to collect her took her passport, a bad sign. "President Doe now send for you," one soldier informed her.

Through the humid July streets they drove before arriving at the Mansion, where Doe awaited Ellen at his desk. He was surrounded by generals and top ministers.

Turning to T. Ernest Eastman, his minister of foreign affairs, he ordered, "Read the speech."

The words that had sounded so smart to Ellen when she was delivering them in Philadelphia now sounded reckless as Eastman's voice steadily rose, complete with inflections at crucial spots. Then Eastman got to the line where Ellen had said "all the nicest words and the biggest promises written by someone trained in the use of the pen and read by someone trained in the use of the gun are taken for what they are—words."

Doe exploded. "Oh! So you sayin' we ain't know book? We just know guns? Tha' wha' you saying?" He jumped to his feet, furious. "They think I stupid! They think I'n't know book!"

When Eastman got to the "idiots" line, Doe exploded again. While he screamed at Ellen, the other men piled on with their own abuse. "You red bitch!" they shouted, and urged Doe to take care of her "once and for all."

By now, Doe was prowling around the room. He accused Ellen of plotting against him, of working with his opponents to engineer his downfall. His ministers egged him on.

Except one—Henry Dubar, a Krahn general. "Chief," Dubar said, motioning toward Ellen, "take time wi' these type of people. You pay too much attention to her, you wi' just make her a hero."

It was wise counsel, but Doe wasn't listening that day. He turned to his minister of justice, Jenkins Scott. "Put her under house arrest," he ordered.

Scott took Ellen back to her house in Congo Town, right next to the house where her mother lived. She was to remain there, Scott told her, under guard by Doe's soldiers. She was not allowed to leave the house. She was not allowed to see her mother. She was not allowed to receive visitors.

It was August 9, 1985.

The days passed with excruciating slowness. Martha Johnson sent her daughter food and supplies every day, and sometimes, standing at the window, Ellen caught a glimpse of her walking past the house. She listened to the radio, to ELBC, where every broadcast seemed to bring a new report of Doe paranoia.

There was a lot of it to report: everybody who ever harbored aspirations of going into politics in Liberia was suddenly a coup plotter seeking to overthrow the government. Breaking off an official trip to Germany a few days after putting Ellen under house arrest, Doe returned to Liberia and announced that he had foiled another coup, this one by Amos Sawyer, a well-known politician. Sawyer too was put under house arrest. "I feel personally disappointed and surprised at the involvement of Dr. Amos Sawyer, a personal friend of mine who seems such an innocent professor, in being implicated in the plot against the state," Doe said in a sorrowful speech.

But the arrest of the popular Sawyer brought students from the University of Liberia into the streets to protest. Doe warned them to stop. The students continued, so he ordered the university closed and fired the administrators. He told his minister of defense to get the students off the streets. Soldiers stormed the university, beating the young men and, of course, raping the young women.

And Ellen? She wasn't scared; she was bored and increasingly defiant. Listening to the news on the radio, she sometimes felt euphoric. She was in the middle of a political movement that was taking over the country. Surely Doe couldn't stand up to the students for long. At some point, she thought, the weight of the people would overcome him.

She tried to sneak out a message to her supporters throughout Monrovia and around the world, giving a folded slip of paper to a servant to give to Chris Maxwell, who handed it to a Doe opponent to give to university students. "To the people," the message began: "Stand firm! Don't give in! Our course is right and we will win!"

But the message was intercepted and landed in the hands of Doe. Within hours, Ellen was taken to the post stockade at BTC and locked up.

In the blink of an eye, Doe turned Ellen into an international cause célèbre. And in that moment—when Doe's soldiers locked Ellen into that tiny cell with the toilet hole in the corner, they unwittingly ignited the women's movement in Liberia.

Chapter 5

GIO GIRL

Monrovia, 1985

In Liberia a woman's place is in the market, selling oranges and potato greens and kola nuts. It is in the hot outdoor kitchen, sweating as she bends over a mortar to pound fermented cassava for fufu. It is in the field, baby strapped to her back as she hacks at the sugarcane stalks that will fetch the money that will pay for this semester's school fees for her children. And it is on her back in the dirt as one, two, three, four drunk soldiers rape her in front of her crying children.

It is in her lover's bedroom, sitting on the mattress, shivering in the air-conditioning and trying to block out the image of her colleagues who were executed by firing squad on the beach days before. It is in the cabinet room of the Executive Mansion as she tries to stem the nausea that rises when she sees those same executioners discussing the budget she put together as they look for loopholes from which they can extract money.

In Liberia a woman's place is not in a jail cell.

There are many things Liberian women will tolerate. They accept that it is their burden to shoulder all of the responsibility for keeping their family fed, whether that means farming alone all day or submitting to gang rape as the price that must be paid to keep their children alive. But jail, for some reason, is a step too far.

Before Dr. Samuel Doe threw Ellen Johnson Sirleaf into a jail cell at the Barclay Training Center, she was, to the developing world, just one of many promising, ambitious West African government bureaucrats. But Doe changed all that when he locked her in the post stockade and charged her with sedition. He turned her from a bureaucrat into a global hero.

Inside BTC, Ellen and her fellow inmates, who included university students who had demonstrated against Doe, occupied themselves by singing and performing mock radio shows. They sang church hymns, they sang patriotic songs like "The Lone Star Forever," an ode to the Liberian flag, which looks like the American flag except it has only one star.

> *The lone star forever!*
> *The lone star forever! . . .*
> *O long may it float o'er land and o'er seas*
> *Desert it? No! Never!*
> *Uphold it? ay, ever!*
> *O shout for the lone-starred banner, All Hail!*

Once a day there was rice, the Liberian staple. Sometimes it was dry rice, and sometimes, for flavor, there was a little palm oil and smoked fish; Liberians call this bonny because of the little bones. The days passed excruciatingly slowly. Ellen and her cellmate, a university student named Lucia Massiley, lived in constant fear of the rapes and beatings they were sure were coming.

After a week, Doe announced that Ellen would be tried before a military tribunal for sedition. It was late August 1985.

He really should have listened to General Dubar, who weeks before had warned him against turning Ellen into a martyr. When word spread that Ellen Johnson Sirleaf, the Citibank vice president, the former World Bank bureaucrat, the former finance minister of Liberia, and, above all, *a woman* was now in a Liberian jail cell on political charges, the reaction was swift.

The *New York Times* began running news stories and editorials about the political prisoners in Liberia. Other newspapers followed suit. Citibank demanded Ellen's release. The U.S. Congress passed a resolution to block all foreign assistance to Liberia if Doe failed to release all political prisoners. The Reagan administration, under pressure from Congress, temporarily suspended approximately $25 million in aid and made the release of Ellen a requirement to lift the ban.

But it was the women of Liberia whose mobilization would prove most effective. It is ironic, given the epidemic of gang rapes and sexual assaults by drunken soldiers since the 1980 coup, that it took an arrest, not a rape, to bring a storm of female protest. But the refrain on the streets quickly became "No, no, they can't keep that woman in BTC."

It is true that in the days after the 1980 coup, a handful of women had been arrested and taken to BTC, including Ethel Dunbar, a former member of the legislature, and other women with connections to the Tolbert government. Beyond those initial arrests, the many other atrocities committed against Liberian women usually took place out of the public eye. When the thirteen-year-old daughters of former Tolbert government ministers were hauled out of their homes, taken to the beach, and gang-raped by Doe's drunken soldiers, those crimes were not reported; no mother was going to broadcast that her daughter had been raped. When nine-year-old Gio and Mano girls were sodomized in their village by newly promoted generals, the people didn't run to the police station. Why bring additional shame to an already brutalized young girl?

But if Liberian women seemed willing to accept that violent sexual crimes would be committed against them every day, they couldn't stomach the public crimes. Doe's decision to put Ellen in a cell at BTC for an extended period—and then to brag about it on the radio and finally to haul her before a military tribunal—struck Liberian women as official sanctioning of female persecution. Women who never before even thought about engaging in politics got organized. University women drafted market women to join the cause. Going door to door, they collected more than ten thousand signatures calling for Ellen's release. They petitioned the government, warning Doe that if he didn't listen to them, they would take to the streets to protest.

The trial began on Thursday, September 5. Each morning, Ellen was escorted on foot by police officers and soldiers from BTC through the streets of Boozy Quarters (so named because so many Boozy people—an ethnic group, not a bunch of drunks—lived there) to the Temple of Justice, across the street from the Executive Mansion. Women came out in droves to cheer for her. The atmosphere was festive, with Ellen's police escorts smiling and waving at the assembled crowds that lined the streets.

General Dubar's prediction was coming true. During the time that Ellen had sat in jail with Lucia Massiley singing "The Lone Star Forever" with the other dissidents, she had become a kind of folk hero. But still Doe did not listen.

At the trial, which lasted a week, government representatives read the long list of charges against Ellen. She had plotted against the government. She had not demonstrated proper respect for the institution of the government. She had willfully tried to incite the public. She had called the president an idiot. After a week, on September 13, she was found guilty. In Liberian style—which acknowledges that it is the president, and not the courts, who holds all the power—Ellen politely thanked the court for having given her the chance to defend herself and then asked the Idiot for clemency.

She hadn't actually made an attempt at insurrection, she told the court, and wasn't that what sedition was supposed to be about? Ellen implored the judges to think about what they were doing. Liberia needed all of her people and all of their talents if it were to succeed. She tried not to appear defiant—this was hard for her—but she was also determined not to be apologetic. She wasn't really worried yet. During the trial, she had known that she would be found guilty; Doe would have lost face otherwise. But she also believed that once she was found guilty, she would get a slap on the wrist and be sent home.

"All rise," the judge said, and then he read the sentence: ten years of hard labor at Belle Yalla maximum security prison.

Ellen swallowed. Not a slap on the wrist, then. Belle Yalla was a place so notorious that parents had long used it as a threat to misbehaving children. Deep in the bush and accessible only by air or on foot, Belle Yalla had always been, in essence, a death sentence disguised as a hard labor camp. Prisoners sent to Belle Yalla rarely came back. The few visitors allowed over the years reported prisoners so physically disfigured by their treatment they resembled people from the Stone Age.

Stunned, Ellen stared at the judges. She knew that if she went to Belle Yalla, she would die.

But the harshness of the sentence would prove to be Doe's undoing. As soon as the news hit the radio that afternoon, the women's groups announced they would protest in the streets of Monrovia. Young girls who had never heard of Ellen Johnson Sirleaf now began singing songs demanding her freedom. The international pressure increased, and newspaper editorial pages, nongovernmental organizations, and Western governments called on Doe to release her.

In the days following the verdict, Ellen sat on the floor of her concrete cell day and night, feeling anxious. Incongruously she found herself fretting about Citibank, which she knew had taken up her cause. By getting involved in politics, she had violated the bank's code of conduct. And still Citibank was lobbying both the American and the Liberian governments for her release. She felt guilty about the worry she was causing her mother, her family, and her friends. Someone had smuggled a note from a friend into her cell that read, "We'd rather have a live ant than a dead elephant."

Ten days after the verdict, the door to her cell opened and a soldier appeared. Doe had caved. Just like that, she was free to go.

But her freedom came at a price. Before releasing Ellen, Doe met with the members of her fledgling political party. "Ya'll gotta expel her," he told them. In exchange for dropping Ellen from the ticket on which she had planned to run as vice president, Doe allowed the LAP to register for the upcoming elections. The party leaders quickly acquiesced, releasing a statement condemning her "seditious" activities. The irony is that they abandoned her just as quickly as she had abandoned her Tolbert colleagues after the 1980 coup.

An angry Ellen left BTC on the day of her release. Doe's officials had called her brother Carney to try to get him to promise that Ellen would withdraw from politics and leave the country. Carney knew better than to make that promise on behalf of his sister. It turned out to be a smart move on his part because on the same day she got out of prison and found out that she had been dropped from the LAP ticket, Ellen announced that she was going to run anyway—for the Senate.

Released from jail just three weeks before the scheduled October 15 elections, Ellen did not have a lot of time to campaign. In any case, Doe was not making campaigning easy for opposition candidates. Those not on his ticket were routinely harassed and beaten up by soldiers and subjected to extortion. Local jails across the country filled with people running on tickets that opposed Doe. There were so many illegal searches of the homes of campaigning politicians that at one point the Special Elections Commission established by Doe himself and filled with his hand-picked allies ordered the searches to stop.

A few days after Ellen got out of jail, soldiers again showed up at her house. Doe wanted to see her at the Mansion.

She found him in his office, looking tired.

"I want you to leave the country," he said. "Just leave quietly. Before the elections. You can have your passport back, we wi' leave you 'lone."

Ellen looked at him. Was he kidding? She had already paid the price for daring to run for office when he put her in prison; now he wanted her to leave without collecting the reward? "Sorry," she said. "I want to stay."

Doe seemed annoyed but resigned, and she started campaigning. She traveled throughout several counties, promoting herself as well as other LAP candidates, especially Jackson Doe, who was running at the top of the ticket. She even campaigned for Emmanuel Koromah, whom the LAP chose to replace her as its vice presidential candidate.

She visited the markets, where she had long conversations with the women who minded the stalls. She took solace in the international observers and reporters following her around, telling herself that Doe wouldn't rearrest her with the international spotlight shining so brightly.

Still Doe was making it difficult. While roughly 30 percent of Liberia's people lived in Monrovia, 70 percent were "up country," as everything outside the capital was called. Any politician who ventured out of Monrovia could mine votes in Nimba and Lofa and Grand Gedeh and Sino and Margibi and Bong counties. Doe knew he could be defeated in the hinterland, so he required that parties be granted permission from the Ministry of Internal Affairs and the local county superintendent to hold so much as a simple campaign rally. In the meantime, all the public facilities were booked by Doe's party, and opposition rallies were routinely dispersed by the police. For instance, the Margibi superintendent broke up a simple gathering in Kakata for local Unity Party supporters to welcome their candidates on the grounds that it constituted a secret meeting. In another case, the LAP was required to stop campaigning in Margibi County on the day Doe was scheduled to pass through the area.

Not ones for subtlety, Doe and his allies let it be known that there would be violence if Doe didn't win. On Election Day, Colonel Harrison Pennue, one of the original participants in the 1980 coup and a member of the PRC (Harrison drove a car with license plates that read IKT for "I Killed Tolbert"), said in a radio interview that if Doe didn't win, he was ready to overthrow a new government within three days: "Who want win, I not dead. I will overthrow you. I still leopard. When we started 1980 nobody asked us to vote." The interview was broadcast repeatedly on ELBC, in case Liberians didn't get the point.

Election Day was sunny, hot, and dry, at the end of the rainy season and the beginning of the stretch of dry months. All over the country, hundreds of thousands of Liberians lined up at polling stations. But soon after the voting began, it became apparent that the results were being manipulated.

Doe arrived at City Hall around 9 a.m. to cast the first ballot of the day. People who had been waiting in line for hours stood aside out of respect and let him do so. But later in the day, a riot nearly broke out when his cabinet ministers tried to do the same thing. This time people who had been waiting in the hot sun to vote refused to step aside. It took three hours to calm tempers, but in the end, in this case at least, the people won.

Up country, soldiers in rural areas forced voters to shout out their choice as they dropped their ballot into the box. Polling booths suddenly materialized at BTC and other military barracks. Children of soldiers were casting ballots, and opposition party observers were barred from military polling booths.

When the polls closed, the counting began, and that process continued for so long it became clear that Doe's Special Elections Commission was making up the numbers and manufacturing votes. Although unofficial observers and journalists were on hand, none of them had any say over the handling of the vote count, leaving it up to Doe's Special Elections Commission. The head of the commission insisted that party representation at the counting violated the secrecy of the vote, but after widespread complaints, he yielded and allowed opposition party members to watch the vote count, but from a distance of at least fifteen feet. They could see little from that distance, of course, although, as it turned out, still too much for the commission to bear. Early exit polls taken by the Liberia Action Party showed that Samuel Doe was losing badly all over the country, including in his home county of Grand Gedeh. And once the actual counting began, those exit polls appeared to be accurate; the few tally sheets the Special Elections Commission allowed the opposition to study showed Doe trailing. One American journalist reported on the BBC that reliable indications suggested a 60 percent landslide for LAP.

Two days into the counting, with all signs pointing to an LAP victory, the head of Doe's Special Elections Commission halted the count. The observers, he said, hadn't obeyed the fifteen-feet rule. The counting would have to start over. He ordered all the ballot boxes to be taken to the government's Unity Conference Center just outside Monrovia and brought in a new batch of hand-picked people to count them. Twenty of the new counters were from Doe's home county. On October 29, two weeks after the elections, Samuel Doe was announced the winner. His Special Elections Commission said he eked out 50.9 percent of the vote.

Most African despots who stage elections and then declare themselves winners did so by announcing that they had won 90 percent of the vote. In an uncharacteristic flash of sophistication, Doe knew no one would believe that, so he took only 50.9 percent—enough for him to win without needing a runoff, but not so excessive that his benefactors in the Reagan administration would cut off aid.

In the parliamentary elections, Doe's commission announced that his party had taken fifty-one of the sixty-four seats in the House of Representatives. In the Senate, Doe's party had won all but five seats. One was Ellen's.

Sitting with some of her friends and supporters at home as they listened to the announcement on the radio, Ellen felt her stomach tighten at the news. A few hours later, an election official came by with an even more stark number: Ellen was the highest vote-getter in the Senate.

Having inadvertently turned her into a cult hero, Doe knew that a win for Ellen, with her international finance bona fides, would give his fraudulent elections a sheen of respectability. Unsurprisingly, Ellen refused to cooperate. She would not take her Senate seat, she announced, because the election results were fraudulent. She and the other four opposition candidates who won Senate seats would boycott.

Doe was furious. So was the Reagan administration, which, eager to move on now that the elections were over, urged Ellen to get on board as well. Chester Crocker, the assistant secretary of state, told a skeptical U.S. congressional subcommittee that the Liberian elections hadn't been so bad. He even praised Doe for claiming only 50.9 percent of the vote, adding that such a modest win was "unheard of in the rest of Africa, where incumbent rulers normally claim victories of 95 to 100 percent."

Ellen recalled later, "The United States felt that my taking a seat in the Liberian Senate would lend the sheen of credibility to Doe's blatantly fraudulent elections. Which was precisely the reason I had to refuse."

Twenty-seven days after the election, on the morning of November 12, 1985, Thomas Quiwonkpa returned home to Liberia. The popular former army chief and famous "conscience" of Samuel Doe had fled the country two years before, but recently rumors claimed he had flown to Freetown, Sierra Leone, where he was planning to mount a coup against the Doe regime.

Quiwonkpa had reportedly expressed outrage that Doe had put Ellen in jail. "Why de man go jail de woman? I wi' free her." Although Doe himself was forced to free Ellen, Quiwonkpa's words would come back to haunt her.

Early that November morning, Quiwonkpa and twenty-four heavily armed men slipped over the Sierra Leonean border into Liberia, where their operation immediately ran into trouble when, in an exchange of fire with Liberian border guards, Quiwonkpa's logistics officer was shot and killed. The rest of Quiwonkpa's men continued on to Monrovia, but now they were launching their coup without a map of their operation or one of their most important generals.

In Monrovia they seized the ELBC radio station and began urging soldiers to join them against Doe. Residents woke up that morning to a friendly male voice on the radio announcing that "patriotic forces under the command of General Quiwonkpa had toppled the Doe regime": "Our forces have completely surrounded the city." What the voice didn't say was that those forces were very small in number and were counting on the Liberian Army to abandon Doe and join their former commanding general.

"We decided to take the ultimate gamble in the tasks of national liberation," Quiwonkpa said at one point. "You shall have free and fair elections and a democratic society. You shall regain your self-respect and human dignity, which have been abused by Samuel Doe." The radio voice even read a list of names—including Jackson Doe, the leader of Ellen's party and presumed true winner of the presidential election—to whom Quiwonkpa would soon be turning over control of the country.

On hearing that Doe had been toppled, the city erupted, with people dancing and cheering in the streets in unrestrained jubilation. Pictures of Doe were stripped from walls, and demonstrators carried huge posters with photos of Quiwonkpa.

The mood quickly soured when, a few hours later, a different male voice was heard on the radio. Samuel Doe was broadcasting from the Executive Mansion.

"The coup has failed."

Ellen had been careening around the streets of Monrovia celebrating with a friend, Robert Phillips, happily trying to find out what was going on, when the second announcement came over the car radio. "Quiwonkpa is not man enough to enter the Mansion," Doe declared. "I am still the commander in chief of the armed forces of Liberia and head of state."

Ellen and Phillips looked at each other in horror. "They see us on the road, they wi' kill us," she said. Quickly, the two concocted a scheme. A former police director had just died; they would go to his house and pretend they were there to comfort the grieving family. Then they'd go home, and if anyone stopped them to ask what they were about, they would say they had come out to offer their condolences to the family of the official.

They stayed at the family's home for half an hour. It was not hard to feign grief—they were both panic-stricken anyway. Eventually the two left, and Phillips dropped Ellen off at her mother's house.

Late in the evening, a Jeep roared into her mother's yard, and Doe's soldiers, poured out and surrounded the house, shooting wildly.

Looking at her frail mother, who had dropped to her knees and started praying, Ellen knew she couldn't let the soldiers enter the house. Quickly, she walked out into the yard. "I know y'all came for me," she told the soldiers. "I wi' go wi' you if you leave my ma 'lone." And she got in the Jeep.

Ellen knew she was in serious trouble. For one thing, she was a member of Jackson Doe's party, whom Quiwonkpa had proclaimed the rightfully elected president. Second, Quiwonkpa had said that when he returned to Liberia he planned to free Ellen. Third, there was a copy of a speech of hers that Quiwonkpa had signed—what if someone found it? Fourth, while she hadn't planned to take an active role in the coup, she had heard rumors of it, and she certainly would have allied herself with Quiwonkpa had he been successful. Fifth, she had danced in celebration that very morning—in full view of dozens of people—when she heard on the radio that Quiwonkpa had launched his coup.

So yes, she was in trouble. *Why the hell hadn't the damn man secured Doe before going on the radio?* Ellen thought.

"Take us to Jackson Doe house," the soldiers demanded.

"I'nt know where he living oh," Ellen lied. The man was probably already marked for death. She wasn't going to speed the process by leading the soldiers straight to his door.

Another Jeep pulled up to them, and the vehicle she was in quickly pulled over. The reaction was so swift that she knew whoever was in the second Jeep was a higher authority.

"We coming from Schieffin. We got instructions to kill her there," said the officer in the second Jeep.

Ellen was pushed out of the car; one young soldier pulled back his leg to kick her, but she quickly jumped out of the way. She was bundled into the backseat of the second Jeep, pressed on either side by soldiers.

As they drove toward Schieffin barracks, on the road to Robertsfield Airport, the soldiers barraged her with verbal abuse. One took a match from his pocket, lit it, and held it close to her hair. A few minutes later, another soldier grabbed her hand and pointed at her gold ring. Saying, "You gwen die, wha' you need ring for?," he pulled the ring off her finger.

Ellen was in a preternaturally calm state that sometimes takes over when people are in absolute danger. She knew only too well what was coming: a lone woman, surrounded by drunken soldiers taking her to an isolated barracks outside of town.

It was dusk when the Jeep rumbled through the Schiefflin gates, but instead of going straight to the barracks, the driver veered away and drove to the beach. "This where de grave at," jeered one of the soldiers crammed in the back with her. "This where we killing you."

The driver spun the Jeep in a big circle in the sand, then headed back to the barracks, to a small building that held only two cells. They led Ellen toward a tiny dank cell, next to a cell with a crush of fifteen or so men. As she walked past them, the condemned men recognized her. This was, after all, the woman who had challenged President Doe, who had won a Senate seat, who had then refused to take the seat she won after accusing Doe of rigging the elections.

"Mama Sirleaf!" one of the condemned called out, adopting the moniker that Liberians use for any woman older than eighteen when they want something from her. "Mama Sirleaf, I know you, I know your ma! Help us!"

Ellen's guards opened her cell door and pushed her in. It stank of urine. In a corner was a stack of sand, meant to be used as a toilet, in the manner of kitty litter.

Next door, the entreaties continued. "Help us, try save us, oh. I hold your foot."

"I beg you."

"I beg you, help us."

Ellen called back, "How I will save you? How I will save you, I here too?"

When night fell suddenly, as it does near the equator, the prisoners in the two cells talked to each other. The terrified men continued to implore Ellen to save them. "Wha' will happen?" one man kept asking. "Wha' will happen?"

Thirty minutes later, they found out.

A swarm of soldiers arrived, carrying rope. They pulled out prisoners one by one and began tying them together. When they ran out of rope, one soldier came into Ellen's cell, screaming, "Gimme your shoe tie! Gimme your shoe tie!"

Shaking now, she untied her shoelaces and gave them to the soldier, who used them to tie the last man to the group.

The men were crying in earnest now, as they were led into the darkness.

The one who had first recognized Ellen turned to her as he was dragged away. "Please!" he cried. "I know Ma Martha!"

The words seized her heart. This man really did know her. Martha was her mother's name.

But what did it matter? Slowly, she collapsed back into a corner, trembling. She could still hear their cries. They continued right up until the rat-a-tat of machine guns took over.

The soldiers returned to Ellen's cell, excited, high-spirited, and mean. "Your time coming," they taunted her. "Ehn you want humbug our Pape?"

"You dry, red, funky woman!"

"Who you think you are?"

Ellen sat in the corner of the fetid cell, her eyes squeezed shut, her lips moving silently as she prayed. Would they rape her before they killed her?

Hours passed. Outside, the soldiers drank and became even rowdier. Then, just past midnight, one soldier walked up to her cell, stood at the bars, and stared at her.

Several minutes passed in silence. Then he said, "I'm going to fuck you."

He opened the cell door, and Ellen rose to her feet, heart pounding.

But just as the soldier was entering her cell, a voice behind him said, "As you were." The soldier dropped his hands.

"Retreat," said the voice.

The soldier closed the cell door, locked it, and moved away.

Her savior stepped forward into the light. He was slightly older than the others, in his midtwenties, with beautiful dark skin and a serious face. Looking at him, Ellen wanted to cry.

"They say you Gola?" he asked her.

"My pa Gola," she replied.

"Say something in Gola."

"Eee-seh."

"Where your pa' town?"

"Julejuah," she said.

Her rescuer stared at her for what felt like forever. Finally, he said, "Okay. I will stay here tonight. Nobody will humbug you."

So on that night, Ellen Johnson Sirleaf was not raped.

But someone else was. A young Gio girl, who also had been captured and brought to Schiefflin, was gang-raped by soldiers there in the early hours of the morning, as Ellen huddled in her cell. Gio and Mano were rivals of the Krahn, and Quiwonkpa was Gio. Whether Ellen's would-be rapist took part as well, she would never know. After brutalizing the girl, the soldiers brought her, naked and crying hysterically, to Ellen's cell, and pushed her in.

She looked to be around nineteen or twenty. She was bleeding and her eyes were wild with fear. Jumping up, Ellen put her arms around her and lowered her onto the floor. In the corner, the two rocked back and forth, clutching each other. Slowly, the girl's cries softened. Her naked body started to tremble.

Leaving her new cellmate for a moment, Ellen went up to the bars. There were a few soldiers milling around, alongside the one who had rescued her.

"Aye man, y'all think about your ma them," Ellen said, her voice shaking.

The soldiers looked at her. She tried again.

"Think about y'all sisters them."

Still nothing.

"I beg y'all, at least please bring *lapa* or something for the child to wear."

Finally, one of the men left and brought back a piece of cloth, and Ellen helped the girl cover herself. For the rest of the night, the two huddled side by side. They did not sleep, just sat and rocked back and forth as the minutes ticked away until dawn, when they came for Ellen.

Busting open the door of the cell, Lieutenant Harris, the officer who had brought her to Schiefflin, strode in and pulled her up by the arm. He and another soldier took her into a room where six soldiers sat around a table. One introduced himself as General Moses Wright, the commander of the Camp Schiefflin Brigade. "Why you causing all this trouble?" he asked.

"I not causing no trouble. I ain't got nothing to do with wha' happened."

"Why youn't want work for President Doe? Just go take your seat in the legislature."

So that was all it would take to get her out? Take her Senate seat? The seat she won anyway? Ellen looked at General Wright for a long time. Then she shook her head. "I sorry," she said. "I can't do it."

The men argued with her for a few more minutes; she didn't budge. Finally, General Wright shrugged. "Tha' your business," he said.

The soldiers took her and her cellmate into the field in the middle of the barracks and ordered them to wash the dirty cooking pans, while the soldiers settled themselves on the ground to jeer at them. Some of their families even came and joined them to watch the show: the well-to-do Ellen bent next to the young, gang-raped Gio girl, washing dishes for the soldiers who had brutalized them.

Ellen was filling a bucket with water, but the pump was slow. "Why you taking so long?" one soldier yelled. "People want eat!"

"I waiting for the water to fill the bucket."

"Then talk to the pump!" came the response. The others, laughing, repeated, "Talk to the pump! Talk to the pump!"

So Ellen talked to the pump. "Pump, can you please pour the water fast so the soldiers them can eat? Hurry up, pump."

"Hurry, pump."

The soldiers were in hysterics now. Finally the bucket was full, and the two women began to wash the rice.

Then Lieutenant Harris rode up in a Jeep. "I came for my prisoner," he told the men. And to Ellen he said, "I carrying you to President Doe."

Now, suddenly, came the terror.

Ellen had taken solace in the hope that she was too well-known a politician for the soldiers at Schiefflin to kill her. They needed some kind of formal authorization. Now the man who would grant that authorization, the man she had publicly called an idiot, was sitting at the Executive Mansion, waiting for her.

As she walked to the Jeep, Ellen looked at her young Gio cellmate. The two women had spent less than twelve hours together. One was now going to face the man she was certain would be her executioner. The other was staying with the men who were certain to rape her again.

The Jeep pulled away and Ellen turned in the seat to stare at the young girl in the field continuing the painstaking job of washing rice. She would never see the young woman again. But in many ways, that young Gio girl would change the course of history in West Africa. That Gio girl would become another stick of fuel for the fire of the women's movement that Samuel Doe had started.

Chapter 6

CULT HERO
Monrovia, 1985

Little girls do not come out of the womb vowing to become activists for female power. They don't spend their childhood thinking about how they will repair the indignities, large and small, that bleed women daily.

It's a series of things that multiply and turn ordinary women into movements of female determination. You're living your life, sweeping floors at Rennebohm Drug Store in Madison, Wisconsin, when your husband storms in to yell at you in front of your white boss lady. You're huddling with your sons inside your house at night, wondering what catastrophe awaits you, while that same husband sits in his parked car outside for hours. You're stunned by the violent shock of a hand slapping your face, delivered by the man who promised to love, honor, and cherish you till death do you part.

You feel the warm, wet skin of a brutalized, naked, hysterical young woman as she crouches in the corner, bleeding, after being savaged by the men who swore an oath to protect Liberia and her people.

"I wanted to be a schoolteacher, like my mother," Ellen said, looking back thirty years later. Describing that night at the Schiefflin barracks, she would use the mental sleight of hand that is common among survivors of unimaginable horror. She would relay the events of that night with no emotion whatsoever.

The joyride on the beach, which the soldier told her would be her execution site.

The useless pleas from the condemned men, that she find a way for them to be spared.

The overwhelming terror of men who know they are about to die.

The overwhelming terror of knowing you are about to be raped.

The gut-clutching anger of holding a young woman after she has been raped by soldier after soldier after soldier after soldier.

"That's what I wanted to do, when I was young," Ellen said. "To teach."

The young Ellen, the pekin who would na' be easy oh, may have started off wanting to teach, but this was not a woman who was destined for the granular. Hers would be a different destiny, one launched in a Jeep by the young Gio girl who had been her cellmate.

As Ellen and her captors drove away from Schiefflin, she was struck by the silence. Unlike the drive the day before, with its soundtrack of sadistic taunting, this time there were no jeers. No insults. Nothing.

Everyone in the Jeep knew what was about to happen. An unhinged Samuel K. Doe was waiting at the Mansion for his prisoner. The soldiers knew they were about to see the execution of a woman. But women were for raping, not for killing. If they died from being raped, so be it. But executing a female political prisoner? This just was not done. The same men in the Jeep who had taunted her with execution just the day before—that was just horseplay, after all—were now quiet as they drove her to Doe.

For forty-five minutes, they drove through the deserted city, passing trucks of soldiers as they patrolled in the aftermath of the Quiwonkpa coup attempt. Quiwonkpa still hadn't been found, and the soldiers were looking for him, going from house to house.

Finally, the Jeep arrived at the Mansion, and Ellen's stomach tightened. This was it.

The head of Doe's Executive Mansion guard, Colonel Edward Smith, walked up to the Jeep and looked at Ellen. After a long silence he asked, "Why you making all this trouble in this country?"

In a daze, Ellen repeated her now stock answer: "I not making no trouble." Even in her fear of what was coming, she was not giving in. She had witnessed Doe's brutality firsthand. A political compromise was out of the question. Taking that Senate seat would mean sanctioning what those soldiers had done to that Gio girl at the Schiefflin barracks.

Smith sighed. He seemed weary. "We all one people here. Why we fighting this way?"

He turned to Lieutenant Harris. "You can't take her to the president. We know what will happen if you carry her to him."

After a pause, Smith ordered an alternative: "Carry her to BTC."

But as the Jeep started to pull away, Smith stopped them. He looked at Harris. "Tell them I said don't hurt her. Just put her in prison. Don't do nothing to her. On my command."

Intense relief flooded Ellen as the Jeep turned around and headed back up the hill, away from the Executive Mansion, finally turning left onto Capital Bypass. She stared unseeingly out of the window as they passed the Temple of Justice, then Boozy Quarters, before the car turned left into the BTC gates.

She was going to live. Colonel Edward Smith had just seen to that.

Samuel Doe did not just crush the attempted rebellion. He obliterated it.

Besides Ellen, Doe had his soldiers round up opposing politicians from all over the country, including Jackson Doe and Edward Kesselly, another presidential candidate. With Quiwonkpa still in hiding, Doe's soldiers went on a search-and-destroy mission across the capital, killing members of Quiwonkpa's Gio tribe and the Mano people who supported him, looting the homes of opposition candidates, and, of course, raping the women who crossed their path. Monrovia residents reported truckloads of dead bodies rumbling through the streets, en route to various mass graves around the city.

Doe went on the radio to announce another dusk-to-dawn curfew. Everyone, including foreign diplomats, was subject to the curfew. "If you are caught one minute after 6 o'clock, you will be executed," he promised.

It took Doe's soldiers three days to find Quiwonkpa, hiding in a house eight miles outside of town. They paraded his body, riddled with bullets, through the streets and took it to BTC, where they put it on view in a public show. A jubilant Doe, holding a rifle, rode in an open car to BTC to view the corpse.

Even after Quiwonkpa was killed, Doe's soldiers didn't rest. They cut up his corpse like meat and paraded the pieces through Monrovia.

Doe launched his ethnic retaliation campaign, focusing his efforts on the Gio and Mano people of Nimba County, laying waste to entire villages, in a purge that set the stage for the civil war that would engulf Liberia five years later.

Ever since the so-called Congo people had come in 1822, the importance of ethnic background had hovered over Liberia's people, differenti-
ating the haves from the have-nots. The 1980 coup had reversed the status
of Congo people and country people, but only briefly; after Doe's initial
purge, the Congo people still had enough money and education to either
escape to America or stay in Liberia enjoying the same—though slightly
muted—lifestyle they had enjoyed in the past.

But now one's ethnic background was a matter of life and death.
Quiwonkpa was Gio and supported by the Mano. Doe was Krahn. The
question "Wha' your tribe?" became the first thing Doe's Krahn soldiers
asked when they stopped young men on the street. The wrong answer
meant the difference between continuing on your way and being shot in
the head.

Other members of Liberia's twenty-eight ethnic groups were desperate
to show they had no dog in this fight. When stopped by soldiers, they
spoke Bassa or Kpelle. Gio boys stammered to speak a different language,
desperate to prove they weren't Gio. It worked for some; others were hauled
out of the backs of pickup trucks and buses and shot on the spot.

Doe also went after people with connections to Sierra Leone. Furious
that Quiwonkpa had crossed over the border, he recalled Liberia's ambassador to Freetown and threatened to cut off diplomatic relations with his
neighbor. And his soldiers went to work on the opposition candidates they
had rounded up.

From rumors and news reports that reached her fetid cell in Monrovia
Central Prison, where she had been moved, Ellen learned that Jackson
Doe, the true winner of the 1985 presidential elections, was also in prison.

On January 6, 1986, Samuel Doe was again sworn in as Liberia's president. As a gesture toward reconciliation—belated, of course, as he had
already killed thousands of people—he released eighteen political prisoners who had been arrested during the attempted coup. But not Ellen
Johnson Sirleaf. Instead, she was formally charged with sedition, a crime
that carried the death penalty.

Once again, her international contacts sprang into action. In the
United States, Jennie appeared on television news reports to talk about her
courageous sister, imprisoned unjustly. The U.S. Congress again pushed the

Reagan administration to threaten to cut off aid if she was not released, and newspaper editorials rallied behind her.

On the Liberian airwaves, too, there were broadcasts about the woman—*a woman, my people*—who was sitting in Monrovia Central Prison because of politics. All the broadcasts carried the Doe administration's version of events: that Ellen had been plotting to overthrow the government. But few people believed that. All they saw was a tiny, feisty woman, losing weight by the day, imprisoned by the government over "ashtray"—Liberian English for "nonsense."

But as Ellen lost weight on the anemic prison rations, she grew in stature in the eyes of Liberian women and girls.

One girl paying attention to the radio broadcasts was Grace-tee McGill. At nineteen years old and weighing only ninety-five pounds, Grace-tee had graduated from Tubman High School and was living at home with her parents, getting ready to start classes at R. C. Lawson Institute. She spent her days listening to the ELBC broadcasts about the woman in jail who had become a hero to her.

Here was a woman fighting for Liberia, Grace-tee thought. Here was a woman unafraid to stand up to Doe. All day Grace-tee talked about Ellen to anyone who would listen. "Why is Ellen Johnson Sirleaf in jail?" she asked. It was a question repeated around town by young girls and marketeers and Holy Ghost women, on the streets of Monrovia, in newspapers around the world, and, most significant for Doe, by the American officials who wrote the checks that kept his government afloat.

Finally, after nine months, Doe had had enough.

On a soggy July day in 1986, soldiers arrived at Monrovia Central Prison and told Ellen to get in a pickup truck with other political prisoners. As suddenly as she was taken into custody, she was being freed.

The soldiers told her to ride in the front while the male prisoners would ride in the back. They didn't realize that in the year since Doe had first thrown Ellen Johnson Sirleaf in jail, the big-mouthed banker had become a political icon. And that political icon knew how to make a statement. Ellen wasn't about to get in the front seat for what she knew would be a ride watched by all of Liberia. Oh no. She climbed into the back with the men being released. The back of the truck took on a celebratory air, as the newly released political prisoners looked out at the crowd that was forming in the streets.

After nine months in jail, Ellen was looking Rasta. She had cornrowed the roots of her hair and pulled it back. She wore a striped wool hat, despite the intense tropical heat. Her tight T-shirt was emblazoned with the words PEACE and SHALOM and two doves; it was a shirt her mother had brought her when visiting her in jail. In the back of the pickup truck, she was instantly recognizable—and instantly iconic.

As the truck slowly began to move, one soldier walked up and put his hand on her arm. It was Lieutenant Harris, who had taken her to Schieffelin. He reached into the front pocket of his uniform shirt and took out her gold ring. Ellen stared at him and took the ring back.

What a dreamlike place, Liberia.

ELBC broadcast the news "Ellen Johnson Sirleaf is free!" again and again. Electrified, women rushed to the streets to cheer, following the pickup truck as it made its way from Monrovia Central Prison.

Soon word went out that Ellen was headed to her political party's headquarters. While she was in jail, LAP had joined the Unity Party to form a grand coalition. Now her first stop out of jail was to the Unity Party headquarters.

Grace-tee McGill was in the kitchen, cooking potato greens and rice as her mother had asked her to, when she heard the announcement on the radio. She ran outside; people were streaming through her family's yard, using it as a shortcut from Camp Johnson Road, Johnson Street, and Capital Bypass. She joined the crowd, leaving the pot of potato greens on the stove to burn. Grace-tee didn't care. She wanted to see the woman who had survived prison, the bold woman who had stood up to Doe. Grace-tee let the crowd sweep her along to Unity Party headquarters.

When she got there, she found the place packed with people. The soldiers who had escorted Ellen from jail had stayed on to celebrate with her. Unity Party members were dancing; Monrovia police officers were looking on, some of them smiling. And Ellen, jubilant and defiant at the same time, was in the middle of it all.

Her eyes bulging, Grace-tee pushed to the front. When Ellen climbed up on the table to talk to the crowd, Grace-tee was convinced her icon was looking straight at her. She pushed in closer.

"My fellow Liberians!" Ellen shouted at the crowd.

The place got quiet.

"In union strong, success is sure, we cannot fail."

Grace-tee realized she was mouthing the words as Ellen recited the second stanza of the Liberian national anthem, "All Hail, Liberia, Hail."

"With God above, our rights to prove, we will o'er all prevail!"

The two women, and all the other people in the crowded hall, kept going.

"We will o'er all prevail!"

Ellen didn't notice the young woman. All she saw was the sea of people cheering and crying with her—people, she determined to herself, whom she would one day lead.

The stage was now set for the revolution that would overturn gender politics in West Africa.

But the men still had one more act to play. And it was a doozy.

Chapter 7

IT'S FOR YOU, SIR

1989

Good-looking, short of stature but long on ambition, Charles Taylor had burst onto the international scene in spectacular fashion in September 1985, when, in a feat so extraordinary that no Liberian believed he did it without help from the U.S. government, he cut his way out of a Plymouth, Massachusetts, jail with a hacksaw blade and slipped out of the window using a rope made of bedsheets.

The former chief of government procurement in the Doe administration, Taylor, like his friend Quiwonkpa, saw his relationship with Doe go sour. In 1983, when Doe accused him of illegally procuring $900,000 in government funds, Taylor fled to the United States.

But $900,000 was serious money, so Doe appealed to the U.S. government, which put the FBI on the case. In May 1984, Taylor drove his Volvo to visit one of his girlfriends, who lived in Somerville, Massachusetts. A federal marshal appeared at the door claiming to have accidentally run into a Volvo in the parking lot. When Taylor came out to check on his car, he was arrested and taken to the Plymouth House of Corrections.

Doe demanded he be extradited to Liberia, but Taylor had hired Ramsey Clark, the former U.S. attorney general under Lyndon B. Johnson. Caught between the two factions and having little confidence in the validity of the claims against Taylor, the U.S. government balked at rushing him back to Liberia, where he would likely be executed. So Taylor sat in jail for sixteen months, until September 1985, when he and four other inmates made their daring escape.

There are many different versions of how Taylor managed this feat. The man himself has offered two differing accounts.

Taylor version #1: After getting out of jail, he hid out in the underground parking lot of the apartment building where his girlfriend Agnes Reeves lived, while the FBI interrogated her. Then the two drove across the country, crossed the border into Mexico, and stayed with a Mexican drug-dealing family.

Taylor version #2: The CIA helped him escape. After fifteen months in the Plymouth jail trying to avoid extradition to Liberia, Taylor said he got a visit from Harry Nyguan, a Liberian, "and he briefs me on what is being put together" by the CIA. A couple of days later, a guard asked him if he could get out of the country quickly once released. And a few days after that, the same guard opened his cell and took him from the maximum security side of the jail through several gates to the minimum security side. There they met two other men. "These guys took a sheet. We tied it on the bars. We came down and got over the fence."

A car waited outside for him, with two men inside. "They had instructions to take me as far as New York, where I wanted to go."

Taylor said the car was "a kind of government car." He didn't know the men who drove him. News reports followed, stating that Taylor "had broken out of jail": "I am calling it my release." From there he segued to his escape route: Washington, Atlanta, Texas, Mexico. On his own passport. From Mexico City, he flew to Belgium and then Ghana.

By the time Taylor arrived in West Africa at the end of 1985, Quiwonkpa's coup had failed. The purge that followed intensified the anti-Doe sentiment; in the Liberian expat community in West Africa, it seemed everyone was plotting to overthrow Doe. From Accra to Abidjan, Conakry to Freetown and Ouagadougou, and as far away as Tripoli, Liberian dissidents were huddling together over red palm oil and rice as they hatched insurrection plans.

The failure of Quiwonkpa and his unit of twenty-eight men had cemented conventional wisdom in the community plotting to overthrow Doe that a large force of armed guerrillas would be required to get the job done. In Accra, groups of former Doe associates-turned-foes plotted. In Abidjan, General J. Nicholas Podier, who had been with Doe and Quiwonkpa scaling the walls of the Executive Mansion to kill Tolbert in 1980, had also fallen out with Doe and was plotting to topple his former friend. Doe grew so worried about Podier's plans that he contacted him from Paris and begged him not to try to kill him, and then promised him he could return to Liberia as vice president. (Podier did return a few months later, sneaking over the border with two Americans. He was promptly caught, tortured, and executed by Doe's soldiers. The Americans were eventually freed under pressure from the U.S. State Department.)

The Ghanaians weren't happy to have Taylor, now an escaped convict, in their country plotting against Doe, so he started looking for another base. He settled on Burkina Faso, a leftist haven. His girlfriend Agnes introduced him to Burkina's ambassador to Accra, who, it turned out, was an ally of Blaise Compaoré, a close associate (but about to turn Brutus) of President Thomas Sankara.

Taylor moved to Burkina in 1987, where he began a friendship with Compaoré. On October 15, Sankara was brutally murdered and dismembered by armed gunmen, and Compaoré took over the presidency. His friend and ally Charles Taylor now had a home base for developing his plan to overthrow Doe. In Burkina, and eventually Libya, Taylor trained disgruntled men for his coming war. He sent messengers over the Ivorian-Liberian border to recruit young soldiers for training. He found fertile ground for his efforts among the disaffected Gio and Mano people, who had seen friends and family members killed in Doe's pogroms after Quiwonkpa's coup attempt.

Taylor also reached out to the wealthy Liberian expat community in America and Europe and found fertile ground there too.

The most fertile of all that ground, it turned out, was Ellen Johnson Sirleaf.

Not long after she got out of jail, Ellen had returned to Washington. But she kept her eye on Liberia, waiting for any chance to aid in plans to topple Doe. She was working for Equator Bank, having finally begun the job she accepted in 1985 during her one-day stop in Connecticut before going on her ill-fated trip to Liberia. She had built up her contacts within the expatriate network of Liberian dissidents, including Tom Woewiyu, a close associate of Taylor's. Woewiyu had testified before the U.S. Congress on her behalf when she was imprisoned for her "idiot" speech.

In Paris on a business trip in 1988, Ellen received a phone call from

Woewiyu. He too was in Paris, along with someone he wanted her to meet. Might she be free to have breakfast? They agreed to meet in the restaurant of Ellen's hotel.

While waiting for them to arrive, Ellen sat at a table reading a book by Thomas Sankara, the murdered Burkina leader. She lay the book on the table when Woewiyu walked up accompanied by Charles Taylor.

Ellen had met Taylor years before, during the Tolbert days, when he was agitating against the president and she was a Finance Ministry official. Even back then he had been charismatic. In Paris, he was both charismatic and brash. "You mean people still talking 'bout that boy?" he asked, pointing to Ellen's book.

Ellen was taken aback. "Everyone da' praise him for the things he did in his country."

Taylor made a dismissive gesture. "Well, he gone now."

Taylor said that during that meeting, he showed Ellen photos of rebel soldiers he was training in Ivory Coast and that she was "very pleased." When Ellen suggested ordering breakfast, Taylor asked her to give him her food money instead. She did, and he and Woewiyu left.

Despite that less than auspicious beginning, Ellen resolved to keep an open mind about Taylor. In fact, many well-intentioned people kept an open mind about Charles Taylor when he initially burst on the scene, in large part because they were so tired of Doe. The majority of Congo people hated Doe because he had upended their rule and executed their families and friends. A growing number of native Liberians also hated Doe; they felt they had simply exchanged Congo rule for Krahn rule; they had seen their country deteriorate economically during his reign and had witnessed the bloodbath after the attempted coup. It had become a widespread belief that the country was in a freefall for which Doe was responsible.

Ellen's own life was in upheaval as well. Her mother had died earlier that year in Alexandria, Virginia. Martha had slowed down considerably in her last few months; after dinner one night, she went to her room, went to sleep, and did not wake up again. The family buried her in Alexandria, as taking the body home to Liberia was not advisable.

Chris Maxwell tried to comfort Ellen. After three decades, their relationship had become platonic. He eventually married, and Ellen was a frequent visitor at his home in suburban Maryland, where she and Maxwell sat in the basement talking politics. One night in early 1989, with Maxwell recently out of the hospital, they discussed Taylor's efforts to train a group of men to take up arms against Doe. "He has to go," Maxwell said. "We have to find a way."

Back at her home in Alexandria the next morning, Ellen received a phone call from Maxwell's wife, Janet. He had passed away in the night. In the surreal world that is Liberian society, Janet asked Ellen to write his life sketch to be read at the funeral.

Days later, Ellen sat back and listened as her words describing the man she loved were read aloud. There was so much she could have written about Chris Maxwell: how he had helped to rescue her from an abusive marriage, how he had given her a haven to turn to, a reason, beyond her four boys, to enjoy life. But that was for the two of them.

Ellen, now fifty-one, threw herself into her work with the expat Liberian dissidents in an organization that called itself the Association for Constitutional Democracy in Liberia, along with Amos Sawyer, Tom Woewiyu, and other fairly high-profile critics of Doe. As Taylor's ragtag forces, the National Patriotic Front of Liberia, trained in Libya, the big question among the ACDL was whether they should provide financial support for what was clearly going to be an armed insurgency against Doe.

Ellen argued in favor of violence. She invoked Malcolm X; his refusal to embrace nonviolence had scared white America into listening to Martin Luther King Jr. Her argument came with the powerful backing of her cult hero status. She had been imprisoned by Doe, had been sentenced to Bella Yalla, had won and then refused to take a Senate seat because the elections were fraudulent. People paid attention when Ellen Johnson Sirleaf talked.

The ACDL decided to back Taylor. Soon they were sending him $10,000.

On December 24, 1989, Charles Taylor and 170 insurgents crossed the Ivorian border into Liberia, launching Liberia's civil war. It would last fourteen years and snuff out 200,000 lives.

The ramifications of that war still aren't fully known. Who can say, three decades later, what lives would have been led by the children who were turned into soldiers at the age of eight, drugged up on amphetamines and marched into the bush on orders to kill, maim, and dismember? Who can know what demons haunt the dreams of the former child combatant, teddy bear backpack strapped over his shoulders, who sprayed a village just outside Monrovia with his machine gun while the severed head of his boyhood friend lay on the asphalt beside him, broiling under the hot sun? Or the woman who fought and screamed while her two boys were taken away by drunken rebels clad in Halloween masks, who then threw her to the ground, mounted and raped her, all the while keeping their Halloween masks on?

Almost three decades after the start of the Civil War, Liberia is still a country of the walking wounded, one of those places where every single person of a certain age has a war story to tell, a story so grisly that your stomach turns and you want to vomit. How do people come back from that?

But if the ramifications still aren't known, they certainly weren't foreseen back in 1989, when Taylor's forces attacked a frontier post at Butuo near the Nimba County crossing point. Back then, all anyone knew was that someone with a legitimate chance of defeating Doe was on the march.

Many of Doe's soldiers guarding the post fled when they saw the approaching rebels, a pattern that would repeat itself in the days to come. Securing the border posts in Nimba allowed the Taylor forces to raid the ammunition stores. The Nimba County residents, brutalized by Doe, welcomed Taylor's forces, and soon young men and women were joining the fight. Mano and Gio people were particularly quick to sign up; they had been gunning for Doe ever since the Quiwonkpa purge.

"They thought we had a multitude," Taylor bragged later to the journalist Denis Johnson, referring to Doe's dispirited soldiers. "It was dark, and they just assumed. Their guilt and their corruption magnified their enemies in their sight. . . . They ran without a fight."

But the fight would come.

Word quickly reached Monrovia, where Liberians were in the middle of the Christmas holidays. The news didn't break on the government-run ELBC radio station or in the newspapers, where so many editors and reporters had been harassed and jailed. Instead, Liberians—and the world—learned about the incursion from BBC Africa, which carried regular reports about Taylor's successes from his frontline bases in the bush.

Doe sought to reassure the population that he still retained control of the country. But he also dispatched two well-armed battalions to Nimba to quash the invasion by attacking civilian Gio and Mano people there. The soldiers moved quickly and brutally against villages in their path, killing, looting, raping, and terrorizing. One woman reported that Doe's soldiers wrapped her mother in a gasoline-soaked mattress and burned her to death.

Doe didn't limit his reprisals to Nimba. On January 4, 1990, he sent his death squad to the home of Ellen's friend Robert Phillips, who had cavorted around Monrovia with her on the day of the Quiwonkpa coup. Phillips too was a political opponent of Doe's, but rather than fleeing as Ellen had done, he was still in Liberia duking it out with the president. Phillips was murdered and dismembered, an act that was becoming increasingly common.

But the brunt of Doe's early retaliation was Nimba County. His forces made no distinction between fighters and civilians; the bodies of men, women, and children littered the roadsides, as Doe's soldiers opened fire indiscriminately on one village after another. Terrified villagers fled into the bush and over the borders, beginning a displacement and a refugee crisis that would last more than a decade.

The Liberian leader's excessive response would seal his own fate. Taylor's rebels saw their numbers swell, at first by hundreds, then thousands, as surviving Gio and Mano youths, bent on revenge, joined. Eventually, Taylor would recruit children kidnapped from terrified parents, but in the early months, hatred of Doe was so strong he didn't need the extra help. However, unlike in the early days of the invasion, when he commanded a (relatively) tight group of trained men, he was now the head of a revenge-obsessed army over which he had no control. Or, at least, that is what he claimed when word started getting out about atrocities committed by his National Patriotic Front of Liberia.

Yet Liberians continued to give Taylor the benefit of the doubt, as reports of NPFL atrocities multiplied. There were other warning signs about Liberia's new conqueror, including the bizarre practice among his soldiers of wearing wedding gowns and wigs—juju to protect them in battle. But because Doe's soldiers were retaliating tenfold for every atrocity committed by the rebels, the fog of war made it easy for Taylor to disguise his own misdeeds under cover of Doe's bigger ones.

For both sides, the enemy was less the opposing army than a civilian population that had to yield for victory to be secured. The result was a living nightmare for virtually all ordinary Liberians.

Parleh Harris, a young office worker, was feeding her two-year-old son in their Bushrod Island house in Monrovia in 1990 when she heard yelling outside. Motioning her son to stay inside, she went to the front step. A young boy who had been hawking gas was being harassed by a group of Doe's soldiers in her front yard.

With businesses shuttering because of the war, all Liberians had become market women, selling whatever goods they could muster on the side of the road. The young boy was offering gas by the gallon in plastic milk jugs. Gas hawkers got their supplies from filling stations on the outskirts of town, then peddled the fuel in the heart of the city. The boy, who looked to be around thirteen, wanted $2 for a gallon. Minus the dollar he had spent on the gas, this meant he could buy rice and dried fish at a time when food was becoming increasingly scarce.

Doe's soldiers, barreling into Parleh Harris's front yard, had other ideas. "They wanted his gas," she recalled later. "He wouldn't give it to them. So they took it."

Taking the boy's gas wasn't enough, however. One of the soldiers grabbed a grenade, pulled out the pin, and threw it at the young gas hawker. It detonated right in front of him, blowing him into pieces in Harris's front yard.

The force of the blast knocked her over, and shrapnel rained across her front porch, accompanied by the smell of smoke and burning flesh. Inside the house, her two-year-old was screaming hysterically. His shoulder, hit by a piece of metal, was bleeding. Sobbing and bleeding herself, Harris crawled across the floor to her child. She grabbed a piece of cloth to try to stem the blood from his shoulder while her eyes darted around wildly, wondering if it was safe to go outside to try to get to a hospital. In the upside-down world of the Liberian Civil War, the answer was yes, it was safe, because Doe's soldiers, having blown up an adolescent boy for $2, had driven away.

Harris and her son ended up at JFK Hospital. From her hospital bed, she spoke angrily to the journalist from the radio station who came to talk to her. "There is no discipline," she shouted. What kind of country had government troops come to people's houses and blow up a thirteen-year-old over a canister of gasoline?

Some 122 miles away, in Gbarnga, Masawa Jabateh screamed in horror as Taylor's rebels tied her grandfather to a pole and set him on fire. Again the Liberian air filled with the smell of roasting flesh and brutally painful death. But for Jabateh, that horror was only the beginning. Soon her three-year-old daughter, who Jabateh had given to her mother for safekeeping, would be dead as well, from malnourishment.

"I'nt know how to mind baby," the teen had told her mother.

"Leave me de baby," her mother replied. But her mother's experience couldn't replace food, and the baby withered and died.

The fate of Famatta Sherman Nah was so awful that even the fog of war couldn't obscure it. Particularly not for Bernice Freeman, Famatta's cousin, who lived nearby and had grown up viewing Famatta as a sister.

As Taylor's forces were bedeviling Doe's up country, Famatta, eight and a half months pregnant, was home with her husband, Johnny Nah, and her two stepchildren, Hilaria, twelve, and Johnny Jr., fifteen, when she heard banging on the front door. This was wartime, when sudden visits from Doe's soldiers usually bore ill.

"Come out, Johnny," called a man's voice.

Famatta opened the door. "We came for your husband," the men said.

"Why?"

"To go to the Executive Mansion."

This was an order, not a request.

The entire family, Famatta, Johnny, Johnny Jr., and Hilaria, got in the car, escorted by soldiers. Bernice Freeman, a few blocks away at her own house, saw her cousin go by. It was the last time she would see her.

The soldiers took the family toward a swamp in Chugbor—nowhere near the Executive Mansion. "Why we going this way?" Famatta asked.

"We going come back."

Famatta started saying the Lord's Prayer: "Our Father, who art in heaven . . ."

As the car slowed down, Johnny Jr. saw his chance to escape and took it, throwing open the car door and running into the swamp. The soldiers opened fire on the fleeing boy, who went down.

The soldiers then shot and killed Hilaria and her father and gutted the pregnant Famatta with a knife.

Doe's soldiers had done this to thousands of other Liberians—people who disappeared in the night and were never seen again. Like theirs, the murder of the Johnny Nah family would have gone unreported except that on this night the soldiers had not been thorough. Unknown to them, they had left Johnny Jr. alive.

Shot in the leg, he crawled from the swamp and through the bush and made his way to Catholic Hospital. There he ran into a family friend, Flomo Washington. He told Washington what happened, and Washington hustled him quickly to the Swedish Embassy, knowing that the moment Doe's soldiers heard that the boy had not died, they would be back to finish the job. It was Washington who then went to the home of Famatta, where Bernice was with Famatta's parents, and told them what had happened to their pregnant daughter.

These were the stories that gripped the Liberian diaspora during the first months of the Taylor invasion: stories of the heinous acts committed by Doe's soldiers on the civilian population. Taylor's forces were unleashing their own acts of violence, but those stories were slower to circulate. When they did get out, many Liberians, praying for the demise of Doe, uneasily dismissed them, blaming the troops. Surely the rebel commander couldn't be held accountable for everything done in his name.

Back in the United States, Ellen continued to raise money for Taylor, while giving interviews to the foreign press saying it was time for Doe to go. A friend who had served in the U.S. Army, Elmer Johnson, was going to Liberia to join Taylor. He would work to bring discipline and professionalism to the Taylor forces, he told her. "You should go," she encouraged him.

One morning, her telephone rang.

"This Charles Taylor," the voice said. The line was scratchy. "We've got this tiger by the tail. I want y'all to know we're going to bring this thing down, and we need all the support we can get."

Ellen asked him about Jackson Doe, her friend and political ally, fearing his death by the rampaging Doe troops. He had slipped behind Taylor's lines, seeking refuge, and offered to join Taylor.

"Yeah, we know," Taylor said. "We arranging to take good care of him. Don't worry."

Reassured, Ellen hung up the phone.

What Taylor didn't say—and what few people in Monrovia or outside of the areas of fighting were aware of—was that in February, one of his deputies, Prince Johnson, had angered Taylor by executing a handful of men for theft and desertion. Then Johnson had broken away from Taylor and formed the Independent National Patriotic Front of Liberia, which was now weaving its own westward path toward the capital. In retaliation, Johnson's parents were quickly found and murdered by Taylor's forces.

In May 1990, wanting to see the situation firsthand, Ellen used a meeting of the African Development Bank in Abidjan to sneak into Liberia and meet with Taylor. A few British reporters were hanging around the meeting and asked to tag along. Ellen agreed, and the group set off into the bush.

At the border, a group of Taylor's soldiers, wearing fatigues, appeared. "He say you can come," one told Ellen, "but you can't bring nobody wi' you."

Nobody was brave or stupid enough to challenge that decision. The reporters watched as the global bureaucrat gingerly picked her way behind the soldiers into the bush.

At one point, crossing a stream, Ellen looked at banks that stretched in both directions. There, lined up in rows, were dozens of Taylor rebels, male and female, all staring at her with red eyes.

The red eyes terrified her.

Deep in the bush, the specter of the silent, drugged, and heavily armed rebels was designed to frighten, and it did. These were guerrillas, and this was war, a Liberian-made war in which no rules applied and you lived or died at the whim of a maniac fueled on revenge, superstition, and 150 years of instability. In the afternoon, with the sun struggling to emerge from the rainy-season sky, darkness pervaded the air.

As Ellen followed her escorts to the camp, she felt the red eyes tracking her. She tried to imagine what they were thinking: *Whe' de one comin from?* She felt the sweat coming out of her skin and sticking to her cotton shirt. It collected on her face, on her neck, under her arms.

Finally, after another half-mile or so of trekking, they reached the base of the camp. There were a few small buildings clustered around a yard that was packed with the machines of war: guns, artillery, handheld rocket launchers, grenades, all carefully watched over by soldiers as far as Ellen could see. Hundreds of soldiers, leaning against the buildings, squatting in the bushes, crouched near the trees.

Her guides ushered her into one of the buildings, and eventually she was taken into the main room, where Taylor sat, surrounded by bags of rice and deep in conversation with a Lebanese man. When she walked in, the conversation stopped and the Lebanese man stood up and walked out. Ellen sat down and listened to Taylor as he unveiled his plans for Liberia.

Like the Liberian people, he was tired of Doe's abuses. He would redeem the country for all of the people. Certain radicals had destroyed the country with their "radicalism." He rose and gestured for Ellen to join him, saying, "Come, let me show you how strong we are."

The two walked into the yard, and Taylor pointed to a huge mountain of weapons: AK-47s, M-16s, shoulder-fired rockets, grenades, rocket-propelled grenades, rifles, pistols. "I got these guns from Doe them," he said proudly. "Now I will use them against him."

Then his tone switched from warmonger to man of peace, and he continued sketching out his vision for a better Liberia. "When this thing is over, I'd like to see Judge Walser—Emma Walser, Rudolph Grimes—in charge."

Huh? Emma Sherman Walser was a venerable women's advocate with a long history of activism. Joseph Rudolph Grimes was a former secretary of state under Tubman who founded a law school at the University of Liberia. *He is not fighting this war, with all those red-eye people behind him, just to take the government and turn it over to Emma Walser and Rudolph Grimes,* Ellen thought.

It was getting dark, time for her to get the hell out while she still could. She made her way through the bush to the Ivorian border, then back to the United States.

And yet, despite all she had seen in the bush, she was still backing Taylor. The reprisal killings that Doe's forces had launched couldn't be tolerated. How could Taylor be worse?

People ran for their lives from the coming assault on Monrovia. Those with money fled by air, first from Robertsfield Airport and then, once Robertsfield was captured by Taylor's forces, from the tiny James Spriggs Payne Airport in Sinkor on the edge of downtown. Those without money were fleeing on foot, creating refugee crises in Guinea, the Ivory Coast, and Sierra Leone.

Monrovia was emptying out. The great battle for the city was coming, and a pervading sense of doom hung in the air. Doe holed up in the Executive Mansion with a shrinking number of loyal Krahn soldiers. His cabinet members, his chief of staff, his political advisers—all had abandoned their president. Some, including the minister of information, cultural affairs, and tourism, had officially gone to Freetown for peace talks and then, after earning for themselves a death sentence back home for calling on Doe to resign, prudently opted to stay in Sierra Leone. The replacement minister of information lasted a few weeks, then crossed rebel lines to Taylor's side, where he was immediately executed.

Doe's soldiers continued their rampage, lobbing missiles daily from the grounds of the Executive Mansion, indiscriminately destroying entire swaths of the city. There were daily skirmishes between Doe's soldiers and the rebels. One morning, Grace-tee McGill—the young woman who had lionized Ellen Johnson Sirleaf back in 1986—woke up to find that she and her family were in the middle of an assault.

The McGill family was living on Benson Street, trying to wait out the coming invasion. They mostly stayed out of sight, venturing out only when they ran out of food. Until the morning that several armored carriers full of Doe's soldiers arrived in front of their house.

Grace-tee could hear the young men outside talking; the soldiers seemed convinced her house was a nest of rebels. Then she heard the terrifying order, "Take down all these buildings them."

The soldiers opened fire on the McGill house. Of course there were no rebels hiding there—just Grace-tee, twenty-three, and her parents, grandfather, brother, five sisters, and a handful of war orphans. As the firing started, the terrified residents dove to the floor, covering their heads.

Crawling on her stomach, Grace-tee felt a torrent of bullets whizzing over her, then heard a cry of pain. One of the young orphans had been hit. Grace-tee crawled under a bench, trying to cover her head with her hands, as if her hands could stop a bullet. In between the rounds, she could hear the commands that signaled a new volley was about to begin. "Ready? Fire!" And then more bullets.

After several hours, the firing stopped. Grace-tee and the others—now minus one—silently filed out of the front door, their hands on their head to show they were unarmed. The soldiers allowed them to pass, and they walked out onto Benson Street. They passed the night a few blocks away, in a pastry shop on Carey Street, before escaping the next morning across the bridge to Bushrod Island, which Grace-tee's parents deemed a safer place to wait out the siege.

But Grace-tee's situation was not nearly so dire as that of fourteen-year-old Josephine. Taylor's forces descended on Tubmanburg, where Josephine lived with her family, like a spectral blanket, complete with fright masks, wigs, and wedding gowns, and laid waste to vast segments of the population. Boys were kidnapped, drugged, and forced to join the rebel ranks. Girls were taken as "wives," passed around, and raped by men three times their age. "Come, you coming cook for us," one rebel soldier told the teenager, after he and six of his comrades had raped her mother in front of her. Josephine did cook for them, over the camp coal pot, in the bush. But she was also raped, four to five times a day. The worst, she recalled, was when new soldiers joined the group she was with. "Anyone who came was allowed to have me," she said, her voice flat. "They would say, 'It's for you, sir. It's for you, sir.'" She stayed with them for eight months. Then, suddenly, they let her go.

At the same time that Josephine was taken, Katoumba, seven years old, was taken as well, by a rebel commander who took a shine to her dimples and her big, wide eyes. Her parents were dead—at the hands of the same rebels—but this commander decided that she would be his "play daughter."

His paternal feelings toward Katoumba meant he didn't allow her to be raped; instead he gave her a pistol and made the seven-year-old his aide de camp, taking her with him from battle to battle. Katoumba watched regularly as her "play pa" survived skirmish after skirmish, unhurt. She began to believe that he was invincible and could not die. Until, inevitably, her play pa's own soldiers turned on him and executed him in front of her.

The siege of Monrovia was coming. Taylor now controlled enormous swaths of the countryside and the Monrovia suburbs. He had warned residents that he was headed their way and there would be a nasty fight. The only way to get rid of Doe, he said, was for the Taylor forces to come get him. Doe had refused to leave, barricading himself in the Executive Mansion. Prince Johnson was also making his way to Monrovia. Doe didn't realize it, but he would have to contend with two advancing rebel armies.

The foreign embassies evacuated their citizens, and the Americans sent four warships to the coast, sending the hopes of Liberians skyrocketing that the United States had come to bail out its stepchild. It had not: the marines on board were there solely to protect American citizens.

From her house in Virginia, Ellen was still rooting for Taylor. In early July, she got a call from a BBC reporter who asked her what she thought about the chaos in her home country. Taylor was approaching the Mansion; Doe was refusing to leave. Might Taylor destroy the Mansion—and implicitly the city—just to bring Doe down?

"If they burn the Mansion down, we will rebuild it," Ellen told the reporter.

"What if Taylor wins this war?"

Ellen was feeling feisty and flip. She replied, "Well, we are nearing July fourth. On July fourth, we'll drink champagne."

Two months later, on September 9, 1990, Samuel Doe emerged from the Executive Mansion for the first time in months. His destination: the Monrovia Freeport, where Nigerian-led peacekeeping forces under the acronym ECOMOG (for Economic Community of West African States Monitoring Group) had recently installed themselves. Doe wanted to pay a visit to the ECOMOG commandant. The port was firmly in Prince Johnson territory and had been shelled by Taylor's forces just the day before.

But after weeks of cowering in the Mansion, Doe needed to show that he was still a force in Liberia. He also believed the peacekeepers would protect him.

It was an unusually sunny Sunday in Monrovia. This was still the rainy season, when rain clouds hang over the city. But on this day, the sun had made a brilliant appearance, casting a bright sheen over the half-starved, war-ravaged populace.

Doe, in his heavily armored motorcade and accompanied by an entourage of around seventy soldiers, including Harrison Pennue, one of the few members of the original coup plotters whom Doe hadn't executed, raced over the Bushrod Island bridge as shocked civilians looked on. Sirens blaring, Doe waved jauntily back at the starving people who yelled angrily at him from the side of the road.

The peacekeepers made Doe's solders disarm on entry, and Doe headed up the stairs to see General Arnold Quainoo, the peacekeeping force commander.

"There was a great commotion outside," recalled Elizabeth Blunt, a BBC reporter who happened to be at the port when Doe made his surprise visit, in an interview years later. Doe's visit, she said, "was totally unexpected."

Blunt settled down to wait, hoping to snag an interview with Doe before he left. But within minutes, Johnson and dozens of his men, heavily armed, burst into the compound, shouting and yelling.

The peacekeepers did not make Johnson's soldiers disarm.

Soon Blunt heard an ominous sound: the clicking of dozens of guns being cocked. She fled into an office to hide under a table. Two peace-keepers lay on top of her to try to protect her. And then, she recalled, "all hell broke loose."

Johnson had run up into the force commander's office, where he confirmed for himself that Doe was actually there. Then he ran downstairs and shouted an order to his men, who opened fire on the Doe soldiers. From near Doe, a voice shouted, "Rebels!" It was Pennue, Doe's close friend and the commander of his death squads. Within minutes, Pennue was shot in the head.

The shooting went on for more than an hour, as Blunt hid under the table. At one point, she heard Johnson call out for a beer.

110

In the chaos, Doe tried to run and was shot in the legs. The peace-keepers had done nothing to rein in Johnson's soldiers; instead they had taken cover themselves. More than seventy people—most of them Doe's soldiers—were killed.

Blunt heard the soldiers dragging Doe outside. He begged the fighters for mercy but also seemed to be admonishing them. "Please, please, I beg you, I beg you, you are embarrassing us," he said.

Johnson and his soldiers bundled him into their convoy and roared off to their headquarters in Caldwell, a few miles away.

What happened next is well documented; Johnson himself helpfully had his rebels videotape it, and then shared the recording with journalists and the world. Even today, anyone who googles "execution of Samuel Doe" can watch what followed.

On the screen, Doe sits on the floor in his underwear. His shirt is open, his hands are tied behind his back, and although his legs are bleeding, he is still tied at the ankles. He looks flabby; his breasts are folded over his stomach. Behind him, soldiers are yanking his shirt off, while another thrusts a microphone into his face.

It's hard to make out what Doe is saying. He is pleading, then suddenly he blinks and smiles. "If you loosen my rope," he says, "I can talk to you."

"I will kill you," Johnson tells him. Then, just as quickly, "I told them not to kill you."

Johnson is drinking a beer. Some of his men—boys, really—have poured beer over Doe's head.

Johnson rants continuously, about ECOMOG, about how he's a humanitarian. He asks repeatedly what Doe did with the Liberian people's money. Someone comes over and starts to fan Johnson's face.

"Plee' loosen my hand," Doe begs.

Johnson is sitting, leaning back, at a desk now, in front of Doe, who is still sitting on the floor. "I say, Doe, ehn you say no gun can kill you? Wha' happen now?" he taunts.

Doe is begging: "Plee' loosen me so I can tell you. . . . My hand swell up."

The video seems interminable. Now Johnson is going on about initi-ating the gunfire. A woman fans Johnson with a towel. He continues to rant.

The soldiers around Doe shout, "No retreat! No surrender!"

"Let me tell you something," Doe says. "Whatever happened was ordained by God."

An order comes from Johnson: "I say, cut the man ear."

More chatter. "Cut the man ear. . . . Y'all hold the man, cut the man ear."

Doe lets out a guttural scream as two boys hold him down while another cuts off first one ear, then the other. One boy presses his foot down on Doe's neck, holding him to the floor.

Johnson sits at the desk, sipping his beer, nodding. Earless, Doe sits up, and one soldier puts his foot on his shoulder in a victorious pose; he lifts his hands in the air and grins, as if to say "Take my picture."

So ends part 1 of the video.

In other videos, Doe is shown naked except for a wet rag covering his crotch, sitting by a river. He is earless and in and out of consciousness. When he can speak, he begs to have his hands untied. Johnson isn't in this scene, which obviously occurs after the first one. The men with Doe are still asking him what he did with the Liberian people's money. Doe loses consciousness, and the soldiers pour water over his head. He wakes up and begs again, "If y'all spare me I wi' tell you everything."

A final scene also appears to have been taped after Doe's ears were sliced off. He is sitting in a yard, bound, naked, and bleeding. "Varney, I dying," he says.

"Nineteen-eighty-five," comes the reply. The elections, Quiwonkpa, the purge that followed.

Another man says, "We are asking you in a polite manner now: What did you do with the Liberian people's money?" Doe doesn't say, and the man pulls out a knife.

"My penis. No, please, not my penis."

Grace-tee McGill thought the death of Samuel Kanyon Doe would end the slaughter in Liberia. Instead, the slaughter intensified.

Ever since the attack on their house, Grace-tee and her family had stayed on the other side of the bridge, sleeping at Ricks Institute, a boarding school on the outskirts of Monrovia, on the way to Cape Mount. The family had barely any food to eat; they had all lost weight. Grace-tee's

112

father's trousers were so loose he wore them wrapped around his body like a woman's *lapa*.

When her sister got sick, the family left Ricks and began the slow walk back to Monrovia, hoping to find medical help. They made their way past Brewersville, past the road leading to the Hotel Africa, where Johnson's soldiers had recently murdered the owner by throwing him off the fourth-floor balcony, past the empty stalls of what used to be the Duoala Market.

The family sought solace at an aunt's house, and Grace-tee's forty-eight-year-old mother went out to forage for food. She was quickly accosted by Johnson's soldiers, ran from them, and in running, terrified, she had a heart attack. Eventually someone brought her home, and Grace-tee and her father took her to Redemption Hospital, but there were no beds. Soon she died.

International aid organizations air-dropped food for the ravenous population, but Grace-tee never saw any. She continued to lose weight and to lose strength. One afternoon she was out with a friend, scrounging for food, when she blacked out. Her friend put her in a wheelbarrow; there was no chance of getting her into a car. She came to, but she couldn't walk and could barely talk. Her friend was trying to wheel her home when they were stopped by some of Johnson's soldiers. It was getting dark.

"Wha' your name?" one soldier asked, looking at Grace-tee.

She told him.

"You lying!" he said. "You Charles Taylor sister!"

And, just like that, he grabbed his gun, trained it on her, and cocked it.

Still in the wheelbarrow, she looked into the barrel. She was too weak to do anything. Not that it would matter.

The silence extended. Then a young woman came running to the soldier. "Commander, commander, commander! The meat over there that y'all said the people mustn't take! They taking it!"

The commander took off at a run. Grace-tee's friend grabbed the wheelbarrow and took off in the other direction. Grace-tee never again saw the woman who had saved her life.

The atrocities continued unabated. All over Monrovia, headless bodies littered the sidewalks and streets, and heads with no bodies piled up at one end of the runway at Spriggs Payne Airfield.

By now, everyone knew: there were no good guys in this war. Doe was gone, but the two men left vying for the presidency were just as bad, if not worse. Johnson had gained a reputation as a cruel man, but Taylor was even worse.

For Ellen, safe in Virginia and glued to television reports and phone calls tracking the war in Liberia, the realization that Taylor was no liberator came when she learned of two brutal murders committed by his forces, those of her friends Elmer Johnson and Jackson Doe. Both men had joined Taylor because they believed he was an ally who wanted to rescue Liberia.

Johnson, a U.S. Marine originally from Liberia, had gone back home and joined Taylor's National Patriotic Front of Liberia, ostensibly to instill discipline in the troops before the oncoming siege of Monrovia. But soon Taylor became worried that he would become a rival; reports were coming in that the former marine was now very popular with Taylor's rank and file. Johnson was killed in an ambush in Buchanan; while Doe's government took credit for his death, later reports documented that the orders came from Taylor.

In the case of Jackson Doe, Taylor had promised Ellen in a telephone call that he was protecting the onetime presidential candidate. Yet once again, the fear of a potential rival gripped Taylor, and, in this case, it was a fear based on very real facts. By all accounts, Jackson Doe—not Samuel Doe—had won the Liberian presidential election in 1985. So Jackson Doe could be considered the rightful president if Taylor ever succeeded in getting rid of Samuel Doe.

According to testimony given by Tom Woewiyu, Jackson Doe had crossed over to Taylor's side in the summer of 1990, led by joyous Taylor fighters in Kakata. "There was a big festival in the middle of the war to celebrate that a leader of our people had been saved; a leader who [President Samuel] Doe wanted dead was saved." Jackson Doe was then escorted to Harbel, where Taylor received him. Woewiyu said that Taylor ordered him to inform Ellen, Amos Sawyer, and other political leaders in the Liberian dissident community that Jackson Doe was safe, "only for me to arrive in Harbel one week later and he could not tell me where Jackson Doe was."

Where he was, as it turned out, was dead—assassinated on Taylor's orders, according to Woewiyu and other Taylor associates—hacked to

114

death, in fact. The murder didn't become known for several weeks. International reports remained fixated on the purges by Samuel Doe's forces all over Liberia.

When Ellen heard of Jackson Doe's death, her mind flashed back to a careless remark she had made a few weeks before, which she suspected may have gotten back to Taylor. She had suggested that Taylor might get more Liberian and international support if he allowed Jackson Doe to become the public face of his insurgency. "Jackson Doe won the election in 1985. If Taylor concedes to him, people will flock to Taylor," she had said.

Now Jackson Doe was dead.

For Ellen, his death marked the death of her alliance with Charles Taylor. She had supported Taylor against the advice of those who cautioned that no one knew his true nature. She had advocated on his behalf, had submerged her own suspicions that he was not the savior the country needed. And she had been spectacularly wrong.

Jackson Doe was dead. Elmer Johnson was dead. Hundreds more Liberians were dead; thousands more would be joining them. Ellen had backed the wrong man.

It was still only the first year of what would turn out to be a fourteen-year war. Many more Liberians had yet to be killed.

And Ellen? Safe in her perch in America, she started to campaign against Taylor.

In November 1990, at a peace conference in Bamako, Mali, attended by Charles Taylor, Prince Johnson, and the remnants of Samuel Doe's army, the three sides ostensibly agreed to a comprehensive cease-fire. A transitional government, led by Amos Sawyer, had been set up a few months before, but the conference didn't formally recognize the interim government.

Not that it mattered anyway. This was just a show, a time to regroup. Taylor and his forces retreated—but only as far as Gbarnga, three hours from Monrovia, where he set up a government-not-quite-in-exile. He still controlled 90 percent of the country, and his NPFL forces were soon fighting Sierra Leonean and Guinean soldiers on Liberia's borders.

Ellen, still in exile in the United States, supported Sawyer's interim government; she had even toyed with the idea of joining it, before deciding she was better off on the sidelines. The government set up shop in Monrovia's hilltop Ducor Hotel, a massive, once-stately edifice that was now surrounded by war refugees and squatters. But the interim government existed only because it was backed by ECOMOG, which launched a series of futile initiatives and diplomatic accords in various West African capitals meant to rein in the violence in Liberia: the Banjul Joint Statement (December 1990), the Lomé Agreement (February 1991), and the Yamoussoukro Accords (June–October 1991).

None of these went anywhere. The population began splintering again, while Taylor, ensconced in Gbarnga, ruled over what he started calling "Greater Liberia." He made himself president and appointed a cabinet. He started a radio station, printed up stationery with a presidential seal, and collected taxes, including from Firestone, also part of Greater Liberia.

Of course, both Greater and Lesser Liberia were a ravaged mess. In Monrovia, previously fat women were now so malnourished they joked that they had the figures of teenage girls. In a place where chubbiness had long signified prosperity, the general citizenry looked anything but. Thirty-year-old Rosanna Hungerpiller Sehaack, who lost her job at Lamco in Nimba County after the mining operation shuttered following Taylor's invasion, had decamped to Monrovia's Ma Barclay neighborhood with her husband. Now she scrounged for food to feed her four children. At around five feet, four inches, Rosie now weighed ninety-nine pounds. Her breasts had virtually disappeared and she had stopped menstruating. Malnourished, weak, and fighting desperately to keep her children alive, she, along with her entire family, saw their bodies shift into starvation mode, as their cells hoarded every scrap of everything they ingested.

In Monrovia, the interim government—rulers of Lesser Liberia—worked with a handful of NGOs to eventually get food to the starving populace, which slowly started trying to put their lives back together, adapting to new scavenging rules. The ECOMOG peacekeepers patrolled the city and manned checkpoints. People uneasily waited for the return to war.

The ruler of Greater Liberia, meanwhile, was printing up his own currency, called Liberty dollars. He began exporting iron ore, mahogany, ebony, and diamonds to the international market. And he used the lull in the fighting to take the money he got from his export business and turn it into more weapons for his troops.

Finally, in October 1992, rested and resupplied, he launched an all-out campaign—Operation Octopus—to do what he had nearly accomplished two years before: he broke the cease-fire and went after Monrovia. And, grabbing international attention again with a vengeance, his troops brutally murdered five American nuns. Taylor later said they were killed in cross-fire, but the nuns, who were all from the same order, were killed in two separate incidents three days apart.

The peacekeeping forces responded by targeting Taylor, but in doing so, they also allied themselves with other warring factions in Liberia that had emerged since Taylor's invasion and now were part of the free-for-all that the Civil War had become. The peacekeepers bombed Taylor's forces in Gbarnga, then inexplicably pulled back, then bombed him again, then pulled back. They never were able to do damage that Taylor couldn't repair and replenish with his seemingly unending supply of drugged-up young-sters to fill out his ranks, and he regrouped during the lulls in the bombings.

Besides stocking up on weapons, Taylor had used the two years of the cease-fire to take on more children for his army. Whether you call it recruitment, abduction, or rescue, the result was always the same: young, uneducated, and orphaned youngsters fought in the army of the man they called Pappy.

Howard French, the *New York Times* reporter who covered the war, wrote of the young fighter he met who emerged from the bush to greet him when his car was stopped on the road to Taylor's headquarters in Gbarnga. The young boy told of how Taylor's forces had slaughtered his entire family, leaving him alone. "Then," French wrote, "in the next thought, without irony or self-consciousness, he added: 'But I joined them because they are the best.'"

Others had more horrific stories to tell: of being forced at gunpoint to kill their own parents, and then being dragooned into Taylor's army; of watching as their mothers and sisters were raped by six, seven, eight drunken rebels, who then slapped them on the back and dragged them into the forest to fight alongside them.

In October 1994, Taylor's forces entered the Bong County town of Zoweeta wearing red cloth masks over their faces. They massacred dozens of civilians, men, women, and children. Seventeen of the fighters raped a young woman named Rebecca. She died after the seventeenth man violated her—raped to death.

Some of the children who weren't killed that day were forced to join the rebels. Months and years later, the ultimate breakdown of society occurred as orphans who had watched beloved family members killed went to work for, and professed to love, the man responsible for their deaths.

Ellen would soon face that same astounding irony. But for now, safe in the United States, she instead dealt with Rwanda. She had landed a job at the United Nations Development Program with responsibility for Rwanda and Angola. It was the perfect bureaucratic landing strip for her. And while there, wrapped in the warm and welcoming embrace of her global bureaucratic family, she put her experience in Africa to work on the civil war and genocide in Rwanda, where Hutus had unleashed their unthinkable horror on Tutsis, slaughtering some 800,000, as the world watched.

Chapter 8

OF HELL AND FURY
1995–1997

On a crisp fall evening in 1995, Ellen left her office at the United Nations Development Program, where she had been promoted to lead the Africa Bureau, at the Manhattan complex on the East River. She got in her car and began the hour-long drive to her home in suburban Larchmont, New York. It had been a punishing day—par for the course—filled with meetings and phone calls as the entire continent of Africa, from Somalia to Rwanda, not to mention Liberia, seemed to be going to hell all at once.

In this newest and most important job, Ellen was ostensibly not allowed to engage in Liberian politics, and so far, she was toeing the line, spending the bulk of her time on daily UN business and leaving her assistants telephone messages at midnight. She had developed a friendship with Under-Secretary-General Kofi Annan, who would soon become secretary-general, and even had him over for dinner.

The United Nations had sent her to a six-week intensive course in French in Aix-en-Provence, and when she got back one of the first things she did was to require all her staff in the Africa Bureau to speak French on Fridays. She had gotten proficient enough to stumble through conversations with the Francophone heads of state.

She was on the front lines of African affairs on the international stage. Her job came with very high highs and abysmal lows. High: At an OAU summit, she shoved her way to the front of the queue and got a photo and ten minutes with Nelson Mandela, telling him that he had inspired her. Low: She sat across the table from the Angolan warlord Jonas Savimbi in a meeting, battling a strange fear as she watched him quietly monitoring the discussion. There was a familiarity about him that gave her pause; he reminded her of some of the Liberian warlords. Low: She was one of the first outsiders to visit the scene of the mass murders in Rwanda, flying by helicopter to Kigali, Byumba, and Gikongoro. She saw bloated decomposing bodies, covered in flies. Looking away did no good; everywhere her eyes turned, there were more bodies.

Unsurprisingly, she saw similarities between Rwanda and Liberia. Both places had allowed huge cleavages in their society. Like the Congo people, the Tutsis had embraced the idea that they were the superior group, better educated and richer than their Hutu countrymen. The resentment felt by the Hutus recalled the resentment of the native Liberians.

Still, she was playing by the UN rulebook and keeping out of Liberian politics, as Taylor continued his rule over Greater Liberia and the Civil War raged on.

That night as she drove home from the UN, rush hour was already dying down, and as she turned onto FDR Drive, an eagerness tempered her exhaustion. Her son Adamah was coming to visit; he should be at her house by the time she got home. She allowed herself to bask in pride over Adamah's accomplishments. He was a full-fledged doctor now, an emergency room physician. She couldn't wait to see him.

Adamah's car was in the driveway when she got home, and she entered the house to be met by none other than her ex-husband, Doc.

What the hell?

Ellen had seen Doc from time to time over the years—they shared four sons, so some exposure couldn't be helped—and in the past, they had managed to keep things cordial. But for some reason, on this night, she was not feeling forgiving.

Leveling an angry look at her son, she demanded, "Wha' you brought your pa here for?"

Before Adamah could answer, she turned to Doc: "Wha' you doing here?"

As her ex-husband looked at her in surprise, Ellen found words—fueled by more than three decades of pent-up fury—spilling out. "Oh, that's now you na come to see me?" she demanded. "Look where you are, look where I am. After wha' you did to me? I was seventeen years old. Seventeen years old, when I went to your house, when you married me! And look at wha' you did to me! Now you come into my house?"

120

On and on she went, finally, after years, releasing the store of anger she had carried deep within. She had always been resistant to making Doc look bad in front of their boys, but now, on that dark night in Larchmont, she found herself unable to hold it in any longer. This man had stolen her childhood. He had beaten her; he had threatened her; he had pointed a gun at her; he had wrapped his hands around her throat; he had terrorized her when she was most vulnerable. And now he was standing in her house, as if he was welcome?

Finally, spent and heaving, Ellen quieted down. Doc looked at Adamah. "Let's go," he said. "I'nt want stay here."

Shaking, Ellen stood in the kitchen as she heard the car drive away. That would be one of the last times she saw Doc. A few years after this incident, Doc Sirleaf died of a heart attack while traveling in the car with Adamah.

Ellen spoke at his funeral. And in the years after that, she felt a twinge of guilt whenever she thought of that night in Larchmont, when she told off her ex-husband. "I guess I was angry," she said. "For a long time, I had been angry."

In early 1997, as Liberia settled into its seventh year of civil war with its attendant rapes, dismemberment, and massacres, Ellen went on a Caribbean cruise.

Jennie had dragged her sister aboard one of those giant monstrosities that ply the sea south of Miami. The extended family came along to celebrate Jennie's sixtieth birthday on the well-appointed cruise ship.

Ellen hated every minute of it. She couldn't stand cruises to begin with—all that enforced confinement and shuffleboard, with no terra firma below her, just deep blue sea surrounded by old people. But with the whole family captive at sea, it was the perfect time to announce the decision she had been chewing on for the past few months.

For the first time in twelve years, Liberia was again headed toward elections meant to give the people, if not real democracy, then at least some say over their own future. Or at least that's what the politicians and international community were saying in their speeches and radio addresses.

In truth, Nigeria and Ghana, which supplied the bulk of the ECOMOG peacekeeping forces, had grown weary of the endless mess. Seven years had failed to uproot Charles Taylor, nor had some fifty-odd peace conferences and a dozen joint declarations and communiqués. Thousands of Liberians were dead; 1.8 million were in need of humanitarian assistance; many thousands were living in refugee camps in neighboring countries; and sporadic fighting continued between Taylor and other armed groups supported by various warlords. The peacekeepers had accomplished nothing; Taylor remained the ruler of Greater Liberia; his army continued to force children to fight; the populace remained terrorized. Yet Liberians somehow managed to drift through daily life as if the situation in their bifurcated country— with Monrovia nominally governed by peacekeepers and the international community and the rest of the country patrolled by marauding Taylor forces—was somehow normal.

Enough was enough. Nigeria and Ghana wanted their soldiers out, so all sides summarily declared that the country was safe and ready for elections. These would happen, the ruling powers decided, in July 1997. Taylor, convinced this was the only way he would get his prize, agreed. He agreed as well to disarmament.

Thousands of fighters showed up at points all over the country to comply with the latest plan, which required them to surrender their weapons. Of course, there was no way to check that the fighters hadn't held back their best armaments, and Taylor kept much of his arsenal. But instead of discussing the Civil War, the people were now preoccupied with presidential campaigning.

Still, when Ellen made her big announcement on the cruise ship that evening, her family looked at her as though she were insane. They had just finished singing "Happy Birthday" to Jennie.

"I'm returning to Liberia, and I'm going to run for president against Taylor," Ellen said, instantly becoming the proverbial skunk at the garden party. Then she sat back and waited for the explosion.

"Wha' wrong with you?" Jennie asked her in disbelief.

"I know how y'all gonna respond," Ellen replied, "but I'm not asking you. I'm telling you." She made it clear that this was not a negotiation. "If y'all agree with me, that's fine. If you don't, sorry."

Not a single member of her family supported the decision. For all the defiance she was showing, Ellen had convinced herself that once she told her family, they would rally around her as they always did. But not this time. "They could not understand at all," she recalled. "I had never in my life felt as isolated as I did that day on that ship. I felt as if my family were disconnecting from me and from all the things I had been working for all those long and difficult years."

Jennie wasn't feeling too charitable either. "Here I was thinking she had come on the cruise because of me," she muttered bitterly years later. "I should have known better."

For all the opposition, Ellen felt something else propelling her: a need to differentiate herself. Who can understand what drives people to think that they, above everyone else, are qualified to lead a nation? What well of confidence does that come from? Struggling to explain herself, Ellen was left with this: "At Citibank, at the United Nations, I was in good jobs, yes. But thousands of other people could do those jobs. If I ran for president of Liberia, I knew, there were not thousands of people who could do that."

Reprising the same stunt she had pulled a decade before, she flew to Liberia without telling her bosses at the United Nations of her plans. She was already resigned to the fact that she would not be able to continue working at the UN if she ran for president, but she wanted to lay the groundwork before she told Annan. Soon after arriving in Monrovia, however, she was found out when a BBC reporter learned of her presence and asked her if she was working with the Unity Party.

Once the news leaked that Ellen was running, she got a very angry telephone call from UN headquarters in New York. Annan's chief of staff was blunt. "You're in Monrovia," he said. "We understand you are there politicking. We understand you may be a candidate for president of Liberia. We wish to know your intentions in this regard."

Ellen confirmed her intentions, and with that, cut the umbilical cord. "I'll be returning as soon as possible to New York," she said. "Please tell the secretary-general I will have to resign."

In New York she cleaned off her desk, then returned to Liberia to launch her campaign and immediately proceeded to do everything wrong.

Speaking to a war-weary populace that had been devoid of electricity, running water, a functional economy, and any of the societal rules that usually govern civilized people, she announced a complicated-sounding Five Point Plan that included strengthening regional alliances with Guinea, Sierra Leone, and other West African countries. She traveled to Ghana, the Ivory Coast, and Nigeria to drum up support in a move that many Liberians viewed as further proof of her overreliance on the outside world at the cost of her domestic support.

She came across as too international, too sophisticated, too Western. What did this pencil-pushing bureaucrat know about the past seven years, while she was sitting in conferences at the United Nations or in board meetings with Equator Bank?

She held rallies in Monrovia and a few up country, and they were well attended. There were long marches and big parades, sometimes with large crowds. There were even times when Ellen's supporters roughed it up with Taylor's people, yelling back at his supporters who heckled her rallies from the sidelines: "Wha' you know 'bout Ellen Johnson Sirleaf, you dirty rogue?"

But rallies don't win elections, and Ellen had no ground game. Many of her supporters showed up in the streets and danced and cheered for her but missed the deadline to register to vote, oblivious to the fact that they would need a voter ID card when showing up at the polls on Election Day.

During the campaign, the former U.S. president Jimmy Carter, there to observe the elections, visited Ellen in Monrovia and asked her if she would support Taylor if he won, since it was pretty clear to everyone except Ellen that Taylor was the leading candidate. She wouldn't entertain the possibility, leaving Carter to describe her in his report to the Carter Center as truculent: "Under our questioning about accepting the results of an honest election, she only became more vehement."

To outsiders it seemed obvious that Liberians should support Ellen. But inside Liberia, a strange dynamic had taken hold. For all the death and destruction he had heaped on Liberia, Taylor somehow had the support of a great many people. Those supporters—including the masses of young boys singing and dancing for their Pappy in the streets—adopted the unofficial campaign slogan "He kill my ma, he kill my pa, I will vote for him." To most Westerners, that made little sense, but to Liberians, it was a perfectly understandable extension of Darwin. Taylor had proven to be the strongest at war; he had survived the ECOMOG bombings, the Samuel Doe rampages. The man had even escaped jail in America.

Beyond that was a belief even among people who weren't his supporters that after seven years of civil war, he deserved his shot at the presidency. "He spoil Liberia—so let him fix it."

Taylor ran a serious campaign. He controlled KISS-FM, the only radio station that broadcast up country, and used the airwaves to exhort people to go to the voting booths; in some places deep in the Liberian interior, villagers had never even heard of the other candidates. He distributed bags of rice at his campaign rallies. He chartered a helicopter to take the Liberian national football team to Togo to play a match, managing to harness patriotic fervor at a time when many Liberians were scrambling to dump their citizenship and find a new country to which to belong.

In July 1997, Taylor won 75 percent of the vote, crushing his nearest competitor, Ellen, who got around 10 percent. No one else was even that close.

At a speech a few months after the elections, Taylor was perhaps most eloquent on explaining why he had won. He said his victory showed that Liberians had wanted him to defeat Doe way back in 1989, when he first invaded, and that the seven years of war that was prolonged by the intervention of the ECOMOG peacekeeping forces did not sway the people from that initial conviction. "In the final analysis, when the people had the opportunity to come out and speak in the last elections, they said 'you've wasted our time for six and a half years.' We've always wanted this man to lead us; you did not give us the chance to express it, you came and dictated your policies, now we are speaking: that's the man we want."

For all the complaints about voter intimidation, including ones lodged by Ellen, the reality is that Taylor won fairly. Liberians wanted the architect of their destruction to lead them out of the hell he had created.

The victorious Taylor sent an emissary to ask Ellen if she would join his government and lead the social security agency. She turned him down flat. "He wants me to take care of the people while he steals the money? Thanks, but no," she said.

When Carter visited her again in the weeks after the election and asked her to work with Taylor, she spurned the former president and remained fixated on her belief that there had been electoral fraud. (If there had, no one thought it was enough to have changed the election results.) She told Carter he should be speaking out against fraudulent elections, not trying to get her to join Taylor's government, further angering the former president, who again returned to the United States criticizing her.

But Carter had decamped from Washington back to Georgia, so his lobbying effort to help Taylor's new administration rebuild Liberia did not go very far. There were other power players in Washington for Ellen to woo. Bill Clinton was president now; America controlled the purse strings of the International Monetary Fund and the World Bank; an American, Paul Wolfowitz, ran the latter, and close friends of Ellen's in the international financial circuit ran the former. She had kept her friends and allies at the UN as well. She reminded these people again and again what she thought of Taylor.

Taylor may have won the presidency, but Ellen would do her damnedest to see to it that he couldn't do anything with his prize.

She soon moved to Abidjan, where she set up a consultancy. From there she could keep a close eye on Liberia and work to undermine Taylor.

It turned out to be an easy task.

Ellen understood that, after seven years in the interior away from his prized Monrovia, Taylor was expecting that the country's treasury would finally be opened to him. He anticipated a Marshall Plan for Liberia, with a big influx of foreign money to help rebuild his broken country. And surely Liberia's mammoth $3 billion in debt would be forgiven? The United States would come to the rescue? The World Bank? The IMF?

Not if Ellen could help it. The only way Taylor could possibly get additional IMF loans or World Bank aid was if Ellen—Liberia's emissary to the global financial world—backed him. She did not, helping to create the ultimate catch-22 for Charles Taylor: without international aid to help Liberia get out of its financial trench—the country hadn't had electricity or running water since 1990—Taylor was stuck. To unstick himself, he turned to a tried-and-true method which, while lucrative, would eventually so enrage the same international community that it would bring about his downfall: commodities and arms dealing.

Desperate for cash and cut off from aid, Taylor organized a criminal empire from Monrovia. He replaced the American businesspeople who ran Liberia's lucrative Maritime Agency—the one that collected money for all those Liberian-registered tankers—with a few of his American friends. The agency accounted for around $24 million in annual income. Taylor transformed it into the Liberian International Ship and Corporate Registry and channeled the money to nongovernmental as well as government bank accounts, giving himself the option of diverting revenues wherever he chose to put them.

He handed out large concessions to friends and crooked foreign companies for a fee. Liberia's rich minerals and natural resources were now available for plunder. The London-based watchdog Global Witness accused Oriental Timber, a Malaysian company, of clear-cutting forests; the company's chairman, a close associate of Taylor, would later be convicted of selling arms to the Taylor government in violation of a UN embargo.

In Abidjan, Ellen marshaled her resources against him.

In 1998, she walked into the penthouse restaurant at Abidjan's famous Hotel Ivoire for a board meeting and lunch with Africa fund managers. She had spent her professional life cultivating relationships with the people seated around that table. The chief executive of Archer Daniels Midland was there, as was the chief financial officer of Citibank and several other big-company types who wanted to do business in Africa. Steve Cashin, Ellen's friend from her Equator Bank days, was there as well. Since then, Cashin, tall and garrulous, had become a big player in the world of African investment banking. In 1998, he had just become head of the Washington office of Modern Africa Fund Managers, responsible for identifying investors to work with the U.S. government's Overseas Private Investment Corporation on Africa projects.

Ellen walked in late, accompanied by Martha Nagbe, a market woman dressed in her full glory: elaborate head-tie, long silver dress, bangles down her arm. Alarmed, Cashin looked around the table at the men staring at the two women. There was only one seat available, for Ellen.

He caught Ellen's eye; she raised her eyebrows and nodded her head at her market woman friend, in a motion Cashin decided meant "Get her a seat." Abruptly, he shoved himself up and went to find a waiter, whom he asked to set another place at the table.

Cashin was becoming used to Ellen showing up with stray market women. Martha Nagbe had known Ellen for years, and as a market woman she traveled frequently up and down the West African coast, from Monrovia to Robertsport to Freetown and back. That morning she had shown up to see Ellen, who had simply invited her to join her at the lunch with the bankers. Ellen was building up her support network. Years later, she would turn to women like Martha Nagbe.

From Abidjan, Ellen started slipping into Liberia whenever she could to make public statements and chat with reporters about how awful Taylor was. For journalists writing about Liberia, she was catnip. This was Ellen Johnson Sirleaf, the former presidential candidate, the former United Nations administrator, the political dissident who was jailed by Doe for eight months. Reporters looking for a credible source to quote on Taylor flocked to her.

And Taylor gave her much to work with. Just a few months after the elections, Samuel Dokie, a former Taylor ally who had broken with him and run unsuccessfully for the Senate on Ellen's Unity Party ticket, was arrested near Gbarnga, along with his wife, on orders from Taylor's security chief, Benjamin Yeaten. The Dokies' charred and mutilated bodies were discovered two days later, in their car in the countryside. Taylor denied knowledge and ordered an investigation. But Yeaten kept his job.

Ellen kept the Dokie case alive in the media both inside and outside Liberia. Similarly, she kept alive the case of Norwai Flomo, a Taylor critic who was dragged from her home and killed by his security forces. The years of civil war had obliterated the gentleman's agreement that "women were for raping, not killing" observed by Liberia's military men. From Abidjan, Ellen spoke loudly to anyone in the international community who would listen: Taylor, she said, was leading Liberia to disaster.

But nothing would help make her case more forcefully than Taylor's own foray into the civil war in Sierra Leone. Less than two years after he had launched his own war in 1990, armed men led by a former Sierra Leonean army officer named Foday Sankoh started an insurrection. From the start, the Revolutionary United Front was backed by Taylor and fought just like the NPFL rebels did: child soldiers were forced to rape and kill their own mothers, civilians were killed. Except the RUF used even more imaginative tactics, including cutting off the hands and feet of their opponents.

As president, the diamonds Taylor got from weapons sales to the RUF would help fund his already failing administration. While the West was willing to overlook atrocities against his own population—these were internal affairs—the international community wasn't willing to overlook cross-border outrages.

Moreover, by vigorously pursuing relations with Taiwan, Taylor had angered Beijing, which killed his chance of keeping the United Nations Security Council out of his business. Soon he was operating under a UN arms embargo, which was in part greased by Ellen. And suddenly Taylor was the pariah of the world.

In 1999, President Clinton's undersecretary of state, Thomas Pickering, went to Liberia to deliver a blunt warning to Taylor. There would be "severe consequences," Pickering said, if Taylor didn't stop interfering in Sierra Leone. Taylor called the warning an effort to "muffle this country" and denied he was aiding the RUF. Soon he, his family, and his aides were subject to an American travel ban.

Shortly afterward, Sierra Leone's minister for mineral resources told a special UN panel that Liberia was exporting forty times more diamonds than the country's own diamond mines were capable of producing. Taylor's foreign minister, Monie Captan, said the accusation was baseless. But Captan found himself going up against Richard Holbrooke, America's envoy to the United Nations, a storied diplomat fresh from the Dayton Peace Accords. Comparing the Liberian president to the Butcher of the Balkans, Holbrooke declared in an interview with the *New York Times*, "Taylor is Milosevic in Africa with diamonds," a comparison that electrified the press and destroyed whatever illusions Taylor nurtured about being accepted in the West. "[Taylor] is fueling the conflict in Sierra Leone for his own benefit. . . . He is threatening to destabilize western Africa."

George W. Bush's assumption of power did nothing to change U.S.

policy toward Liberia. In March 2001, after strong lobbying from the United States and Britain, the UN Security Council passed another anti-Taylor resolution, banning any export of diamonds from Liberia and expanding the travel ban against Taylor to include 130 of his family and associates. Taylor was now permitted to leave the country only to attend conferences of the United Nations, the Organization of African Unity, or the Economic Community of West African States. Liberia's president was essentially under house arrest.

As it happened, he had plenty to occupy him at home. While he had been battling the United Nations and the global community over blood diamonds, another group had emerged to battle him.

There is something about an insurgency group called Liberians United for Reconciliation and Democracy whose acronym makes it hard to take them seriously. But LURD, a disparate group of anti-Taylor men, was very serious about removing Taylor from power. Taylor accused Ellen of backing LURD, and she issued a passionate denial from Abidjan. "I defy him to expose details. . . . If he is a true Darkpannah, let him reveal this little bit of what he calls 'fact,'" she said, coming perilously close to the world of Harry Potter in an outrageous use of Taylor's adopted middle name, with its connotations of dark African magic.

LURD had plenty of help from some of Ellen's allies, including President Lansana Conté of Guinea, who hated Taylor and who, as early as 1992, had tried to brand Taylor's NPFL a terrorist organization. With help from Conté and others, LURD attacked and overran Taylor forces in Lofa County, then they gunned for the Taylor stronghold of Gbarnga, and after that, LURD's guerrillas turned their attention to Monrovia.

With Taylor under siege, Ellen went to work cutting the last thread of his support in the outside world: the one between Taylor and the president of Burkina Faso, a Taylor friend since Compaoré's bloody takeover in 1987. Taylor had stayed under Compaoré's protection in Burkina while he plotted to invade Liberia in 1989. The two were brothers in arms.

But now Compaoré was president of Burkina and intent on polishing his image before the rest of the world as a statesman, not an assassin. What better way than if he somehow managed to negotiate a peace deal that saw the end of fighting in Liberia and Sierra Leone?

Ellen decided the Burkina leader was ripe for a turnaround. She visited Ouagadougou and met with Compaoré, appealing to his ego. "You're moving your country forward," she stroked. "Our country is moving backwards."

For weeks Ellen worked on Compaoré, using a friendship she had developed with George Soros, the multibillionaire founder of Open Society, to prod Compaoré to host a reconciliation conference in Burkina meant to bring peace to Liberia. Open Society would fund the conference, and Compaoré would host it in Ouagadougou and gain status in Africa. Taylor would be invited—after all, the travel ban did allow him to go to regional conferences. The date was set for December 2001.

Ellen convinced Compaoré that this conference could bring a negotiated settlement: she and the other critics would accept Taylor's right to rule Liberia; in return he would stop "behaving like a warmongering commando" and all would be well. So Compaoré invited his friend to his peace conference.

But Taylor did not come. Nor did he send a delegate or representative. What he sent instead was a message, which his old and now very miffed friend relayed to the other attendees: "I have God and I have guns. I don't need anybody else."

And so ended the relationship between Taylor and his last remaining West African ally. For Ellen, it was mission accomplished.

By 2002, Taylor was considered a top-tier war criminal. As if to further drive home the point, the United Nations sponsored the Special Court for Sierra Leone, and in March 2003, the court's judge green-lighted the indictment of Taylor on seventeen counts of war crimes. The indictment wasn't immediately made public.

It was near the beginning of the rainy season, and LURD had reached the edge of Monrovia. Liberia was now at the center of a vicious cycle of diamond-fueled wars in Ivory Coast, Guinea, and Sierra Leone, as guns for hire in all four nations roamed the countryside and terrorized the populations. Each country fed the wars in the next. Taylor used Ivory Coast to launch his war in 1989, when he crossed over the border at Danane. And he allied with the RUF as they raped and mutilated their way across Sierra Leone and into southern Guinea. Eventually Ivory Coast succumbed to chaos after a failed coup sent that formally stable country tumbling. And that Ivorian turmoil eventually rebounded into Liberia.

Throughout all of these blood-soaked years of horror, it was the women of those countries who suffered the most. There are, after all, far worse things than dying. Dying is easy: the clap-clap of a machine gun, the slicing of a cutlass, the nothingness that comes after. Living can be harder. To live with the image of your children being dragged away, knowing they will become killers and will then be killed themselves. To be raped so often by teenagers wearing Halloween masks that you can't close your eyes without imagining a bewigged monstrosity looming above you. And to see your rapist take off his mask and reveal his face—and that face is your son's.

In Liberia, the war turned every woman into a market woman. Rich and poor, elites and native women, educated and illiterate, the overwhelming reaction of the Liberian women to all that was going on around them was to make market. Whatever functional economy existed in Liberia during those black years existed because of the market women.

Women with college degrees began collecting kola nuts to sell on the side of the road. They made caustic soda soap, placed the bars in buckets atop their head, and walked from village to village. Some, like Lusu Sloan, a widow with three children, braved bullets, machine-gun fire, rocket-propelled grenades, and the penises of insane marauders to walk through the bush, from Monrovia to the Guinean border, to get sugar and flour and bouillon cubes to bring back to the markets in the starved and wasted capital city.

The market women had carried the country on their backs for years, making market through war. But now they realized that market alone was not going to be enough. Reality had become untenable.

In Monrovia, market women wearing white T-shirts began holding peace demonstrations. Some gathered in front of the Executive Mansion, looking terrified but determined. They demanded that Taylor attend peace talks in Accra, Ghana, meant to bring an end to the fighting.

For days on end, the women occupied the large expanse of the no-man's-land in front of James Spriggs Payne Airport. Bernice Freeman, whose pregnant cousin Famatta had been murdered by Doe's forces thirteen years before, joined the women at "Airfield," the name Liberians gave the expanse. Wearing a white T-shirt over her loose skirt, Bernice knelt down in the sandy dirt and joined the other women to pray for peace.

The women wore no adornments to beautify themselves—just the white T-shirts and the loose clothes. They sang, they fasted, and they prayed. The Holy Ghost women moved in and out of the group, leading prayers and chants and songs. The days turned into weeks, and the women still came, every day, to Airfield.

Stationed so prominently between Airfield and Tubman Boulevard, the praying women were the first thing international visitors saw upon arriving in Liberia. Soon they became too much of an eyesore for Taylor, and he sent his hated and feared security chief, Benjamin Yeaten—the one who had ordered the murder of the Dokies and so many others—to remove them.

It was around 1 p.m., and the sun was hot. Louise Yarsiah was leading the prayers, and the hundreds of women in white T-shirts were on their knees in the sand. Five pickup trucks pulled up, and Yeaten, accompanied by around fifty soldiers, jumped out. Yeaten was a slim man; Bernice immediately recognized him, but she said nothing, just stayed on her knees. So did the other women.

Yeaten and the soldiers assumed firing position. One by one, the women heard rounds being chambered. Still they remained on their knees, praying.

The silence deepened, as the men waited for the order to fire.

Finally, Yeaten said, "As you were." Even for Taylor's most feared henchman, it turned out, there was a line he couldn't cross. As Yeaten and the men walked away, Bernice heard him saying, "We can't do this."

And the women kept praying.

Under the gun, with LURD rebels engaging in periodic strikes on Monrovia, an embattled Taylor finally agreed to attend peace talks in Ghana in June. There, in a surreal scene, he found out about the war crimes indictment against him. The United Nations had waited three months to unveil the indictment that accused him of "bearing the greatest responsibility" for a decade's worth of murders, mutilations, and rapes—in Sierra Leone.

Not Liberia. Sierra Leone.

Even stranger, the indictment was announced just after Taylor declared that he would step down by the end of the year. It was a stunning diplomatic drama in which Taylor, in the space of mere minutes, was transformed from statesman to fugitive. The delegates at the peace conference applauded his announcement, then news of his indictment came out, and Taylor abruptly left, catching a plane home rather than risk arrest.

Back to Monrovia, where a million people endured a humanitarian crisis, cut off from food, water, and medical supplies. Mortars—some from the rebels, some from the government—pounded crowded neighborhoods. Spent shells collected on the pavement, settling beside dead bodies. People ran frantically through the streets searching for safety, and dozens were killed just outside the fortified American Embassy in Mamba Point, where they had gathered to seek shelter. LURD leaders said they would stop fighting only if Taylor left; Taylor told his supporters, "Fight on."

"Your survival is my survival," he said on the radio. "My survival is your survival."

In late June, preparing for his first ever visit to Africa, President George W. Bush called on Taylor to resign for the sake of peace. Taylor said he wouldn't leave until international peacekeepers came.

LURD began a fresh assault on Monrovia.

And in the sand and dirt in front of Airfield, Bernice Freeman, Louise Yarsiah, and the hundreds of other women in white T-shirts continued to gather and call to God to end the war. They sang "We Shall Overcome."

We shall overcome, we shall overcome
We shall overcome someday;
Oh, deep in my heart, I do believe,
We shall overcome someday.
We are not afraid, we are not afraid
We are not afraid today;
Oh, deep in my heart, I do believe
We are not afraid today.

Chapter 9

ELECTORAL COLLEGE

Accra, July 2003

In 2003, Liberia was dubbed one of the world's worst places, among a small handful of countries that combined "warfare, banditry, disease, land mines and violence in a terminal adventure ride."

Not Iraq, where American forces had overrun the capital but were soon to spark a bloody insurgency that would leave almost 5,000 Americans and 100,000 Iraqis dead.

Not Afghanistan, where the Taliban had begun to stage a comeback, and Pashtun, Uzbek, and Al Qaeda warlords were battling CIA contract agents and U.S. Marines simultaneously for control of South Asia's famous graveyard of empires.

Not even Somalia, where Islamic gunmen drunk on their own power had turned the streets of Mogadishu into a hellscape.

Monrovia had them all beat. Liberia, pronounced Robert Young Pelton in his irreverent travel guide, *The World's Most Dangerous Places*, was "a chaotic backwater where an escaped prisoner trained by Qaddafi plunders to the sound of American gangster rap."

In one week alone, in July, more than six hundred Monrovia residents were mowed down by machine guns, rocket-propelled grenades, and mortar fire. Tubman Boulevard was lined with bodies. One woman squatted on the side of the road, rocking back and forth and chanting incomprehensibly in front of the bullet-ridden body of her teenage son as he lay in the fetid air.

Women dragged the dead bodies of their children and lined them up in front of the fortified American Embassy in Mamba Point. The bodies lay there for two days, in the pouring rain, until finally the women picked up their dead children and took them away.

On July 5, market women turned out for a peace rally at the fish market in Monrovia. In Accra, Liberian women dressed in white T-shirts demonstrated outside the center where peace talks were being held, demanding that delegates not leave the talks until there was a real peace deal.

Although Taylor wasn't at the meetings, he had representatives there, and there were representatives from LURD and other warring groups. Ellen was there as well, furiously telephoning the United Nations envoys, chatting up the Ghanaian president, and simultaneously berating the Bush administration for sending a low-level delegation to the talks. She even got an op-ed published in the *New York Times* during the peace talks in which she aired two decades' worth of grievances against the United States, criticizing the Reagan administration for giving its official sanction to the crooked Liberian elections back in 1985, which, she said, helped pave the way for the carnage in 2003.

Of course, she had given her official sanction to Taylor in the beginning, a decision she would have to live with for the rest of her life.

On the floor outside the negotiating hall, two hundred Liberian women, led by the charismatic Leymah Gbowee, staged a sit-down protest, continuing their demand that no one leave until they reached a peace deal. When one of the LURD warlords, General Joe Wylie, tried to leave the hall, the group blocked him.

When Wylie kicked at the women, Nigeria's former president General Abdulsalami Alhaji Abubakar became furious. "I dare you," he told Wylie. "If you were a real man, you wouldn't be killing your people. But because you are not a real man that is why these women will treat you like boys. I dare you to leave this hall until we have negotiated a peace with these women."

And still, the fighting continued.

As LURD rebels advanced swiftly into Monrovia, shelling buildings and spraying bullets, a terrified twenty-eight-year-old Mary Warner strapped her four-year-old son on her back and ran from place to place, finally ending up pressed against a gate outside the United Nations compound, desperately seeking shelter. "Anywhere we go, they say 'place full,'" she told a reporter with the *New York Times*. "We don't have anywhere to go."

Finally, after eight weeks of haggling in Accra while Monrovia burned, the warring sides reached a peace agreement. All combatants would disarm. West African peacekeeping forces would enter Liberia and would be replaced in a few months by a United Nations peacekeeping mission, complete with international troops. A transitional government would be set up, whose job would be to pave the way to democratic elections in Liberia.

Charles Taylor would leave. Nigeria, after years of losing its own blood and human treasure in Liberia, stepped forward and offered him a safe haven.

On August 11, Taylor appeared before a crowd of Liberian politicians, foreign officials, and journalists in a room at the Executive Mansion. "History will be kind to me," he said. "I have accepted this role as the sacrificial lamb."

Appearing to be losing his already tenuous grip on reality, Taylor likened himself to Jesus. He blamed international forces for his downfall. Then, as required by the peace deal, he turned the government over to his vice president and longtime ally, Moses Z. Blah, who would be charged with steering the country until a transitional government could take over in a few months.

Dressed in white, the man the world had accused of sparking the worst fighting and bloodshed in West Africa's history got into his car and rode through the streets of Monrovia to Robertsfield Airport. Along the road, Taylor's supporters waved and wept, while LURD rebels, many of them stripped naked to resemble the monkeys to which they likened their opponents, jeered and waved their machine guns.

Just after 5 p.m., waving a white handkerchief at the crowd and escorted by President John Kufuor of Ghana, Charles Taylor boarded a Nigerian jet and left Liberia.

Three American warships showed up on the horizon off Mamba Point, while two helicopters ferried goods from the ships to the American Embassy. It was all for show, but the traumatized Liberian population ran to the beach and cheered the warships anyway.

Fourteen years of civil war had come to an end. The prayers of the market women who had knelt in front of Airfield in the hot sun for weeks had been answered.

The market women ran to the beach too. Wearing their white T-shirts, they cheered and danced and sang hymns. The men representing the various rebel groups and political factions were already maneuvering to see who would be the next to take over. They didn't know it at the time, but the market women had plans as well, and the embodiment of those plans was sitting in Accra at the peace talks—Liberia's equivalent of Yalta—where the transitional government was being carved up and handed over to the warring factions.

No matter. The real battle would be coming soon. The men had ruled the war. Now the women were getting ready to rule the peace.

From the beginning, the men put up a fight. In Accra, it was time to choose an interim chairman for the transitional government. The person elected would be critical to positioning the country for real democratic elections, the kind in which the motto of one of the candidates isn't "You killed my ma, you killed my pa, I will vote for you." Whoever won the position would have two years to rule Liberia, a critical period to begin the job of turning child soldiers, whose entire lives had been a close study in abandonment, violence, depravity, and survival, into people again. Whoever won the position would be barred from running in the presidential elections in 2005, but the winner would get a two-year window to begin dragging Liberia from the abyss to something resembling a functional civilization.

After complicated rules were established to determine who among the representatives of the warring parties was eligible to vote for the interim chairman, ten men and one woman put their names forward for the position.

Ellen won the most votes, receiving thirty-three. Next was Rudolph Sherman, who was believed to be close to Taylor; he received eighteen votes. Third was Gyude Bryant, a fifty-four-year-old businessman and a member of Ellen's former party, the Liberia Action Party.

But for women, apparently, it is not enough to win the popular vote.

After the vote, representatives of the factions declared themselves an "electoral college" and asked for the names of the three highest vote-getters. From those three, they would choose an interim president, they said. Meanwhile, in the hallways outside the conference, businesspeople wanting to curry favor with a new Liberian government baldly offered cash to the various power players.

That night, Ellen huddled with one of her advisers and came up with a plan: she would join the cash-for-votes practice and would bribe one of the warlords to talk the rest of the men into pushing for her; she was the top vote-getter, after all, she reasoned.

A LURD chief was summoned to Ellen's makeshift headquarters in Accra, where she gave him $10,000 in cash that she got from a wealthy friend, in return for his vote. The warlord took the money and left to attend the meeting.

In African politics—like politics in the Americas, Europe, and everywhere else—there are always two worlds. One is the aspirant world, where leaders talk about good governance and anticorruption and spout platitudes about the importance of staying clean and walking the high road. In some places, maybe Sweden, some even manage to do so. And then there is the real world, where aspirant leaders—even one who cut her teeth at the World Bank and the United Nations—offer cash under the table to a warlord for his vote.

Ellen played in both worlds.

"Delegates at the Liberian peace talks in Ghana have chosen Gyude Bryant, a 54-year-old businessman, to head a two-year National Transitional Government that will take over from Interim President Moses Blah on 14 October," the IRIN news agency reported the next day. The men making the selection said that Bryant was politically neutral and therefore acceptable to all the warring parties.

The LURD chief returned the money to Ellen, saying, "I'm sorry we did not select you."

The men had won that battle, but they had set themselves up to lose the war. Ellen wouldn't get first crack at trying to turn her blood-soaked home back into a country again, but the coast was now clear for her to run for president in 2005.

She asked to head the Contracts and Monopolies Commission, a deceptively arcane-sounding position from which she would be able to track questionable side deals between the Liberian government and shady businesspeople. "Beyond your reach," Bryant told her. Instead, he made her head of the Governance Reform Commission, a nebulous entity charged with promoting good government in Liberia, a place where a real government had not functioned in more than a decade.

There was another cabinet position that appeared largely useless to the men who were setting up Liberia's interim government: the Ministry of Gender. Who cared about the Ministry of Gender? Clearly whoever Bryant gave that position to would have to be a woman; the ministry focused on issues involving women and children, infant feeding programs, malaria prevention, and maternity health, issues in which the men maneuvering for positions of power were barely interested. So the men concentrated on Defense. (Rebuild the army.) Finance. (Control the purse strings.) Foreign affairs. (Travel to world capitals.) To the Ministry of Gender they delegated Vabah Gayflor, on the advice of Etweda Sugars Cooper, one of the women peace activists who had been harassing them at the Accra peace talks.

Gayflor had studied economics at the University of Liberia, but like just about every other Liberian woman, she had become a market woman during the war years, selling fried potatoes on the side of the road. While the country's various rebel groups pounded each other in the bush and the cities, she was getting up early in the morning with the rest of Liberia's market women to find anything she could get her hands on to sell to feed her children. Hiding out near Bong Mines during one bombing campaign in 1990, she had noticed a line of women disappearing into the bush every morning and returning in the afternoon with goods to sell. One morning she followed them and discovered that the women were gathering potato greens, okra, bitterballs to fill the buckets they put on the top of their head and brought to the market. Soon Gayflor was doing the same thing and gaining some allies who would eventually prove very powerful.

One of the women gave her a diamond she had dug out of one of Liberia's diamond mines. "You know book," the woman said. "You can help me sell it, and you can eat some of the money." Gayflor sold the diamond for her friend, and they split the money. After that she started skirting the edges of the diamond mines herself, looking for strays. She asked her brother if he wanted to come with her to help look, but her brother refused. "And get bitten by snake? I beg you, ya." Instead, he stayed home and ate the food his sister bought with the money she made selling diamonds and potato greens.

"I got so pissed off," Gayflor recalled later. This was just so typical, a perfect illustration of the Liberian parable "monkey work, baboon draws." She and the other women were scouring the bush to put food on the table so their children—and their men—could eat. They started commiserating with each other, and these bonds, forged in the backbreaking work of making market with a baby on your back, cemented them into a movement. Vabah Gayflor, the university-educated economist turned market woman, now had a network of women up country with whom she had survived the war and whom she now viewed as the vehicle upon whose backs the country could rise or fall.

Meanwhile, at the Governance Reform Commission, Ellen began holding public forums where ordinary people showed up and registered their complaints. She collected suggestions about how they would like to be treated by their government, and she and her commission made suggestions, including one about how too much of the government's anemic stash of money was being spent on security services for Gyude Bryant. But her recommendations went nowhere. So she began making plans for a time when people would pay attention to her critiques.

Liberia in 2004 was a postapocalyptic place slowly awakening to the possibility that the war might actually be behind it. But its population was ravaged. In the streets, young women wearing long wigs, with no family, no prospects, and no training, patrolled the side of the road hoping to be picked up by men with money—UN bureaucrats, NGO workers, returning Congo men—anyone, really, willing to pay the price of lunch and maybe a trip to the hair stylist for a cheap thrill. Girls as young as fourteen were being squired around town by seventy-year-old men, former and present government ministers, who saw nothing coercive about exploiting teenage war orphans with no other means of support. At a wedding reception, a mature man of means and former government minister bragged that his current "girlfriend" was getting too old for him. "She just turned seventeen," he said, laughing. People around him shook their heads in a "boys will be boys" way.

The lot of life for women and girls in Liberia mirrored their lot all over Africa. In 2004, the worst place on earth to be a woman was Africa. In

Bukavu, Congo, old women with huge bundles of bamboo sticks on their back, their burdens larger than the backs carrying them, trudged up one hill after another on their long walk from village to market. In Sierra Leone's countryside, young women and girls sat in front of village huts bathing their sons, daughters, brothers, and sisters in rubber buckets, with no idea what electricity was or what running water felt like. In Guinea, the market women in their colorful dresses huddled together on the side of the road selling oranges, hard-boiled eggs, and nuts, knowing that what coin they produced on any given day was all their family could depend on to eat that night.

As Ellen traveled around Liberia collecting input from ordinary women for her job on the Governance Reform Commission, she met woman after woman who, against all odds, still clung fiercely to the trappings of daily life, no matter how difficult it was to obtain those trappings. She saw young girls walking miles down dirt roads with buckets of water on their head. She saw women who had been dragged from their home during the war, raped in the forest by multiple men, abandoned by their family. Forced to bear the children of their rapists alone and frightened in the bush, they strapped those same babies on their back and hacked with cutlasses as they tended their farms, cultivating pawpaw to sell at the market.

While she was organizing her public forums, Ellen passed through village markets attended by the women who had kept selling dried fish, cassava, and kola nuts even through the war years. They all had stories to tell her: of their daughters who had disappeared in Monrovia and who were now engaged in funny business with big men; of their sons who were taken from them; of their husbands who abandoned them after they were raped.

Ellen had been largely living an expat life in America, in Abidjan, and in the World Bank and United Nations conference rooms where bureaucrats talked about microfinance and rural empowerment and the need for development dollars to go to small businesses. But now she was seeing the need firsthand.

These women. The prostitutes in front of Samuel K. Doe Stadium on the road to Robertsfield. The women with dirty fingernails at Rally Time

Market across the street from BTC, where Ellen had been jailed all those years ago.

The women who had walked from door to door during her prison term collecting signatures demanding her release. The Gio girl who huddled next to her in that dank dark cell in Schiefflin after being raped by the soldiers. The young girl who had gone to the Unity Party headquarters the day she was released, who could still remember, with tears in her eyes, Ellen reciting the second stanza of the Liberian national anthem.

Grace-tee McGill, who had become Grace Kpaan after getting married during the Taylor war. Bernice Freeman, who last saw her pregnant cousin Famatta as she was being driven away by the Doe soldiers who would execute her and her baby. Parleh Harris, who crouched with her two-year-old son watching Doe's soldiers blow up a young gas hawker in front of her house. Masawa Jabateh, who witnessed Taylor's soldiers tie her grandfather to a pole and burn him alive. Josephine, who cooked every day for the Taylor soldiers who raped her. Katoumba, who, at seven, was taken by a rebel commander after his soldiers killed her parents, who called her his "play daughter" and protected her, only to be executed in front of her.

All of these women, and thousands upon thousands more. These were the women who would become Ellen's base.

To all appearances, Ellen looked like she was making a valiant effort at doing her job as head of the interim government's Governance Reform Commission. But anyone who knew her knew what she was really doing: preparing her base for the fight of their lives. Elections were coming in October 2005.

It was time to make history.

Chapter 10

VOTE FOR WOMAN

Monrovia, 2005

> You selling your bitterballs and your okra? We will mind it for
> you. Go register.
>
> —Etweda Sugars Cooper, speaking to
> Liberian market women, June 2005

The biggest and most significant battle of the 2005 election began long
before the campaign season started, when Vabah Gayflor woke up on the
morning of May 2 to discover that her women had not been registering to
vote.

Voter registration for the presidential elections was to take place for
one month, from April 24 to May 24, after which no one without a voter
ID card would be allowed to cast a ballot in October. This was the first
hurdle for any candidate hoping to motivate supporters to actually vote.

A slew of men were tossing their hats into the ring for the presidency.
They included Charles Brumskine, a former Taylor ally turned foe, whom
the *Washington Post* had recently dubbed a "real contender" for the presidency. There was Winston Tubman, the justice minister under Doe. He
had made a last-ditch, unsuccessful effort in 1990 to try to get the Americans to help Doe when the Taylor and Johnson rebels were advancing on
Monrovia. There was Varney Sherman, a Harvard-trained lawyer. George
Weah was a world-renowned football player. A star in Europe when he
was a striker for the Italian team AC Milan, in 1995 Weah won the Ballon
d'Or and was named the FIFA world player of the year, and had even been
voted by sports journalists as the African Player of the Century, an honor

he shared with the incomparable Pelé, who won as the South American Player of the Century.

Two Weah goals in particular stood out. One was against Bayern in 1994 when he played for Paris St. Germain and embarrassed not one or two but three Bayern defenders with his quick pivots before letting rip a gorgeous sally into the near post. The other goal was for AC Milan in 1996, when Weah destroyed the Verona midfield as he singlehandedly slalomed his way down the pitch, twisting, turning, bucking, and weaving all the way to the Verona goal in a legendary performance that Liberians, who watched it using their makeshift Tiger batteries to generate power on their television sets since there was no electricity, still talked about a decade later.

At thirty-eight years old, Weah was beloved by young Liberian men, who live, eat, and drink football and who saw in him the embodiment of that rarest of things: a Liberian who was famous on the world stage for something other than killing people. Yet many Liberians were angry at Weah because in 2002, when he coached the Liberian football team to the edge of qualifying for the World Cup—Liberia's Lone Star team needed only a tie with Ghana to qualify—Weah let the players get drunk and preemptively celebrate the night before the crucial match, losing the next day 1–0.

Still, unlike his rivals, Weah was not tainted by any association with the maniacs who had run Liberia into the ground over the past two decades.

That Weah had no college education (he claimed a bachelor of arts degree in sports management from Parkwood University in London, which was an unaccredited diploma mill that awarded certificates without requiring actual study) did not bother his youthful supporters, who countered that the Verona goal showed its own education.

At the other end of the spectrum among the contenders for president was Ellen Johnson Sirleaf. Finance minister under Tolbert; dissident against Doe; United Nations, World Bank, and IMF pedigree; ally-turned-foe of Taylor. The woman who had morphed from an abused wife, cowering and hunched in the front seat of Doc Sirleaf's car while he slapped her, to an international bureaucrat and iconic political dissident was now attempting to do something no woman had ever done before: win, by popular vote, the right to lead an African country.

Often when the press, both international and local, wrote about her these days, they described her as "the sixty-six-year-old grandmother." Taylor, who had numerous grandchildren from his fourteen children, most of them bestowed with names that have some version of "Charles" in them—Charal, Charishma, Charmilah, Philip Charles, Charles Emmanuel, Charlyne, Charlize—was never described as a grandfather.

To the Weah supporters, there was no contest. Grandmother versus football star? But to Vabah Gayflor, Bernice Freeman, Grace Kpaan, Etweda Sugars Cooper, and the Liberian women in the white T-shirts, there was likewise no contest. Harvard-trained economist versus football player? Get real. "You will take our country, our baby, and throw de baby away to football player? I beg you, no," Gayflor said.

In appearance and manner, Gayflor was the antithesis of Ellen. Mouthy and spontaneously passionate, she exuded a robust energy that contrasted with Ellen's calm reserve. Sure, Ellen could turn on the fire when she was on the stump, but in one-on-one meetings, she didn't blow up at people. Gayflor, on the other hand, was quick to ignite.

The two women barely knew each other, but to Gayflor, that didn't matter. She knew Ellen's résumé. Gayflor had lived in Liberia throughout the Taylor and Doe years. She knew what she wanted—and more important, what she did not want—for her country in the years to come.

As the head of the Ministry of Gender, Gayflor's job was supposed to be about helping women and children get access to health care, school feeding programs (in a postwar country with hardly any schools), antimalaria drugs, maternal support groups, rape support groups, and more. But Gayflor did not view her job that way. She had decided that all those nice programs for women would be available only if there was a woman at the top to supply them. So she decided her job as minister of gender was to get a woman elected president. And on the morning of May 2, she was not happy with the news she had just gotten from the National Elections Commission: of the 100,000 Liberians who had registered to vote in the first week of the monthlong registration drive, only 15 percent were women.

Who was registering instead? Former combatants—from LURD, Taylor's NPFL, and all the other armed groups. Gayflor was appalled.

Ellen had not yet announced her candidacy, but everyone knew she was planning to run, and she had already resigned from the Governance Reform Commission. In any event, huddling with Etweda Sugars Cooper, the women's activist known throughout Liberia as "Sugars," after the first week's dismal registration count, Gayflor knew they had to take action fast, whether or not Ellen was formally in the race.

"We will put our country devil there and dress it later," Cooper told the group. Translation: We'll worry about the actual election when October comes; first, just make sure the women register so they'll be able to vote.

"We had three weeks. The first week was already gone," Gayflor recalled.

The men were holding mass rallies to urge their supporters to vote. But market women didn't have time to go to mass rallies. They were busy trying to make a living. Gayflor and Cooper realized they were going to have to try a different strategy.

Quickly they and Parleh Harris, another Gender Ministry official, organized a group to use the radio stations to plead, "Women, oh women! Y'all gotta register to vote." They fanned out to the Monrovia markets, from the Rally Time Market across from BTC to the Nancy Doe Market in Sinkor, corralling the women who had set up shop to sell potato greens, kola nuts, soap, and bread.

At first, some of the women balked; they had their wares or their babies to tend. But Cooper was ready for them. "You selling your bitterballs and your okra?" she asked. "We will mind it for you. Go register." And young aides dispatched by Cooper and Gayflor tended their stalls for the women while they left to register. For young mothers who said they couldn't register because they had children to mind, Harris had nannies at the ready. "Bring your baby," she said. "Let me hold your baby. Go register."

Masawa Jabateh, the teenager whose baby had died from malnourishment during the Taylor war, joined them. She was a grown woman now, thirty-three years old. She had had another child, this time a son, also born during the war years. This one had survived. But Masawa remained haunted by the loss of her three-year-old daughter. And that despair mixed with a blinding fury when she thought about the elections: "Those men want put some grona boy in the chair who don't know what he doing? So we can go back to war again? No." Masawa's thought process was straight-forward: "Woman will not go get boyfriend. Woman now bury plenty of her children them. I voting for woman." So she joined the women, going door to door, to get women in Monrovia registered to vote.

But it wasn't enough to register the women in Monrovia. The Liberian bush loomed, large, imposing, and filled with village women. "We got to get out of the city because if we don't do something up country, we are doomed," Gayflor said.

They bought bullhorns and scattered their troops along the road to Cape Mount, to Gborpolu, to Margibi, to Gbarnga, all the way to Nimba, along the traditional pathways used by market women to bring their wares into the cities. "Women, oh women!" they yelled into the bullhorns. "Go register."

Up country, Gayflor asked the officials at the local registration office to set up mobile registration stands in the villages deep in the bush, to take the registration process to the people. They agreed. So she and Cooper and other women activists walked three, five, seven hours into villages deep in the bush, with their mobile stands, to register women to vote. Men came to register as well, and Gayflor and Cooper didn't turn them away. But they focused on the women.

It was almost like a party at times, the women dancing and singing behind their leaders, who bellowed into their bullhorns for all to hear as they entered each village: "Women, oh women! Come register."

It was the start of the rainy season, and the holes in the roads up country were quickly filling with dirty brown water. Gayflor was trying to sleep one night in an unfinished and abandoned house, lying on the floor with the other women activists as the rain seeped through the cloth someone had hooked over the open window. They were not far from Gborpolu, in a place with no plumbing, electricity, running water, or even a Tiger battery to charge their cell phones. That night, the women had become itinerant squatters, finding a place to sleep in a building long ago abandoned. Gayflor lay on her back in the dark, wondering why it had become so important to her, this goal of getting women to register to vote.

A rat ran across her face.

She jumped up, her stomach heaving, her body trembling in revulsion. "Wha' happen?" asked the woman sleeping nearby.

"Rat," Gayflor answered. "Rat now run over me."

She spent the rest of the night sitting up near the window in a plastic chair as the rain beat down outside, her eye trolling the dark room for rats.

Why was it so important, this business of registering?

Then she thought about the war, and remembered why.

When she went back to Monrovia at the end of the registration period, she tried one more time to sway the registration commission. Could they, she asked, please extend the registration period for another week? Just give people a little more time? They said no, but they released the final figures: 1.5 million Liberians out of the country's 3 million population had registered to vote.

And they released an even more important number: 51—the percentage of registered voters who were women.

On the damp Saturday morning of August 13, 2005, Liberia's Electoral Commission announced the candidates who were cleared to run in October. All thirty seats in the Senate and seventy-three in the House of Representatives were up for grabs. The commission cleared 206 candidates to run for Senate; they included Prince Johnson, the former rebel leader and killer of Samuel Doe, who was running in Nimba County; another former warlord, Adolphus Dolo, nicknamed General Peanut Butter, a Taylor loyalist running against Johnson for the Nimba seat (his slogan: "Let him butter your bread"); and Jewel Taylor, the wife of Charles Taylor, for the Bong County seat.

The commission cleared 503 candidates to run for the House of Representatives and announced the twenty-two candidates it had cleared to be on the presidential ballot. Besides Brumskine, Tubman, and Sherman, they included William Vacanarat Shadrach Tubman Jr., the son of President Tubman, who, for obvious reasons, had shortened his name to "Shad"; Togba-Nah Tipoteh, the former minister of planning who had botched the Citibank meeting in 1980 with his inflammatory verbal assault on the old and recently murdered Liberian guard; and Sekou Conneh, the former LURD rebel leader.

The commission also cleared George Weah to run, despite grumblings that he had taken French citizenship when he was playing football in Europe during the war years. After all, what Liberian in their right mind hadn't lunged for any foreign country that would have them during that time? Weah's supporters quickly adopted a new slogan for their man. It sounded familiar, though: "Did he kill your ma? No! Did he kill your pa? No! Vote for Weah!"

And the commission cleared two women to run. Both of them had double-barreled surnames in a poignant reminder of a fledgling feminist generation—though not so feminist that Ellen could get rid of Doc Sirleaf's name—taking baby steps toward independence. Margaret Tor-Thompson was a little-known activist and occasional Holy Ghost woman. She was not considered a potential force in the election. The other woman, though, was a different story.

Campaigning began two days later, on Monday, August 15.

Weah quickly became the show, riding down Tubman Boulevard in a convertible, waving at the thousands of supporters who lined the street, singing and shouting. Anyone who has ever been in Liberia knows that it takes a special kind of chutzpah to ride in a convertible, what with the rain and mud during the rainy season and the dust during the dry season. Weah's supporters loved it; the boys who led his convoy stood on cars moving slowly ahead of their man, while others played football in the streets, tying up traffic for hours.

Ellen started more quietly but more deliberately, putting her international contacts to work. She went to an old friend, Larry Gibson, a Maryland lawyer with interests in African politics; he had recently run a successful campaign on behalf of the president of Madagascar. After interviewing hundreds of ordinary Liberians all over the country, Gibson had come back with simple advice: Weah had a lot of support among young men—remember the Bayern and Verona goals—but that was about it. His support had a ceiling of around 25 to 30 percent. Liberia's election rules dictated that a winning candidate had to get 50 percent of the vote—a quirk that practically guaranteed that in a crowded field of twenty-two candidates, there would be a runoff. So the key for Ellen was to survive the first round without alienating the supporters of the other candidates, whom she would need to flock to her side when the second round came.

Gibson had Ellen sit at her house for a photo session for her campaign poster. She changed into a succession of outfits, both Liberian and Western, striking different poses. As soon as she announced her candidacy, she started wearing colorful African Fanti dresses and suits, complete with head-tie, the better to connect with native Liberians. But Gibson had a specific pose in mind for her; he remembered an old black-and-white photo of her after she got out of jail in 1986. Fresh out of prison and surrounded by supporters, Ellen had on her Rasta hat and her hippie "Peace Shalom" T-shirt and had pumped her fist in the air, looking for all the world like a young and sexy avatar of black power. This was the pose Ellen would replicate for her campaign poster, next to the original 1986 just-out-of-prison photo, just in case anyone needed reminding that she was a fighter. In one fell swoop, Ellen would be declaring that, sure, she had been in the government before, but she had also fought the government and had paid for her activism in prison.

Gibson flew to China to print up 850,000 posters and to buy 20,000 rain ponchos emblazoned with the words "The rain will not stop Ellen and the Unity Party." When the posters finally went up in Liberia, people were electrified.

Old Lady was old. But Old Lady knew how to fight, oh!

Ellen also turned to one of her best friends, a feisty woman called Mary Broh. The two had hung out together when Ellen was at the United Nations. Mary was still in New York, still working as the shipping and logistics manager at the toy division of Marvel Entertainment. She asked for a two-week vacation and flew to Monrovia, bringing with her a hundred Spider-Man backpacks. She donned one herself and gave the other ninety-nine to women who would be going door-to-door to campaign for Ellen.

And off they went, Mary Broh and her minions, hitting communities in Paynesville, markets in Sinkor, houses in West Point and New Kru Town.

"Ma people, we here oh!" Mary yelled, hopping off a bus in New Kru Town one afternoon, wearing her Spider-Man backpack. As women clus-

152

tered around her, she launched into her spiel: "Y'all know the Old Ma. The Old Ma got connections, oh! She will bring jobs here. She will make sure the banks them will come here, they will give you credit. You will be able to make good market."

For two weeks straight, the dogged Mary Broh and her spider-women campaigned. Then, her vacation time up, she flew back to America.

The country was now gripped by election fever. Every car, taxi, bus, building, lamppost, and yard seemed to sport a campaign poster. There were rallies every day, in churches, on the streets, in town halls across the country.

Early on, Ellen found herself in a debate with Brumskine, the *Washington Post*'s "real contender." Brumskine had huge support among some religious organizations and had been going around saying that God had ordained him to be president.

Liberia is a seriously religious country, with a church on every corner and piety brandished openly. Holy Ghost women fast and pray for days on end; Ellen herself had a core group of such women who were, even now, clad in white T-shirts and holding days-long fasts to pray for her candidacy. In Liberia, pious sayings come from the most incongruous places, including from the lips of dissolute men who live to sin. Married Liberian men will sit in bars next to their sixteen-year-old war-orphan "little friends" and go on and on about how homosexuality is wrong in the eyes of God.

So for Brumskine to proclaim that God wanted him to be president was serious business. Ellen knew she was supposed to make nice with her opponents so as not to alienate their supporters come runoff time, but this was too much. During a joint campaign session at a Baptist church, when Brumskine repeated his God-wants-me bit, Ellen offered up her own, delicately worded reply. "I do believe in God and His messages," she assured the audience. "Maybe He does want Brumskine to be president." She paused. "Just not in 2006."

Ellen had been dubbed the "Iron Lady" already, a reference that most people believed stemmed from her having survived imprisonment, multiple brushes with death, and the vagaries of working with and against Liberia's various strongmen. But in the two months between the beginning of campaign season in August and Election Day in October, the aides around her came to realize that the nickname actually referred to her constitution. Her *physical* constitution.

The Iron Lady never got tired. She decided early on that she would visit each of Liberia's fifteen counties. The country is only the size of Ohio, but with a few exceptions, there are no paved roads outside of Monrovia. And there are very few dirt roads. And the dirt roads that do exist are barely passable during the dry season, being pockmarked with crater-size holes and bridges held together with miscellaneous car parts. In the rainy season, most become unusable.

And yet Ellen insisted on using them. "I have to *be* the show," she told her aides. She drove all night and campaigned during the day. They were long, painful drives, with her convoy going excruciatingly slowly to navigate the potholes, the mud, and the pools of rainwater that collected in the middle of the road. Sometimes Ellen, along with everyone else in her convoy, got out and pushed the cars through the mud. Where there were no roads, she took canoes—sometimes paddling herself—to cross a river to visit a village.

Everywhere she went up country, Ellen was confronted with stories of survival. Everyone she met, in fact, was a survivor with a story to tell of escape from some sort of wartime atrocity. She heard of entire families who died of malaria because they couldn't get drugs during the war; of people who fled into the bush to escape one militia or another and who survived by eating rats; of girls who were turned into sex slaves and given to various rebel groups, made to serve an entire corps, until they inevitably got pregnant and swollen and were then abandoned to have their babies alone in the bush.

With only seven weeks before the election, Ellen certainly could not go everywhere. That's when her growing army of market women came into play. Ellen now had an army of Martha Nagbes, the market woman she took with her to lunch at the Hotel Ivoire in Abidjan. From village to village, from hut to hut, Martha Nagbe and the troops of Vabah Gayflor and Mary Broh and Bernice Freeman traveled to campaign for her.

Freeman was chatting with some market women one afternoon, trying to convince them to vote for Ellen, when she noticed some boys laughing nearby, waving something white. She looked closer. The boys had taken women's panties, smeared the crotches with tomato paste, and were waving them at the women. Instead of making Freeman and the other women cower in embarrassment, however, the heckling only pissed them off. "You know what?" one of the undecided women told Freeman, looking at the boys in disgust. "We will vote. Don't worry, we will vote."

As the minister of gender, Vabah Gayflor was supposed to be neutral. She was not, technically, allowed to show favoritism for any candidate, let alone campaign on her behalf. So she and Sugars Cooper devised a strategy: they would present their efforts as simply an attempt to empower women to vote. Gayflor wouldn't sully her cabinet position by *telling* the women who to vote for, oh no. (She left that to Cooper.) Instead, she would simply encourage women to exercise their right. She organized women's rallies, where she gave speeches exhorting the crowd to vote. "Make sure you get up early, women!" she said. "Get up early to vote!"

"I'm not telling you who to vote for, women! Just make sure you vote."

Right after Gayflor spoke, using the cloak of government respectability that her cabinet-level office gave her, Cooper—not constrained by any neutrality vows—shouted at the crowd, "Vote for woman!"

From Kakata to Gbarnga to Cape Mount, the women's rallies followed the same script:

Vabah Gayflor: Women, oh women! If y'all gotta tie your baby on your back soon in the morning, I beg y'all, go vote!

Sugars Cooper: Vote for woman!

Vabah Gayflor: Wake up early, women, I beg y'all, and vote!

Sugars Cooper: Vote for woman!

Vabah Gayflor: Even self your baby got poopoo diapers, put it down, go vote!

Sugars Cooper: Vote for woman!

Vabah Gayflor: Even self your husband get vexed, that's his business, go vote!

Sugars Cooper: Vote for woman!

At the rallies, the women passed out plastic bags of drinking water, a rare and precious commodity, especially in the bush, where people regularly drank from unsanitized wells and dirty rivers, one of the reasons the rate of waterborne disease was so high.

At first, Ellen didn't campaign with the market women and the women activists; she kept them at arm's length. "I'm running on my merits," she had told Cooper months before, when the activist came to her house to talk about the election. Rolling their eyes, the market women nonetheless continued campaigning for Ellen, and slowly word of giant rallies for her organized by the market women began to reach her ears. Often, her convoy passed Gayflor on the road, each headed toward the same electoral goal but never going to the same place.

"I'd be going somewhere, would see her coming back from there," Gayflor said.

The separation benefited both women. Gayflor was not supposed to be campaigning for a candidate, but this was Liberia, where everybody was bending the rules. One of George Weah's campaign managers, in fact, was a postal affairs official in the government.

A few days before the election, the two women appeared at the same event. By now, Ellen had come to see how much the market women were doing on her behalf all around the country. Spotting Gayflor in the audience, she sent for her to come sit on the stage. "The minute people saw my face appear beside her, it was news," Gayflor said.

Ellen and the women were feeling optimistic that they could pull off a win. Then, on the Saturday before Election Day, Weah staged a rally in Monrovia. If ever there was a show of strength, this was it. A whopping 100,000 people, mostly young men, showed up at the rally, flooding the streets and bringing the city to a standstill. Wearing T-shirts and bandanas printed with Weah's name and photo, the supporters marched ten, twelve, twenty, sometimes fifty deep from Weah's house to the headquarters of the Congress for Democratic Change Party. "George! George! He play football! He play football!" one group of men sang, running in formation. People waved palm fronds and signs; one of them called Weah "the messiah."

So mobbed was the rally that a forty-five-year-old man died from heat exhaustion and four people were treated at the hospital for dehydration.

Dispirited, Ellen and the women watched the news reports of the rally that night. In a country of more than 3 million people, Weah had gotten 100,000 out in the streets on the eve of the election to support him. How was that even possible? And how could Ellen withstand that kind of raw power?

The rainy season was ending, but the air was still stewy when Election Day dawned. And the heat never went away. Of the 1.3 million people registered to vote, some 900,000—or 75 percent—showed up at the polls. They walked, some of them for miles, from rural villages deep in the bush. They came in wheelbarrows, in wheelchairs. They came with babies on their back. They came the night before, some of them sleeping on the hard ground outside the polling booths so they could vote when morning came.

The line of people at the polling stations stretched as far as the eye could see. So many people showed up to vote that the polling stations had to extend their hours so that everyone could cast a ballot.

Ellen had spent the day before campaigning up country, finally crawling into bed at her hilltop farm in her father's village of Julejuah at around two in the morning. She woke up that morning still tired, but with a nervous energy. She voted at a polling station near Julejuah, ticking the box next to her own name. Then she headed back to Monrovia.

The results began to trickle in that night. As expected, Weah was in first place. But Ellen was right behind him, where she needed to be. Brumskine was in third.

In the week of counting, under the eagle eye of international observers, that order never changed, although at one point Brumskine got a burst of good returns and seemed to be catching up with Ellen. "This is like a roller coaster," Jennie Bernard muttered to herself. But Brumskine's surge wasn't enough. On October 18, the National Election Commission announced the results: George Weah, 28 percent. Ellen Johnson Sirleaf, 20 percent. Brumskine came in third, Tubman fourth, and Sherman fifth. But only the top two got to go to the runoff.

The Elections Commission set the date for the runoff on November 8. Campaigning would start on October 27.

Time for the real battle. The football player versus the now sixty-seven-year-old grandmother.

Chapter 11

COME! BORROW MY BABY

Monrovia, November 2005

The men fell in line behind George Weah and then complained that the women supporting Ellen were sexist.

It was a remarkable display. Given the choice between a football player with no credible college education, but two fantastic goals against Bayern and Verona, and a Harvard-educated development expert, the top male presidential candidates who fell short in the runoff, with the exception of Brumskine, endorsed the football player. Sherman, Tubman, Matthews—all hurried to back Weah.

Years later, Tubman explained his rationale. He endorsed the former football player not because he thought Weah was more qualified to be president than Ellen but because he knew he had a better chance of rising to a top position in a Weah government than a Sirleaf government. "I knew that I could have more influence with George Weah," he explained in an interview in 2013, "whereas Ellen Johnson Sirleaf already had lots of people backing her who were just like me, so my voice would be muted."

Weah, honing his message explaining why he, and not the Old Lady, should run Liberia, settled on an "educated people failed" theme. "You know book, you not know book, I will vote for you," became the Weah runoff slogan. And that theme was endorsed by the failed male presidential candidates who endorsed him. Even Sherman, the Harvard-trained lawyer, was claiming Weah's candidacy represented the future of Liberia.

Liberia had one of the lowest literacy rates in the world. So an illiterate population would identify with a president who dropped out of school, right?

Wrong. What the men who endorsed that strategy failed to realize is how much that very idea was angering the market women. Those women may not have been educated themselves, but they worked day and night in the fields and the market stalls to send their children to school. Now the men were telling them education wasn't important?

Just as the men fell in behind Weah, the women fell in behind Ellen.

It didn't happen all at once. Women political candidates had appeared all over the ballot in the elections, running for Senate and House, on the same ticket as Weah and Tubman and Sherman. Even Parleh Harris had competed in the first round on the Liberia Destiny Party as Nathaniel Barnes's vice presidential candidate.

But once the time came for campaigning for the runoff, those allegiances peeled away even the women who were staunch members of parties that opposed Ellen's Unity Party abandoned the men and took up the now familiar mantra "Vote for woman!"

Door-to-door the market women passed out T-shirts and handing out fliers. They slept on the side of the road at night, curled up on their mats. They walked from village to village, exhorting women to vote for woman.

Weah's supporters responded by predicting that if he lost, the country would go back to war. "No Weah, no peace!" they chanted.

Weah himself fed that view. He suggested that he had actually won the first round, that he had received 62 percent of the vote, and that the Elections Commission had engaged in fraud to keep him from being declared the outright winner. One of his campaign surrogates told supporters that only fraud would keep Weah from winning and that Weah's supporters wouldn't "accept anything less than victory."

Thus the runoff started resembling past elections, like the one in 1985 in which Doe's supporters had suggested the same thing: Vote for Doe or the country goes back to war. Ellen raised a stink against such talk, and members of the international community took up the call, urging Weah and his supporters to refrain from such bullying. But in Liberia, this tactic was how men managed to get their way: they simply threatened the people.

Except that, in November 2005, they appeared to have met their match. Because the women had their own tricks, tricks that would make Weah's threats look like boys' play.

"You want beer? Just gimme your voter ID card, I will buy you beer."

"I say, we buying voter ID cards oh. Ten Liberty dollars for one."

"Who looking for money? Just bring your voter ID card."

The group of women had stationed themselves at a bar near the ELWA Junction, a major intersection in Monrovia along the road to Robertsfield. Armed with Liberian dollars—so-called Liberty dollars—which were virtually worthless on the international market but good for small purchases within the country, the women set to work luring the young men in a time-honored fashion. Except this time it wasn't sex on the table. And this time the women were the ones with the cash and the young men were the ones with the commodity for sale.

"Some of those boys were finish stupid," one market woman recalled with a smirk. She declined to give her name to the interviewer but was happy to go into detail about what she called the women's "crafty technique."

"We were crafty oh!" she said, one silver tooth glinting in the sunshine as she laughed. Many of the young men thought they were done with voting after the first round and didn't understand they would need their ID cards again if their man was to actually assume the presidency. Others knew and didn't care; late in the evening of a muggy hot day, the lure of a crisp, cold, and malty Club Beer far outshone whatever benefits they thought their voter card could bring them.

As for the ones who were too smart to sell their voter card—well, their mothers simply stole them. "Some of those old ma them, when their children had hard head, said they still voting for George Weah, they stole their children' them voting cards," Parleh Harris said, looking sheepish and defiant at the same time.

One market woman, who agreed to be referred to as "the Oma," said she snuck into her son's room while he was sleeping, slipped his voter ID out of his wallet, and buried it in the yard.

Years later there was no shame among the women who stole their sons' ID cards. "Yeah, I took it. And so what?" the Oma said. "That foolish boy, wha' he knew? I carried him for nine months. I took care of him. I fed him when he wa' hungry. Then he will take people country and give it away? You wi' give elephant head to child to carry?"

A few days before the runoff, Gayflor called a meeting at the Ministry of Gender. Tensions were high. Both Weah and Ellen had been bouncing all over the country, campaigning. Ellen was pushing through on a punishing schedule that left her younger aides panting. One morning she left Monrovia before dawn for Buchanan, on the coast, a hundred miles away. A hundred miles on Liberia's dismal roads usually meant a four-hour drive, but it took Ellen all day because at every village, every town, every orange stand on the side of the road, people came out to wave and cheer, and she stopped to talk with them. She avoided mention of Weah and talked instead about what she planned to do to get the country back on track.

Back in Monrovia, she attended Gayflor's meeting in a room at the Ministry of Gender on Gurley Street, notorious as the street where Monrovia's prostitutes worked. Because the minister was not supposed to be holding political rallies, the meeting was billed as a simple women's meeting, meant to encourage women to vote. The list of invitees was long—Gayflor basically invited every female political candidate, no matter what party she belonged to, along with market women, female lawyers, and anyone else she could think of who lacked a Y chromosome. She had even invited the Mandingo women. Liberia in 2005 was too bombastically Christian to elect a Muslim president, but with the Mandingo population at over 30 percent, they were a force. She called it an "interfaith" meeting.

Ellen arrived as the meeting was beginning. Some two hundred women had gathered in the musty hot room. Someone had opened the windows so a little air could get in, but that served only to let in more mosquitoes, and there were sounds of smacking as women tried to swat the mosquitoes before they could draw blood.

When all the women were assembled, Gayflor spoke. "Liberia," she said, "is ready to produce the first female president."

The room buzzed as it sank in that Gayflor was abandoning any pretense at neutrality. Women from competing political parties looked at each other, then at Ellen, who herself looked shocked.

"Women, oh women," Gayflor said, "we are here today because if anyone can change things in this country, it is this woman." And she pointed at Ellen.

One by one, women in the audience stood up and spoke. They pledged their support for Ellen and exhorted others to work on her behalf. "We will campaign in the market! In the hospital! In the church!"

Two women from Weah's party stood up, shaking, and were asked, *Will you support Ellen?*

They nodded.

All eyes turned to Charles Taylor's wife, Jewel Taylor. She had won a Senate seat in the general election a few weeks before, representing Bong County. Now she was asked, *Will you support Ellen?*

And she answered, "Yes."

From the back of the room, one woman said softly, "We will win."

Then another voice joined, and another, and another. "We will win."

Soon everyone in the room, all two hundred women, were standing up and shouting, "We will win! We will win!"

"We will win!"

"We will win!"

Their voices poured out the windows, spilling out onto Gurley Street and onward to Center Street. In Mamba Point, people could hear "We will win!"

"We will win!"

Finally Ellen stood up. Not one for showing emotion, on this night she looked overcome. She struggled to stand upright, then slumped against the wall. Then she got herself in order again.

The room got quiet as the women waited for her to speak.

"If I were a crying woman," she said, "I would be crying right now. You have humbled me."

The repercussions came the next day. Gayflor arrived at work to find reporters camped out on the ministry's steps. She invited them into her office and sat down behind her desk. The microphones and tape recorders hit the desk in front of her, ready to record her defense of her actions. The questions came furiously. Wasn't the meeting illegal? Isn't it a conflict of interest for the gender minister to endorse a female candidate? Isn't it wrong to make the whole election about sex?

Gayflor was past the point of backing down. "When you men were falling behind each other, y'all didn't know it was gender?" she shot back. "When Winston Tubman was endorsing George Weah, that one wasn't gender? When Varney Sherman, all of them, was falling behind the football player, that one wasn't gender?"

She continued, "You take a former football player and give him our country? Liberia is not a learning ground!"

And she had one last shot to fire. "Let me give you a goodbye statement," the soon-to-be-former minister said. "Mrs. Sirleaf will be the next president of this country."

In the streets of Monrovia, the signs for Ellen had changed. Now they read, "Ellen: She's our man."

On Tuesday, November 8, the people of Liberia woke up and went to the polls for the second time in four weeks. There was a real and palpable sense in the air that something big was happening.

Throughout the country, international observers stationed themselves at polling places and voting booths; some 230 agencies, from the Carter Center to the European Union, showed up to chronicle the proceedings. Helicopters from the United Nations mission hovered overhead, a constant presence above the voting booth lines.

Lusu Sloan got up at 5 a.m. She went straight to the polls, sitting outside for three hours, so that she could be one of the first to vote as soon as the booth opened. Then, after voting, she headed to the market at Red Light, just outside Monrovia, to hustle the market women there to go vote. From table to table, stall to stall, Lusu went. "Y'all go vote, oh," she said.

"We coming," the answer came back.

At forty-three, Sloan might as well have carried the entire weight of the market women's burdens on her back. By the time she went to the polls on the day of the runoff, she had more than two decades of making market under her belt. As she hustled from poll to poll, urging the women to vote, she thought about the years that had brought her to this point.

She thought about 1989, when Charles Taylor first entered Liberia, igniting the Civil War. In her heart, she believed that if the market women had not been around then, Liberia would have collapsed. She thought about the times when the market women were the only ones willing to walk to get food. She thought about the weeks when there was nothing to eat in Mamba Point, when all the food to be had was across the city, at Red Light. During those times, Sloan and other market women piled goods into buckets upon their head, ducking and weaving through warring battle lines.

She thought about the time she and several market women walked all the way to Guinea, illegally, because Monrovia had no Maggi bouillon cubes for seasoning, no salt, no nothing to cook with the dry rice.

They ran into a group of rebel fighters in the bush near the Guinean border. "Where y'all going?" the fighters asked, shoving their guns into the women's faces. Sloan and the other market women started begging the fighters. "We just trying to carry food back to Monrovia oh," they said.

One of the fighters pushed Sloan to the ground and climbed on top of her. "I know this woman, she from Bong Mines," he grunted. "She married to soldier. Her husband da Krahn man." The words struck terror in Sloan, since the fighters were sworn enemies of Doe's Krahn soldiers.

She pleaded with the man. Her husband had died years before. He wasn't Krahn. "I beg you, that not me you thinking of," she insisted.

Eventually he rolled off her and let her go.

On the day of the runoff, Sloan thought about another night years past, when she and other market women, returning from Guinea with their purchases, encountered another group of soldiers. This time they were Guinean soldiers, and they surrounded the women as they tried to cross the border. They told the women to lie down in the dirt. Sloan had a bag of coffee on her head; she placed it next to her and lay down, heart pounding.

In French, the soldiers fired questions. The women didn't speak French, but they all started pleading to be let go.

"Oh my people, I beg y'all," Sloan said. "We don't have food to eat in Monrovia. We are your sisters. Please forgive us."

For more than an hour, the soldiers kept the women at gunpoint on the ground. Many times during that hour, Sloan thought she was going to die.

But again the soldiers let the women go.

Years later, on the morning of November 8, 2005, Sloan thought about those terrible nights in the bush, as she went from market to market, stall to stall, to corral her market women friends to go vote. "Y'all remember," she said, "vote for woman."

Sloan prayed that Ellen would prevail that day. She thought about the taunts from the Weah boys, who called Ellen "that Old Ma." One of them, the day before, had said to Sloan, "That Old Ma, she will soon die, oh."

"Y'all must sit down there, that Oma will soon kick the bucket," he said.

But Sloan felt she knew better.

"Vote for woman," she told the women. "Y'all go vote. Vote for woman."

Helpful poll workers at a polling station in Sinkor were allowing pregnant women and nursing mothers to cut to the front of the line, so Bernice Freeman, Louise Yarsiah, and a handful of other women were passing around babies and toddlers.

"You want borrow de baby?" Bernice was grinning at one woman, sneaking a furtive look over her shoulder. "Put de baby on your back." To another woman, she advised, "Act pregnant. If dey think you pregnant you can vote in front."

It was unclear whether the poll workers noticed how many different women were carrying the same baby.

Meanwhile, at her house near Fish Market, Ellen woke up on runoff day, showered, and got dressed, putting on the colorful gown and head-tie she had chosen for this, the biggest day of her life. Her sister, Jennie, and Jennie's husband, Jeff, had moved back to Liberia to support Ellen's campaign, and the rest of the family, including Ellen's brother Carney, were on board as well.

As Ellen always did, she ate breakfast—oatmeal and cassava and fish gravy—in the dining room that overlooked the yard. Then she climbed into the backseat of her SUV, and her driver took her to the polls.

Her name was first on the ballot, in black and white: "Johnson Sirleaf, Ellen (president) and Boakai, Joseph (vice president), Unity Party," ahead of "Weah, George Manneh (president) and Johnson, J. Rudolph (vice president), Congress for Democratic Change Party."

Ellen checked the box next to her name. Then she went home to await the results.

"The Oma in the lead, oh!"

A few miles down the road from Ellen's house, Parleh Harris was with a bunch of women glued to the radio that evening, listening to election news, when an informant came in with the update. The official results weren't in yet; polls had just closed, and the final tally wouldn't be known for weeks. But already there was a whisper in the air from spies posted at different polling places. People weren't supposed to disclose voting trends at the polling booths, for fear of swaying those who hadn't cast their vote yet. But all across the country, Ellen's army of women was finding ways to skirt the regulation.

For Lusu Sloan, the workaround came by reverting to an old nursery school chant used to teach children the alphabet: "S-O So, G-O Go, N-O No." Every Liberian kid knows this chant.

For Sloan on runoff night, the chant took on a new meaning. Hanging outside a polling booth, she nervously asked an informant how the vote was going.

He eyed the voting officials in attendance, then grinned. "S-O So, G-O Go, N-O No," he sang. Then he added, "U-P Up!"

Unity Party, up!

Sloan started dancing and singing in glee: "S-O So, G-O Go, N-O No, U-P Up!"

"U-P Up!"

"U-P Up!"

When the election officials glared at her, she sassed them. "You can't stop me from singing my S-O So!" she said. "U-P Up!"

Across Monrovia, the women took up the chant. "U-P Up!"

They went to bed that night singing.

The Old Lady was in the lead.

On Wednesday morning, she woke up and walked into her living room to find it already full of campaign aides excited about the preliminary returns from Lofa and Nimba counties. She wasn't just in the lead; she was in the lead by a lot: 60 percent to 40 percent.

It was a lead that she never relinquished during the days of counting that followed. Weah's supporters demonstrated in the streets, yelling, "No Weah, no peace." Young men threw stones at the American Embassy to display their ire. But none of that changed the numbers in the vote count.

U-P Up.

For forty-three days, Weah protested the election.

On the Saturday after the runoff, pickup trucks mounted with loudspeakers drove up and down Tubman Boulevard, blasting music and urging Weah's supporters to go to a rally the next day to protest the rigged election.

Weah's protest continued even after all the international organizations on hand to monitor the elections deemed them free and fair. It continued after the heavy hitters on the African political scene, from Olusegun Obasanjo of Nigeria to Meles Zenawi of Ethiopia, issued statements calling the runoff transparent, peaceful, and fair.

It wasn't until December 21 that Weah told a news conference in Paynesville that he was dropping his challenge against the election results, to "allow peace" in Liberia.

His news conference was little-noted because a month before that, on November 23, the National Elections Commission had declared game, set, and match to Ellen. It dismissed Weah's complaints of fraud and declared that Ellen Johnson Sirleaf had been elected the twenty-third president of Liberia. In all of Africa, this was a feat no woman had ever before accomplished.

The Old Lady would be Madame President. Out of the twenty-five years of carnage that was Liberia's descent into hell had emerged a new leader, and that person was a sixty-seven-year-old grandma.

"I felt a chill that day, straight on my spine," Parleh Harris recalled.

Ellen too was feeling chills. Heading back to her house from her campaign headquarters on November 23, she was juggling congratulatory phone calls from officials all over the world.

In the backseat of her SUV, her American friend Steve Cashin turned to her, grinning. "The White House just called. Bush wants to talk to you," he said, then recited a very secure, encrypted phone number. "Call that number."

A minute later, Ellen was on the phone with the American president, accepting his congratulations and best wishes.

Then the phone went dead.

Liberia in 2005 had no landlines thanks to the war, so everyone used cell phones. They paid for service from Lonestar Cell by purchasing scratch cards from grona boys on the side of the road. The president-elect of Liberia had just run out of credit on her scratch card. "I need to buy another scratch card!" she exclaimed. Her driver immediately pulled over to the side of Tubman Boulevard as she and Cashin rolled down the windows and called to the boys, "Y'all plee bring people some scratch cards!"

Soon everyone in the car was frantically scratching out the codes on the cards to plug into Ellen's phone so she could call back President Bush and continue their nice chat.

Turning to Cashin, Ellen smirked. "This isn't very presidential at all, is it?"

When word spread that Ellen's victory was free and clear, the markets of Monrovia emptied as the women who minded the stalls at Rally Time and Nancy Doe and Red Light and Paynesville ran, jubilant, into the streets.

"Go to school, go to school!" some of them yelled.

"Don't play football!"

Chapter 12

ALL PROTOCOLS OBSERVED

Monrovia, January 16, 2006

The hats. Years before the fascinators appeared at the wedding of Prince William and Kate Middleton, the women of Liberia conducted a master class on the ancient art of millinery.

It was to be expected, really. How could the inauguration of the first woman ever elected president of an African country not be the kind of turbaned affair to rival the mad hatters of Ascot?

Liberian women live to dress up and believe strongly that they are not fully clothed if they haven't put some kind of ornamentation atop their head. During the war, they still donned all of their finery on Sundays and trooped to church, to weddings, or to funerals in full regalia, including stockings in the ninety-degree, no-air-conditioning heat. There was no way they would not pull out all the stops for the inauguration of the first female president.

And Ellen set the pace. To take the oath of office on January 16, 2006, she wore an intricate lace and gold-lined long ivory sarong and tunic that perfectly matched her cream kitten-heeled slingback sandals. A single strand of pearls around her neck. Big gold earrings. Dramatic eyeliner and mascara. But what was on her body was completely dwarfed by what sat upon her head: an elaborate, intricate cream head-tie that added almost another foot to her height.

The officials who came from around the world to witness history made their own lower-wattage efforts at headgear. First Lady Laura Bush and Secretary of State Condoleezza Rice had received the memo that the American Embassy sent on what to wear, and both came helmeted and pristine. Despite the muggy ninety-two degrees, both women wore button-down suit jackets over their skirts: Bush in a light pastel green with taupe pumps and Rice in a rust jacket and taupe skirt. Perched precariously upon the head of the American secretary of state was a wide-brimmed sand straw hat, which she managed to pull off despite edging dangerously close to safari territory. The American first lady took it up a notch, matching her hat perfectly to her mint suit and adorning it with a perfectly dyed-to-match flower.

But neither of them could touch the Liberian women for sheer headpiece daring. The women of Liberia had fought, scratched, stolen, borrowed babies, cheated, and bled to get a woman up onto that podium on Inauguration Day; this was their day to drink in their victory, and they were determined to do it up right.

R.L., a businesswoman known by the initials of her nickname, Republic of Liberia, came to the inauguration decked out from head to toe in red, white, and blue, the colors of the flag of the Republic. Her shoes were red and white. Her dress was red and white striped, with a white star over a blue background over her right breast. She had on a blue necklace and a matching blue, wide-brimmed hat.

The Holy Ghost women were all in white, their heads wrapped up in complicated scarves.

One robust-looking woman wore a light-blue lace gown over a floor-length shift cut daringly around her bustline. But who could look at her bosom when her head was grabbing all the attention? For clinging there was an enormous purple balloon-thing trimmed in gold, a cross between a turban and a large air-filled shower cap.

Congo women from elite families wore mile-high headgear. There were feathers, flowers, and even fake birds. Native Liberian women from village markets proudly wrapped themselves in their finest Fanti *lapa*s and head-ties.

Some of the women went so far as to wear *lapa*s, gowns, and head-ties printed with Ellen's photo. There she was, beaming, wrapped around the dancing hips and swaying bosoms of her female base.

All up and down the streets of Monrovia, thousands lined the route that Ellen's motorcade drove down slowly—*with white men in dark sunglasses running beside her car!* Talk about a reason for pride and cheering among war-weary Liberians. Young children—some of them so poor they had no shoes or shirt, sang and chanted and clapped, "We love you, Ma Ellen, and that's a fact!"

It was as if the city had collectively decided to throw a party and invited itself to attend.

On the way to the ceremony, Ellen kept getting out of the car and walking alongside, the better to wave to the cheering people. At times, she looked dazed, as if she couldn't believe this day had actually come.

Women from across Africa had made their way to Monrovia to celebrate this historic event. Abena P. A. Busia, an English professor from Ghana, told a *New York Times* reporter that she would have swum to the inauguration if she had to.

Monrovia itself was tatty, sweltering, and still torn-up-looking after two decades of war, and all of the Election Day bunting did little to disguise that sorry fact: streetlamps remained broken, the steady hum of generators at the Executive Mansion and the capitol grounds where the ceremony was being held gave voice to the fact that the city, like the rest of the country, still lacked electricity. There were hardly any toilets for the VIPs attending the inauguration, let alone the ULPs (unimportant Liberian people).

But none of that seemed to dampen the enthusiasm of the people at the ceremony.

Mr. Executive Horn was there. Gabriel Nyanti Wilson had long walked behind Liberia's presidents, including William Tolbert and Samuel Doe, blowing on a traditional red, white, and blue horn. He followed Ellen to the capitol, his horn lending a charming, festive air to the event.

Miss Liberia was there, wearing her crown and sash.

The audience was a who's who of Africa's formerly all-male club of presidents: Nigeria's Olusegun Obasanjo, South Africa's Thabo Mbeki, Ghana's John Kufuor, Sierra Leone's Tejan Kabbah, Burkina Faso's Blaise Compaoré, Mali's Amadou Toumani Touré, Togo's Faure Gnassingbé. On this day, January 16, 2006, a woman would finally be joining their ranks.

The band from the UN's military mission in Liberia played the national anthem. And then, "All protocols observed," intoned the master of ceremony. Translation: This is serious business here, and we Liberians want all you foreigners to be impressed with our grasp of ceremony.

Ellen Johnson Sirleaf walked to the stage, her oldest son, Jes, beaming beside her, holding the Bible, while her other three sons, Charles, Rob, and Adamah, looked on. In her seat, Laura Bush was surreptitiously wiping the sweat off her face. In the crowd, Liberians who had lived through fifteen years of being a pariah nation abandoned by the world marveled at the panoply of global dignitaries who were actually attending their ceremony.

As Ellen began to recite the oath of office—"I, Ellen Johnson Sirleaf, hereby swear"—a few people stood up to get a better view. "Sit down!" a loud voice yelled. They sat.

". . . that I will support, uphold, protect, defend the constitution and laws of the Republic of Liberia"—she was keeping a straight face, but a smile looked like it was going to burst out—"so help me God."

And then the smile did burst out, as applause erupted, along with a few hoots. That smile turned into a laugh a few minutes later, when the sergeant at arms showed up to put the traditional locket around her neck and couldn't get it over her head, adorned as it was by her elaborate foot-high head-tie. "It can't go, Mama," the sergeant at arms said plaintively and loudly, as Ellen grinned at him. Two of her ladies-in-waiting scurried onto the stage, batting him away, getting the job done themselves. What did a man know about how to get a necklace over a head-tie anyway?

Finally, Madame President stepped up to the podium. The baby girl, the pekin who wa' na easy, oh, whose big mouth had landed her in prison before turning her into a cult hero, was now Madame President. Or, as she was being called around Liberia, simply "Madame."

Finally the place quieted down.

"Fellow Liberians," she began, "the days of the imperial presidency, of domineering and threatening chief executives, are over."

There was a roar of cheers. Outside the VIP-filled ceremony, the ULPs listening on tiny handheld battery-powered transistor radios cheered as well.

"I want to talk to the women," Madame said. "The women of Liberia, the women of Africa, and the women of the world." Her voice grew stronger as she continued. "Liberian women endured the injustices during the years of our Civil War, gang-raped at will, forced into domestic slavery. Yet it was the women who labored, who advocated for peace throughout our region.

"My administration shall endeavor to give Liberian women prominence in all the affairs of the country."

She looked up at the faces of the men in the audience, and then at the teary faces of the women before her: Vabah Gayflor, Parleh Harris, Etweda Sugars Cooper, Bernice Freeman, Mary Broh, Grace Kpaan. The market women, the Holy Ghost women.

"They stood with me; they defended me; they prayed for me," she said. "The same can be said for the women throughout Africa. I want to here and now gratefully acknowledge the powerful voice of women of all walks of life whose votes significantly contributed to my victory."

On this day, nobody knew if the victory would be pyrrhic or total. For all of the euphoria, the task of bringing Liberia back from the grip of madness that had engulfed it for two decades was enormous. Unemployment was so high no one even bothered to calculate the rate; whatever estimates the international community put out were useless in the face of the legions of former combatants and young people who gathered in the streets day after day with nowhere to go, nothing to do. There was no running water; generators were the sole source of electrical power, and the only people who could afford the luxury were the relief organizations and the foreign groups in the country.

Liberians, for their part, lived in the dark: dark houses, kept even more so with dark paint in an effort to keep out the relentless heat. At night, the few people lucky enough to have a cell phone used its light to navigate the dark streets and even darker country roads. Downtown Monrovia at night looked positively medieval; candles in shop fronts cast their dim glow on the ribbons of dirty water that ran down the gutters. People gingerly picked their way through the gloom to their shanties and hovels that clustered on what used to be sidewalks. The smell of feces and urine from gutters that served as public toilets permeated the air.

There were few hospitals, and in those few hospitals there were fewer drugs and even fewer doctors. The health system was barely equipped to handle a routine bout of malaria, let alone an infectious disease outbreak.

The country's HIV rate had quadrupled during the war. Children routinely died of curable diseases: tuberculosis, malaria, measles. Few of the ones who lived went to school. Few of the ones who went to school went to schools that had textbooks.

And the country owed $4.7 billion to the World Bank, the International Monetary Fund, and international donors. Because the previous governments had not paid down that debt, Liberia was no longer considered creditworthy.

This was the country Madame was now supposed to fix.

And yet, on Inauguration Day 2006, none of that seemed to matter. This was not the time to dwell on the massive and looming mountain to climb. As the market women danced in the streets and the children chanted and clapped, the prevailing mood, especially among the women, was a combination of jubilation and utter euphoria, the kind brought on by a desperate population who, after two decades of bloodshed, was hell-bent on seizing a long-awaited moment in the sun. It was a day to celebrate.

"We love you, Ma Ellen," the children sang.

"And that's a fact!"

Chapter 13

MADAME PRESIDENT

Monrovia, 2006

In the first year of Ellen Johnson Sirleaf's presidency, the market women became a monumental headache.

During the war, they were the engines that drove the economy, moving back and forth from Monrovia and the villages to the Guinean, Sierra Leonean, and Ivorian borders to bring food back to their stalls. When fighting disrupted their village markets and rebels tore down the city markets, the women simply installed themselves on the side of the road, selling their oranges, kola nuts, dried fish, dried meat, and rice.

Slowly the actual marketplaces in Liberia disappeared, replaced by makeshift tables and stalls that sprouted along those roads. Monrovia, already heaving at the seams under the weight of 500,000 war refugees, found its streets and roads swollen with stalls and market tables. Drivers didn't even bother to pull over to the side of the road when they wanted to buy goods; they simply stopped in the middle of the already clogged streets and gestured to the market women to bring them five oranges. Pedestrians wandered down the middle of the street, stopping at tables that encroached farther and farther into those streets.

Rally Time Market, Nancy Doe Market, and the market at Red Light continued to operate, but they all sprouted offshoots that stretched along miles and miles of Tubman Boulevard. Need a Lonestar scratch card for your cell phone? Just stop in the middle of Broad Street and gesture to Sis Rosaline, sitting under the umbrella next to International Bank. Feeling peckish? Ma Bindu them on Airfield Shortcut selling plantain chips right on the side of the road. Thirsty? Aye man, just go buy some ice water bags those girls them got in their wheelbarrow in front of the road to Don Bosco.

For convenience, it couldn't be beat. But the result was that Monrovia—

and Kakata and Gbarnga and Salala and Totota—became even more chaotic, trash-strewn, and difficult to navigate. The drive from suburban Congo Town to Broad Street, a six-mile trek, started taking a whole hour, sometimes up to two hours, during the day. The trash left after the market women retired for the night piled up, and no one could conceive it might be their job to clean it up. The flies (around the dried-fish remnants), the maggots (around meat remnants), and the ants (around plastic bags of sugar) converged on the ground beneath the market stalls; dogs defecated at the foot of the same tables where women sold cassava leaves and potato greens by day; gnats hovered around the wheelbarrows jammed with jars of mayonnaise and peanut butter and Spam.

It's not that Liberians are dirty; in fact, Liberian people are fanatical about keeping their body clean, even taking the time to bathe their children in the middle of bombing raids during the war years. But as the stench and squalor of Monrovia grew amid the breakdown of normal social mores during the Civil War, people came to view their own private enclaves—be they one-room mud huts, zinc shacks, or cement houses—as their sole oases for cleanliness. And slowly they came to tolerate the filth, trash, dust, and even feces out on the streets. So they collectively allowed their cities to become more and more dirty. It's as if the population decided that it could tolerate the filth in the street as long as, at the end of the day, they could go home and take a bath.

In particular, the market women seemed tolerant of the trash they generated. Who was going to tell them to pick it up? There were no municipal services, no garbage collection.

Madame swept into office aiming to change all that. Summoning to the Mansion her (female) chief of police, Beatrice Sieh, and her (female) minister of commerce and industry, Olubanke King Akerele, Madame ordered them to clear out the illegal market stalls on the side of the road. The market women, she said, needed to sell their goods in markets, not on the sidewalks or in the city streets.

After weeks of announcements on the radio and visits to the illegal stalls, Police Chief Sieh showed up with a bullhorn and a handful of city officials in March to present the market women with a one-week deadline to move their stalls, wheelbarrows, and tables to the city's established marketplaces, Rally Time and Nancy Doe. "The market people belong in the market!"

Sieh yelled into her bullhorn, as the market women glared at her, fuming. "So I beg y'all, from Monday, everybody got to take their own place!"

Monday came, and none of the market women had moved. Tuesday, Wednesday, nothing; they were still in the middle of the street every morning, selling cartons of cigarettes and jars of corned beef. Randall Street, one of downtown Monrovia's main thoroughfares, swelled with foot traffic and market stalls from Broad Street all the way to the sea.

Madame went on the radio to plead her case, giving an interview in which she sounded woefully clueless about the magnitude of the problem facing her. "In the case of the marketeers, they have the right to sell," she said. "But the motorists have a right to drive on the streets because they buy their license and pay their taxes." So far, so good. But then she veered into delusion. "The market women have been understanding because they know their Oma is with them. I think we're all together right now."

Except that they were not all together. Liberia had been a lawless no-woman's-land for two decades; it would take much more than a couple of public service announcements on the radio and an unarmed police chief with a bullhorn to undo years of habit born out of desperation. A woman who has literally foraged in the forests for years for food to sell, who has learned that she can depend on nothing more than her own wits and grit and wheelbarrow filled with precious jars of evaporated milk and bags of palm kernels to provide her with the dirty Liberty dollars to feed her family is not going to quietly get up and desert a spot she views as a sure thing, out in the open air, for some building two miles away that the government claims will be the perfect place to sell her wares.

The deadline passed, and the women did not move.

Finally, Police Chief Sieh showed up with what passed for Monrovia's riot police: a dozen or so officers wearing hand-me-down uniforms from the New York City Police Department and wielding batons, which they took to wildly swiping at the stalls and wheelbarrows to try to get the women to move. It was an ugly scene, the female police chief accompanied by her small police force swatting at women with rickety tables and wheelbarrows. The police succeeded in tearing down a handful of stalls and running off a few women. But the next morning, all the market women were back out in the street.

Madame called a cabinet meeting to huddle with her advisers over how to proceed. They decided to build a temporary shelter and marketplace for the women. But it quickly became apparent that the minuscule $129 million that was Madame's government budget for the year did not include an allotment to build such a shelter.

"We have to find the money from somewhere," Madame said. Some of her cabinet ministers looked at her with raised eyebrows. Seriously? Of all the basic necessities that Liberians needed right now—water to drink that wasn't filled with parasites came to mind—Madame wanted to spend money to build a temporary market for those women?

As is often the case, the proposed solution pleased no one. The market women were furious that they were being moved and demanded that the government build them proper stalls. Madame's minister of commerce went out to talk to the women and promptly got into a loud and angry fight with them, as they demanded that the government do more to help them set up their tables instead of just pointing them to temporary shelters and telling them to have at it. Angrily yelling at the women, her sunglasses slipping at the top of her head-tie, Commerce Minister Akerele got more and more furious. "We can't do everything! We can't do everything! The government did not promise to fix nobody table!"

As the standoff grew more fraught, Police Chief Sieh called about twenty-five market women to a meeting. It quickly degenerated into a furious name-calling free-for-all, the hot room becoming louder and louder until a frustrated Sieh blew a whistle she had placed around her neck that morning. The shriek pierced through the cacophony.

"We cannot continue with this kind of tension," Sieh yelled. "Fighting and swearing don't solve problem! By now we would have all been rich because we been fighting for long time!

"Now," she continued, "how can we come to one conclusion?" She looked around the room as if that was all that was needed to bring the impasse to an end.

The women looked back at her. That was it? Disgusted, they shuffled out of the room. Within hours they were back on the streets with their wheelbarrows, tables, and stalls.

This was a dicey issue for Madame, and one she was doing a poor job of confronting. In describing the problem in that radio interview as one of marketeers versus cars, she had not drawn a direct consequence from the problem of Monrovia's filthy, overburdened streets to the forces that were holding back the country.

Development in Liberia had all but stopped during the war years. Forget about the aspirations of African countries to lure foreign investment and developmental funds to try to get their anemic economies on the road to industrialization; Liberia was so far behind that it was not even a part of the conversation.

When Madame took office, she was confronted by a country not only mired in debt, but one that had survived for two decades on the black, or underground, economy: trade of ammunition, drugs, illegal natural resources, and other illicit products. The famous Russian arms dealer Viktor Bout registered his companies in Liberia during the Taylor years, but the country was driven by the underworld. Each product created its own environment, and the drivers of the economy were a few people who kept the rest of society quiet with hush money. The result was that the normal drivers of commerce—farming, small-scale manufacturing—were broken by this black economy, which also served to obliterate the country's already nonexistent tax base, leaving Liberia broke, and with no framework from which to rebuild.

For two decades, Liberia had sat on the sidelines while other African countries grew, and even so, Africa was way behind Asia. The postcolonial period had begun with countries in Africa, Asia, and Latin America together at the starting gate, a line of banana republics with enormous natural resource potential but held back by a legacy of European colonial pretensions that had stymied the intellectual growth and development of indigenous minds. Once the Euros packed up their colonial overseers and left, these countries, eager to rule themselves and join the modern age, all jumped on the development ladder—but with wildly differing degrees of success.

The Asian countries got out ahead fast, with the Latin Americans limping behind them. Once upon a time, for instance, Ghana and Malaysia were in the same shape. They had both just become independent from Britain at the same time, in 1957. They both began independence with British institutions, plenty of natural resources and foreign-currency reserves, and annual per capita income of around $750.

But Malaysia quickly outstripped Ghana, as foreign investors flocked to the Asian tiger in part because Malaysia put its money into primary education, raising its literacy rate to 80 percent, while Ghana put its money into elite universities, producing a talented elite class but leaving the rest of the country with a literacy rate of around 40 percent by 1995.

Liberia, of course, was never in quite the same place as the other African countries because it was never colonized by the Europeans but by freed American slaves. The freed slaves came with a dollar or two from the American Colonization Society, but the U.S. government never had the empire-building aspirations of the Europeans and largely left Liberia alone to do as it pleased. This was a blessing in one particular way: Liberians felt inordinately proud that they hadn't been colonized by Europeans and were the oldest independent country in Africa, with the exception of Ethiopia, whose claim to independence dates back to 800 BC. But it was also a curse: Liberians, left to their own devices to make or break their country, didn't just break it; they jumped up and down on the broken pieces and ground them into dust.

All the while, Liberians wondered why their country couldn't be more like Ghana.

The answer was simple: Ghana had finally taken off in pursuit of Malaysia. Tired of its coups and anemic growth rate, Ghana—with a lot of help still from the British government and foreign office—had had four successful elections since 1993 and had actually experienced a peaceful transfer of power between democratically elected governments, a rarity in the neighborhood. The country had a free and vibrant press, steady albeit low economic growth, and tourism. Accra even had shopping malls and a multiplex cinema.

Ghana had finally put money in primary education, and as a result its real literacy rate had passed 60 percent, so farmers were now able to learn new growing methods and a larger slice of the population was able to work in export-oriented manufacturing.

To be sure, Ghana was still a poor place. The country had a per capita income of $421 a year, and most people survived on $300 to $400. Child mortality rates were still high, and a huge gender gap remained in primary school education, with boys far outstripping girls in school attendance.

Not to mention, Ghanaian food couldn't touch Liberian food. Why, the Ghanaians didn't even put ham hocks in their jollof rice, the West African staple that all West African countries believe they are best at, but which anyone with a single taste bud knows is best made by a Liberian cook who knows what she's doing.

Still, Ghana was what Liberians dearly, dearly wanted to be.

The idea that a poor West African country embodied all of Liberia's aspirations for itself shows just how deep in the proverbial hole was Liberia. But Madame had privately set a goal in her head: Ghana in thirty years. She hadn't said it aloud yet, but that was her goal.

To get to Ghana in thirty, she had to first get the market women out of the streets. Because those cars fighting it out against the women on the streets of Monrovia had passengers in them who were foreign investors. More than anything, Madame knew, the country needed more foreign investment. It needed factories, places for all those youths who had laid down their weapons after the war to go and work. It needed the construction work that comes when someone decides to build a bank branch on Tubman Boulevard. It even needed the service work that comes when a rich foreign family moves to town and hires a cook, a guard, and a houseboy. Liberian children needed to see people in business attire walking into their smart-looking office buildings so they could at least have something to aspire to that didn't involve sweeping floors.

But the way Monrovia looked right now scared all but the bravest souls. No one who had not experienced life in Cambodia or the Democratic Republic of Congo or Afghanistan could look at Monrovia and not want to run. How do you imagine, let alone build, a T-shirt factory when the streets are overrun with people, wheelbarrows, mangy dogs, flies, and feces?

By sheer determination, the market women had carried Liberia on their backs during the war, and then picked up Madame and added her to their load, getting her elected by every means, fair and foul, they could think of. Now and over the course of her entire term in office, they would prove themselves to be one of her biggest headaches.

Next up on the list of Madame's early—and prevailing—problems was corruption, an issue that would bedevil her for years to come. She came into office vowing publicly that she would impose a "zero tolerance" policy on corruption in the government. Now anyone who has ever stepped foot in Liberia knows that is an impossible goal. The Liberian mind-set revolves around a simple proposition: You scratch my back, I'll scratch yours. Travelers who arrived at Robertsfield Airport were shaken down the second they stepped off the plane, and by the time they arrived at passport control—to be met by toothy grins from passport officials asking "Wha' you brought for your brother?"—most visitors had already parted with much of their money. Zero tolerance for corruption in Liberia would mean sacking the entire government and then starting again from scratch after performing a countrywide lobotomy.

From the start, Madame's government officials signaled that they planned to pick up where their predecessors had left off: Information Minister Lawrence Bropleh quickly began siphoning hundreds of thousands of dollars into a private account; Internal Affairs Minister A. B. Johnson allegedly went to work diverting government money to build himself a lavish house on Robertsfield Highway; and Police Chief Sieh was indicted for stealing $199,800 from public money that was supposed to buy uniforms and guns for the police, who were still wearing NYPD kit.

Making things worse, Madame appointed her own son Rob to head the National Oil Company of Liberia, charged with navigating the country through emerging oil discoveries. The appointment to such a potentially powerful and lucrative post was so politically tone-deaf that it left even Madame's staunchest backers scratching their heads. With Liberia's history of nepotism, why would she open herself up to the criticism that was bound to follow? She countered that the potential oil riches that could come to Liberia were so vast, and the country so poor, and most government officials so corrupt, that she needed someone at NOCAL whom she could trust to safeguard any potential windfall for future Liberians. But the howls of outrage from critics and allies alike were so loud that eventually Madame was forced to accept Rob's resignation. When asked about it, she shrugged and said, "It became too much of a headache." But by then, the damage had been done.

The contrast between Madame's lofty words of intolerance for corruption and the reality of her officials' actions was stark, and very quickly the euphoria and high expectations of her election gave way to disappointment and a sense that in Liberia, business as usual would always continue as business as usual.

But perhaps no early setback for Madame was as stark as the one posed by the Truth and Reconciliation Commission. Theoretically patterned after the one established by the postapartheid government in South Africa to investigate the wrongs of the past, Liberia's nine-member commission, established under the 2003 peace agreement in Accra, was supposed to look into the long host of atrocities inflicted on a traumatized Liberian population, going back all the way to January 1979, when William Tolbert rounded up political dissidents and threw them in jail. In a place where the idea of justice had long given way to the day-to-day reality that few crimes were punished, the Truth and Reconciliation Commission was supposed to give Liberians a sense of due process, even if it didn't lead to anything.

In announcing the formation of the commission, the president set lofty goals. "We must make collective restitution to those victimized, rehabilitate the victimizers, while at the same time visiting some form of retribution upon those whose violations qualify as crimes against humanity," she said.

The new commission quickly went about the business of collecting testimony. The commissioners announced that they wanted to hear from child soldiers—children who were forced to join the fighting. They described the commission as an opportunity for combatants to seek forgiveness after confessing their sins, but that opened the door for those accused of indiscriminate killing to excuse their actions by simply saying that they were forced (in the case of the boys) or possessed by the devil (in the case of the men).

In most cases relating to the boys, that was the truth: young boys and, to a lesser extent, girls *had* been dragged away from their home, pumped with drugs, armed to the teeth, and told to kill or be killed. But the men? Was it really enough just to confess to slaughter, squeeze out a tear, blame the devil, and walk away free?

Because by and large—with one notable exception so ironic it could happen only in Liberia—the Truth and Reconciliation Commission was not about crime and punishment. It was only about crime: a way to talk about crime, to discuss how it affected you, but with no avenue for punishment. The warring parties at the Accra peace talks had unsurprisingly balked at establishing a war crimes tribunal for Liberia, setting up instead the Truth and Reconciliation Commission to make sure they themselves wouldn't end up prosecuted for what they had done during the war.

The way Madame explained it, the Truth and Reconciliation Commission was a way "to have all those young people who caused so much pain stand before their accusers and face them and apologize and then go on and try to make new lives for themselves." It was a classic technocratic solution to an emotional problem—and Madame already had developed a reputation as a technocrat who veered toward bureaucratic solutions that didn't take into account the impact of so many years of brutality on the Liberian psyche. So the Truth and Reconciliation Commission limped along, satisfying no one, while war criminals—Prince Johnson, who drank beer while his soldiers mutilated Samuel Doe; Mustapha Allen Nicholas, who took part in two massacres; the criminal with the preposterous nom de guerre General Butt Naked—all roamed Monrovia's streets, ran for office, and, in the case of General Butt Naked even opened up a home for wayward boys.

In particular, the case of General Butt Naked demonstrated the inadequacies of the Truth and Reconciliation Commission. One of Liberia's most notorious warlords, he spent the Charles Taylor years leading his infamous Butt Naked Brigade into battle wearing only boots and carrying machine guns. Ritualistic child sacrifice and cannibalism were his calling cards; all told, he boasted that he and his forces killed more than twenty thousand people, mostly children, a stunning, although probably exaggerated number.

General Butt Naked—his real name is Joshua Milton Blahyi—stood up before dozens of people gathered in the hot room in Monrovia's Centennial Pavilion and described his killings. He said that he first started killing children when he was a child himself, eleven years old, and was initiated into what he called a priesthood ritual performed by members of the Krahn people—a ritual that began, he said, when he was brought a young girl as a sacrifice whom he then killed, later eating her organs.

Noisily crying, General Butt Naked testified that after Prince Johnson captured and killed his Krahn tribesman Samuel Doe, he went on a rampage of revenge on behalf of his tribe. The Krahn political leaders looked the other way because they knew that "if they wanted me to fight, they should allow me to make human sacrifices." These sacrifices included "the killing of an innocent child and plugging out the heart which was divided into pieces for us to eat. More than 20,000 people fell victim to me and my men. They were killed."

He ordered members of his Butt Naked Brigade to rape women, but downplayed the evil in that order by explaining that only women who had had sexual relations with Taylor's forces were raped by his men.

Like most of the other killers who came crying for forgiveness to the Truth and Reconciliation Commission, General Butt Naked credited God for turning him back to the straight and narrow—conveniently as the war neared its close. In his case, God appeared before him as he was scampering naked across a bridge in Monrovia during a battle. God told him that he was a slave to Satan and should repent. He asked Liberians to forgive him, saying, "What we did at the time was not of our own but upon orders of evil men."

Next up in the hearing that day was Mustapha Allen Nicholas, a Taylor combatant with the nom de guerre Arab Devil. He told the people in the hearing room about two massacres in which he took part: the Carter Camp massacre and the DuPort Road massacre.

The Carter Camp massacre took place on the night of June 5, 1993, at a refugee camp near the Firestone Rubber Plantation. It was a place where rubber tappers and their families tried to hide during the nightly bombing raids. A subsequent UN-commissioned inquiry found Doe's army responsible, but later accounts conflicted with that verdict. Arab Devil's testimony to the Truth and Reconciliation Commission threw the verdict into even more doubt.

What all agree on, though, is that on the night of June 5, around four hundred men and women and two hundred children were slaughtered at Carter Camp. Gunmen dressed in military uniforms entered the sprawling camp; two Jeeps took up position at either end of the camp to stop terrified residents from fleeing. Then, using machine guns and cutlasses, the men systematically butchered the refugees. Howls of anguish rent the air, mixing with the steady rat-a-tat of machine-gun fire. When the men were finished, they got in their Jeeps and left.

A reporter with The Associated Press who visited the scene soon after the massacre described it: "Strewn through the camp were babies with crushed skulls, mothers hacked by machetes, elderly people butchered like livestock."

Arab Devil admitted to taking part in this slaughter and in the DuPort Road massacre of 1992, which he claimed was orchestrated by Taylor's forces. Only thirty people were killed there, so it was mentioned almost as an afterthought.

Like General Butt Naked, Arab Devil blamed others for his actions and asked for forgiveness: "I am begging all of you to please forgive me. What I did was done under the influence of demons." Also like General Butt Naked, Arab Devil left the commission room to live his life, free and clear, in Monrovia.

General Butt Naked, now president of the End Time Train Evangelistic Ministries Inc., got married and became something of a cult figure in the West after starring in the 2010 documentary film *The Redemption of General Butt Naked* by the Sundance Institute. He provided the inspiration for a couple of evangelical churches in the United States, and even served as the basis for a character in the musical *The Book of Mormon*.

Madame appeared before the Truth and Reconciliation Commission as well, where she was taken to task for her initial support of Taylor. The commission ignored the time she ran against him in 1997 and the fact that Taylor accused her of treason.

Instead, when the commission finally released its recommendations—all toothless—for justice against those who committed brutal acts during the Civil War, it included Madame on the list of Liberians who should be sanctioned. The reason? The commission said she didn't express proper remorse for her early support of Taylor.

And guess who was left off the list of those deserving of justice?

Arab Devil and General Butt Naked. No justice needed there, the commission ruled. After all, they asked for forgiveness.

Chapter 14

THE DARK LORD RETURNS

2006

On March 15, 2006, in a scene reminiscent of America's highly stylized State of the Union presidential address, Ellen Johnson Sirleaf arrived at the U.S. Capitol to address a joint session of Congress. It was an honor unimaginable for any other African leader at the time; only three sub-Saharan African presidents had ever been bestowed such status, and one of them was Nelson Mandela.

The scene awaiting Madame in the chamber was electric. Two months after her inauguration, she was already viewed as a rock star in America, and this was her first state visit there. Some of the most powerful U.S. lawmakers tripped over themselves to shake her hand or get in a photo with her.

Unlike most visits by African presidents, during which American senators and representatives spare a few minutes to listen to the long list of requests for more financial aid before busy congressional staffers usher out the visiting dignitary, on this day the congressmen and women waited and waited and waited in the packed chamber for Madame to speak. For this was a historic visit. This woman had achieved what no woman in America had, and in Africa no less.

There was Vice President Dick Cheney, in his role as president of the Senate, standing before the room, waiting for Madame. Next to him was Speaker of the House Dennis Hastert, holding the gavel.

The dean of the diplomatic corps arrived, then members of President Bush's cabinet. The buzz in the chamber got louder. Finally came the announcement "Mr. Speaker, the president of the Republic of Liberia," and Madame swept in, decked out in show-shopping burgundy gown, sash, and head-tie and flanked by Representative John Boehner and members of her official escort committee.

She took her time reaching the front of the room, stopping to bestow a smile here, a handshake there, a rare hug, as all around her the lawmakers whooped and cheered. At the front of the room, patiently waiting for her, was the junior senator from Illinois, Barack Obama, the only member of Congress with an African parent.

When it came to manipulating America's bigwigs, Madame's political instincts were sharply honed. When she got to Obama, she paused. Quickly the Republican Boehner, who had been walking beside her, melted away— *he* wasn't going to be making this introduction—and Nancy Pelosi, the Democratic house leader, appeared as if by magic. "Madame President, our senator from Illinois," she said, presenting Obama.

Obama thrust out his hand, proclaiming it an "honor" to meet her, as Madame beamed at him.

She then ascended to the podium to begin the most important address of her presidency. Thousands of miles away from Monrovia's dusty roads and fetid air, she knew that this chamber in the Capitol was the mouth of the river from which all of her ambitions for her presidential tenure would flow. She had to nail this for one simple reason, which could be summed up in one enormous number: 4.7 billion. This was the dollar amount of Liberia's foreign debt.

Economists classify external debt by using the debt-to-export ratio: how much debt a country has versus how much income it gets from exports, which would presumably help pay for that debt. The U.S. debt-to-export ratio at the time was around 5 percent. But economists consider poor countries to be wrecks if their debt-to-export ratio exceeds 200 percent. The average ratio for highly indebted poor countries was around 500 percent.

Liberia's debt-to-export ratio was 3,000 percent.

There was no way the country could even begin to pay off its huge external debt, and no way that all those promises Madame made during her campaign could be kept, if Liberia didn't get a huge infusion of cash. But to qualify for new loans, the country needed to either pay back its debt or get that debt forgiven. The government's budget when Madame took over in 2006 was $186 million a year, so paying back the debt was obviously not feasible.

As the largest holder of Liberia's debt, the United States was the first port of call if Madame was to convince the IMF, the World Bank, the Paris Club, and all of the world's other donor organizations and countries to forgive Liberia's debt. Where the United States went, the others would follow. So Madame needed Congress on her side. She needed lawmakers to urge the Bush administration to cut Liberia a break. Just as important, she needed to make sure that no lawmakers would stand in the way if Bush decided to cut Liberia a break.

Standing in front of those lawmakers, Madame did a bit of code-switching, abandoning her Liberian accent for the one she learned in Wisconsin. This was the most important speech of her life, and she was going to make those legislators like her. "Mr. Speaker, Mr. Vice President, members of the United States Congress, distinguished guests," she began, "I am deeply touched by the honor bestowed on my small but proud West African Republic of Liberia."

She went through the obligatory recounting of America's close ties to Liberia—founded, as it was, by freed American slaves—and then took a rare detour. At a time when the public perception of the U.S. Congress was in the cellar, Madame looked out into the chamber of faces before her and told the lawmakers that it was they, from Denny Hastert (who would later be convicted and imprisoned for hush money payments in a sexual abuse case) to Jesse Jackson Jr. (who would be convicted and imprisoned for looting campaign funds), who "brought blessed peace to our nation."

She credited them, the same group the *Wall Street Journal* had recently labeled "a do-nothing Congress . . . the legislative process a travesty," with leadership that "paved the way for the international effort" that brought peacekeepers to Liberia. She laid it on thick. "Honorable ladies and gentlemen, the Liberian people have sent me here to thank you. Thank you for your vision. Our triumph over evil is also your triumph."

She spoke for thirty-five minutes and received thirty-three standing ovations. The next day, the House voted to award Liberia an additional $50 million in supplemental aid as a "democracy dividend."

By all accounts, Madame was a huge success. The city was abuzz with talk of the fabulous female African president. Robin Givhan, the *Washington Post*'s fashion correspondent, wrote about her head-ties: "Those head wraps physically increase her stature. They set her apart. They define her as African. But with her discreet little pearl necklace—so very Western, middle-class, tasteful, familiar—she created as masterful a combination as if she'd worn traditional robes and a tailored blazer. With Johnson Sirleaf, Africa meets the Junior League with stylish ease and quiet dignity."

Madame had vaulted over the first hurdle of convincing the U.S. Congress that with her at the helm, it was time to start thinking about forgiving Liberia's debt. But there would be many more hurdles on the road to solvency, and the next hurdle presented by Congress was extremely high. She was told to apprehend Charles Taylor.

Over the course of fourteen years, Taylor had laid waste to his country, turning the already limping West African backwater into a hell on earth. He had launched a war. His forces had kidnapped thousands of children, fed them alcohol and drugs, and turned them into psychopathic killers. The forces he unleashed left an estimated 75 percent of Liberian women victimized by rape and other forms of sexual violence.

And yet, when the self-appointed dispensers of justice for genocidal maniacs decided it was time to prosecute Taylor for war crimes, they went after him for crimes he committed not in Liberia but in Sierra Leone. And then, as if to further drive home the irony, they demanded that the Liberian government—that is, Madame—be the one to turn him over to the UN-backed criminal court.

Congressman Ed Royce, Republican of California, had telephoned Madame before she even took the oath of office. The chairman of the House's Africa subcommittee, Royce had wanted to add Congress's imprimatur to a message that had already been drummed into her by the Bush administration. "If you want your government to succeed, you've got to do something about this Charles Taylor," Royce told her. The United States would not support her new government "unless that Taylor issue is dealt with."

Taylor, along with his entourage, was presently residing in a seaside villa in the coastal Nigerian town of Calabar. As far as Madame was concerned, he could stay there; the last thing she wanted to do, especially considering the huge number of items already on her plate, was to unleash the human tsunami that is Charles Ghankay Taylor on the Liberian population. Taylor still had hundreds of thousands of fervent supporters in Liberia, many of them still angry that their "papay" had been run out of town. If she made bringing Taylor to justice her first order of business, she would risk reigniting the conflict she hoped had finally been put to rest.

But Taylor had been indicted by the UN-backed Special Court in Sierra Leone for war crimes, and the United States wanted to make an example out of him.

Madame wanted that debt forgiven. The United States wanted Taylor.

President Olusegun Obasanjo of Nigeria had said he would hand over Taylor only if he had violated the terms of his asylum (which Taylor hadn't done) or if the head of a democratically elected government in Liberia (i.e., Madame) asked for him. So the problem of what to do about Taylor was now squarely back in Madame's lap, where she least wanted it to be.

After she addressed the joint session of Congress, President Bush hosted Madame in the Oval Office, and she met with Secretary of State Rice. They threaded their praise for her achievements with a warning: if Madame wanted the United States to pony up much-needed money for Liberia's development and to lead the way to forgiving the debt, she would have to find a way to deliver Taylor to the Special Court.

During their Oval Office meeting, Bush told Madame that he would include a stop in Liberia on his upcoming Africa trip—a huge honor for a country whose airport was still in ruins. He would support debt forgiveness for Liberia. He would throw the full force of the United States behind Madame's efforts at development. But "the president made very clear that the Liberian government needed to act in an aggressive manner on the Charles Taylor issue," a senior Bush administration official said, describing the meeting.

On March 17, two days after her speech to Congress, Madame gave the Americans what they were demanding. She formally requested that Nigeria hand over Taylor. In so doing, she was opening a Pandora's box for herself and her new administration, but there was really no choice. The country needed money. And no Taylor, no money.

But even to the last, after formally requesting the extradition of her nemesis, Madame was still trying to keep Taylor out of Liberia. She suggested that Obasanjo send him straight to Sierra Leone, bypassing Liberia entirely. But the Nigerian president was adamant. He had promised safe passage to Taylor until a time came when either Taylor violated the terms of his asylum or a democratically elected Liberian government asked for him back. He would send the accused war criminal only to Liberia.

During a press conference announcing her request that Taylor be turned over, Madame went out of her way to stress that she and the Liberian government weren't the ones going after him. Liberia, she said, didn't have a formal case against Taylor. Nigeria was releasing him to the international community, to the Special Court for Sierra Leone. It wasn't her fault that the Nigerian president was insisting she had to be the one to hand Taylor to the Special Court.

By this time, the legend of Charles Taylor had assumed almost mythic proportions in the minds of the Liberian people. He had eluded multiple peacekeeping forces and ECOMOG bombing raids during the Liberian Civil War. He had even managed to escape from an American jail cell. There were few people in Liberia who didn't believe that no matter how many guards were watching him, if he returned to Liberian soil he could give Liberia's puny security forces the slip, disappear into the bush, and launch another ten years of war.

In the spring of 2006, the drumbeat from the international community got louder. American newspaper editorials demanded that Obasanjo stop stalling and turn over Africa's Slobodan Milošević. Finally, Obasanjo announced that he would give Taylor to Liberia. But then he seemed to almost taunt Madame: *If you want him, come get him.* Nigerian officials insisted publicly that it was Liberia's responsibility to go to Taylor's villa in Calabar and arrest him. Obasanjo's spokeswoman even declared at one point that Taylor was "not a prisoner," an ill-advised statement that many took as a signal for Taylor to try to escape.

Which, to the surprise of absolutely no one, Taylor did, on March 27, 2006.

"The papay na run away! The papay na run away!"

Liberians woke up on March 28 to the news that their former president was on the loose.

Taylor's disappearance coincided with Obasanjo's visit to Washington, where he was to meet with Bush. The U.S. State Department and the White House had a collective fit over Taylor's vanishing act. Newspaper editorials and American lawmakers urged Bush to deny Obasanjo his scheduled Oval Office visit until the Nigerians had rounded up Taylor.

Obasanjo folded fast. Within a day of Taylor's disappearance, Nigerian officials announced that they had captured him in the remote border town of Gamboru, some six hundred miles from Calabar, as he was trying to escape to Cameroon. They loaded him onto a plane and flew him to Robertsfield.

Taylor's story of his disappearance differs in some key ways from the official Nigerian version. Speaking at his war crimes trial in The Hague, he offered a rambling—although quite believable—tale of how he came to "escape" and be captured. First of all, he said he was never "imprisoned" in Nigeria, so the idea that he fled was bogus to begin with, because he was a free man. He said Obasanjo knew he was planning to travel, but he was focused on his trip to the United States to meet with Bush.

Taylor lamented that there was no map in the courtroom for him to show a bit of African geography, specifically that Calabar was fifty miles from Nigeria's border with Cameroon. Why, then, if he was trying to escape Nigeria, would he have driven a thousand miles north to try to cross the border into Chad, when he could have gotten to Cameroon so much faster? The only rational reason for doing what he did was if he actually was trying to get to Chad, to see his "dear friend Idriss Déby," a fellow warlord-turned-president.

"I was being escorted by Nigerian Secret Service, Nigerian security police, driven by Nigerians in a four-car convoy. Now unless you judges and the world believes I am stupid, which I'm not, I could not have been escaping with Nigerian Secret Service, armed police, driven by them, travelling 1,000 miles. . . . I get to the border and I'm stopped. I am amazed. 'What do you mean I'm stopped?' All of the Nigerian security get out. These border people say they are border security and they are ordered to arrest me. I was arrested."

Whatever the case, on the morning of March 29, Madame received a phone call from the Nigerians: "Taylor is on his way."

She got on the phone to the United Nations officials in Liberia. "Use the Irish troops," she told them. She was so conditioned to viewing Taylor as a charismatic figure that she didn't want any African peacekeeping troops close enough for him to connive his way to freedom.

In the end, the UN peacekeeping force sent Nepalese troops to escort Taylor off the plane when it landed at Robertsfield. It was a rainy afternoon, and Taylor, unshaven, wearing a white tunic and a bulletproof vest, tan pants, and slip-on shoes, looked small.

A helicopter awaited him on the runway. Madame didn't want him spending any time on Liberian soil and had tried to keep the news of his arrival (and hopefully swift departure) out of the media until after the fact. But reporters in Monrovia got wind that something was up and raced to the airport. Just as Taylor landed, though, the skies opened up, dumping sheets of rain on the tarmac, which prevented the reporters from surrounding the plane.

The UN troops frog-marched Taylor from the plane straight to the waiting helicopter. Taylor asked if he could go to the bathroom; the UN commander said no, ensuring that Taylor would not be allowed to find an escape hatch in a Robertsfield urinal.

Within minutes, the rainstorm eased, and the helicopter was in the air, clearing Liberian airspace, headed to Freetown.

In Monrovia, his supporters were furious. "Charles Taylor is Innocent" posters went up all over the city almost instantly, and his backers held press conferences to pronounce their belief in his innocence—although how such a word could be used about such a man is one of those only-in-Liberia head-scratchers.

"We will exhaust every avenue! The man is innocent until proven guilty!" Sando Johnson, who worked for Taylor when he was president, yelled loudly, spittle flying, at a press conference.

"Taylor is better than Madame Sirleaf today," another supporter yelled at a television crew filming the reaction to the news. Across Monrovia's battered, ditch-filled streets and trash-strewn alleyways, the Taylor supporters carried their "Charles Taylor is Innocent" posters, attaching them to trees, poles, and buildings.

Riding down Tubman Boulevard on her way home from work one

rainy evening, Madame looked up and saw one of these posters stuck haphazardly on the wall of a cell-phone shop. She glanced at it as her motorcade drove by.

Then she returned to her BlackBerry, which was actually red, to continue catching up on emails. She had done what the international community demanded. She would make sure Liberia got its payback.

Chapter 15

THE EMPIRE STRIKES BACK
Monrovia, 2006

On a bright morning late in 2006, Madame, peering out of an upstairs window of her home, saw an extraordinary sight: lying on the ground in the parking lot in front of the gate to her house, just to the left of her security guard posts, were around two hundred women wearing white T-shirts and white head-ties.

Madame had refused to take up residence at the Executive Mansion, citing a litany of reasons why she couldn't stay at Liberia's official presidential residence, where her former boss had been disemboweled. So she traveled back and forth every morning and night to her two-story house near the beach just behind Fish Market. Her sister and brother-in-law lived a couple of houses away.

A few months into office, Madame's decision not to live at the Mansion began to look prescient when a suspicious fire broke out there that gutted much of its interior. Luckily no one was killed. After that, she moved her offices to the Ministry of Foreign Affairs next door.

Madame's house was modest. The WiFi was often iffy and couldn't handle enough traffic for conference calls, but there was a swimming pool and a nice palaver hut. A dining table was big enough for her extended family to join her for breakfast, as they often did. Family dinners were more rare; Liberians don't eat a big meal at night, and Madame usually worked until late anyway. A balcony wrapped around part of the second floor.

The women lying in the parking lot were Madame's base, the remnants of the movement of women who demonstrated outside the Accra peace talks, who went door-to-door during the presidential campaign on her behalf, who tended the stalls so market women could go vote on Election Day. For them to show up, en masse, meant something was very wrong.

Madame sent someone out to bring them to the house, and the women crowded into the palaver hut.

"One good thing about her, when she sees us wearing our white head-tie, she will always stop and ask wha' wrong," Bernice Freeman recalled later. "We don't have to ask for appointment."

Soon Madame came out to greet them. "Y'all morning."

Stepping to the front, Freeman handed Madame photographs of the mutilated bodies of five women recently killed in Bong County, in and around Gbarnga. The women had been raped, after which their attackers had cut out their genitalia. They tied the body of one woman, spread-eagled, to branches in a nearby creek and left her there. The mutilated bodies of two other women were left in the bush.

"You see how they coming for us?" one of the women asked Madame, her voice cracking. "You see what they doing to us because of you?"

The women seemed angry, not frightened. They told Madame that everyone in Bong County knew who had committed these crimes; in fact, the men responsible had been bragging. But the police commissioner hadn't made any arrests.

Madame has never been an emotional person—her reserve, in fact, has often led people to call her cold. But on this morning, looking at the photos before her, the tears came. "Don't show these pictures to the press," she said. The news would get out, she knew, but the photos were too horrific to appear in the newspaper or on TV, where other sadistic misogynists could find inspiration. "I need to make some phone calls."

There was never any question that the election of the first woman to rule Liberia would spark a backlash among the men. Africa has always been a deeply paternalistic place, dominated for centuries by a Y chromosome that instilled in generations of men the belief that no matter how many conquerors, European or otherwise, might come to rule them, at the end of the day the men would always at least have women under them. And as long as the women were under their control, many African men believed, all was not lost.

Now Madame and her women had upended that fundamental tenet of African sexual politics. And that sparked the anger that comes from seeing someone you view as your inferior rise above you. For an American reference, just talk to some of those people holding the "We want our country back" signs after Obama was elected president.

With a woman president, a feat engineered largely by women, the doormats that for centuries had cushioned the men from the floor were gone. And the men wanted them back.

But the doormats weren't willing to be doormats anymore.

Ritualistic killings had long been common in Liberia; witch doctors and medicine men and women sometimes cut out the organs of children, leaving the mutilated bodies in the bush, so they could go "make medicine." But cutting away female genitalia was a new twist, aimed directly at the president, a macabre reminder of a belief that no power gleaned at a ballot box could supersede the power of brute strength and a bullet. If Madame let this go unchallenged, she might as well resign.

She phoned the superintendent of Gbarnga and demanded, "I want the people who did this arrested. Before twelve o'clock today, I want to know how these women died." By two that afternoon, the Gbarnga police announced that they had arrested five suspects.

But these were anemic steps. That a crime so heinous could be unaddressed in Liberia's second largest city, until the president herself intervened, said much about the deep disregard for women of many men who were still in power. There they were aided in part by a societal groupthink that shrugged collectively at sexual violence. Rape was both prevalent and widely accepted in Liberia. There was no law that stipulated punishment for it, so sexual predators were never prosecuted.

Within weeks of being inaugurated, Madame, egged on by the women, began a campaign to stigmatize rape, particularly of underage girls. But even before she was elected, in 2005 she and a handful of female lawyers asked the legislature to prescribe sentences for rapists. "Do you know the farthest the legislature would go is seven years?" a disgusted Madame recalled later.

Still, seven years was something. A few weeks after she was elected, reports surfaced that a Nigerian soldier who was part of the international peacekeeping mission in Liberia had raped a nine-year-old girl. Enraged, Madame got on the phone to the head of the peacekeeping operation.

"Don't let him leave Liberia," she ordered. "If he leaves Liberia and goes back to Nigeria, they'll free him."

Then she went on the radio with a warning to all: "I've got grand-daughters that age. Those who engage in rape better know that from now on, we're going to prosecute."

Prosecution for men who rape nine-year-old girls is considered mandatory in many countries, but the Liberia that Madame had inherited was a place where two decades of carnage had broken down social constraints. The population had become so demoralized that the fabric of humanity had stretched past its breaking point. And nowhere did that manifest more clearly than in the backlash against women after Madame was elected president.

On March 28, 2007, the body of Ponawennie Folokula, twenty-five, was found in the St. Paul River in the Sanonyea district of Bong County. Her tongue, breasts, heart, and vagina had been cut out.

On September 4, 2007, the body of Annie Kpakilah, a young market woman, was found in the Lelieh district of Bong County. Her genitalia had been removed.

To be sure, ritualistic killing was not limited to women; hundreds of Liberian men, during the war and before, had fallen victim to heartmen and witch doctors and murderers who believed in carving out organs for good luck. But after the election of Madame more women than ever were attacked.

Except now the crimes were being prosecuted, a change that confused some members of the Liberian press. For instance, thirty-eight-year-old Modesco Nyanti was convicted of the murder of Annie Kpakilah. He was sentenced to death by hanging, leaving the newspaper, the *New Dawn*, to report, "The sentence is a first of its kind to be handed down by the Gbarnga-based circuit court. It is still unclear why the decision of the court was death by hanging because there have been similar murder cases with convicts getting live [*sic*] imprisonment, why [*sic*] others have been jailed for specific number of years."

The Empire also turned to political bullying to strike at Madame. Across Monrovia, former warlords, Taylor disciples, and even run-of-the-mill politicians gave interviews filled with dire warnings that they would take up arms again if Madame and the women didn't watch out. In the words of Alhaji Kromah, who ran unsuccessfully for president against Madame in 2005, "We will reach a point where we will have to intervene."

For their coup de grace, the men returned to familiar gladiators: former members of the Armed Forces of Liberia. Just before Christmas 2006, Madame's first year in office, retired soldiers turned out en masse one morning and blocked the streets of Monrovia in the biggest and most concerted threat to the new government thus far. The men claimed they were due back pay and pension benefits for their service to the country. They were technically correct; the governments of Samuel Doe and Charles Taylor had often fallen behind on monthly salaries for the men protecting them, leaving the soldiers to supplement their pay by extorting and harassing civilians.

So among these were the men who had taunted and abused Madame on orders from Doe and Taylor. They had raped village women and their daughters; they had—often acting on orders from their superiors—gone on rampages killing Gio, Mano, Krahn, or whatever group was unlucky enough to have incited the ire of whoever was ruling Liberia at the time.

Now, on a bright December morning, the former soldiers massed on the streets near Capital Bypass, close to City Hall, the Executive Mansion, and the Ministry of Foreign Affairs, and threatened a return to war if they were not compensated financially for their past fine work in the army.

"Where de Oma? Where de Oma?"

The crowd of men grew, outfitted in every conceivable way. There were simple African shirts with slacks, frayed T-shirts, and, in a grim reminder of the past, a handful of masks and wigs and one bright yellow dress. There were tattooed arms and scary markings from long-ago brandings. The crowd teemed with anger, desperation, and no small tinge of cane juice.

Police Chief Beatrice Sieh's pitifully outfitted officers milled around, looking both helpless and hapless. "Y'all move from here, I beg y'all," one police officer, carrying a fly swatter, yelled at the crowd.

As their numbers swelled, so too did the intensity of the threats coming from the men. "If the president cannot see us now, then these men are going to have to come out into the streets," one demonstrator demanded, glaring at the video camera thrust in his face. "It will be a serious thing. We not going to condone anything here."

Another yelled, "De Oma ain't give us nothing yet!"

Some began chanting, "We want our money! We want our money!"

In a sixth-floor conference room of the Foreign Ministry, where Madame was discussing the issue with her advisers, the bedlam below was easy to hear.

Ever the technocrat, Madame was still trying to apply her bureaucratic solutions to the problem. Looking around the table, she stated the obvious: "We now face a situation in which the AFL [Armed Forces of Liberia], to which we have paid huge sums of money, says they have not been paid."

Both sides were right. The Liberian government had already made some payments to the retired soldiers; the soldiers, however, insisted they were due more. They also sent representatives to tell members of the Liberian press corps that if Madame didn't come up with something, there would be another war.

Another chant began: "No pay, no Christmas! No pay, no Christmas!"

Madame got up from the table, walked out of the room, and got on the elevator. She was going down to the street to talk to the men. Her startled aides hurried after her.

The image of this diminutive old lady walking out to confront the horde of angry men was captured by the multiple clicking cameras. Motioning to the crowd, Madame called out, "Let the leader come. Who's the leader?"

One man pushed his way through the crowd. He appeared conciliatory. "I told them they were here for a purpose," he told Madame.

Angrily, she lashed out at him, slipping straight into raw Liberian English. "Y'all say y'all will make war, and there will be no Christmas, that one—you say that one, that will be a problem!"

"No-ooo," came the denial.

"But that what the paper was saying y'all were saying!"

"No, Ma. No one was saying that."

The two conferred a little longer. Then Madame offered, "As long as you are peaceful, we will sit down together and find a solution together."

"When?"

Exasperated, she replied, "We will do it today." Then she turned and walked back into the Ministry of Foreign Affairs.

The former soldier turned to the wildly cheering crowd of men behind him. "Helloooo! We have finally met the president! And I have a message for you! They will let everybody go in City Hall!"

Sensing victory, the soldiers turned and trooped down the street to Monrovia's massive City Hall building, one of the few places big enough to house the whole group.

Back in the conference room, Madame was plotting strategy with her advisers. "What solution can we offer today? Where can we draw the line in the sand?" Translation: *How little can we give these chuckleheads to get them off the street, while at the same time teaching them a lesson that I'm not going to take this crap in the future?*

The group went back and forth, circling around the question of whether the government could pay the salary arrears, a proposal Madame favored until she heard the amount: $5 million to $6 million. Shock registered on her face; the accent slipped again. "Whoo hoo that's big money oh!" she said, pursing her lips. There was no way the government was handing that kind of money to those men—certainly not all at once, certainly not with the rest of the country still trying to crawl out of the hole those very same men put it in.

Finally, she decided: "We have to say to them the salary arrears will be retired in three years because the government does not have the resources now." The soldiers would get a small installment now, and the rest dribbled out over time.

She had to meet with the men at City Hall to deliver the message. But first, she had to show that she was listening to their grievances. In an interview later with a reporter, Madame gave a bald recounting that acknowledged she knew when to adopt her Old Ma persona and when to cast it off: "I must listen to them in a way that says 'I want to hear you.' That's the 'Old Ma' approach."

When Madame entered the crowded conference room at City Hall, she found a group of around twenty representatives sent to speak on behalf of the former soldiers. Their list of grievances came down to one salient point: Christmas was coming, and they wanted money.

They put it more eloquently, however. "You take the whole army and deactivate them?" one of the representatives asked angrily. Now, he said, everyone from the Liberian people to the United Nations peacekeeping troops "look at us like we are stupid."

Another representative called it a "disgrace" that he hadn't been paid for fighting in the Taylor war.

Finally, after fulfilling the requirements of her self-imposed Old Ma listening time, Madame began to speak, and the room got quiet. Her voice low, she spoke first in American English: "We've got many people out there in the villages who today are saying, 'Y'all paying the same people who beat us?'"

As she got more agitated, she slipped into her tried-and-true Liberian English, paraphrasing how villagers would view government payments to former soldiers: "That de same people who kicked us! That de same people who killed us! Y'all got us in the village, poor, today, and you giving them all de money cos they go in the streets?"

In her persona as president, she continued, "We gotta deal with that too. How do we respond to these people in the villages? The people who got taken out of their homes, because SSS [Special Security Service] and warring factions went into their villages, took all of their things, made all of them run, kill some of their people? Wha' we must tell them?"

Madame paused. Then the words tumbled out of her, fast and furious: "Every time y'all make demands, we give y'all money! Wha' we must tell them? We got to take care of them too!

"*They* were the victims! *They* were the true victims of the war! Don't stand up there and say you're high and mighty. Those are the people who *you* impoverished!"

Quiet and chastened, the men looked at her.

Then, suddenly, Madame smiled. "Anyway, we will see what we can do."

As she rose to walk out of the room, one soldier hustled over to speak to her. "I promise you, Ma, tomorrow you will not see tensions no more."

Chapter 16

BEAUTIFUL DAY
2010

The story of how Madame got the world to forgive Liberia's mammoth $4.7 billion debt is the story of high-stakes poker so intricate that an observer would need a cheat sheet with definitions of the acronyms and abbreviations involved. The story is only truly comprehensible to a faceless international bureaucrat steeped in the arcane minutiae of global finance paper.

It is a story of vulture funds that were publicly shamed by television news cameras, of secretive asides between representatives of America's most storied billionaires (Bill Gates, Warren Buffett), of one very vocal and angry Irish rock star (Bono) and one Hungarian philanthropist (George Soros). (First item on the cheat sheet: vulture funds are private equity firms that buy up defaulted debt at a discount price on the secondary market just so they can sue the debtor for a larger amount than whatever they paid for the debt to begin with.)

The story begins decades before Madame won the 2005 elections. Back in 1984, Samuel Doe stopped making payments on Liberia's debt. No one at the helm in the years of madness after Doe was assassinated bothered to pick up those payments or renegotiate the country's foreign debt burdens. As the interest and lawsuits were racked up, the country saw the arrears on its debt obligations balloon; from $50 million in 1984 they swelled to $863 million in 1988 (on a total external debt of $1.8 billion), and by the end of 1999, Liberia owed the world $2.6 billion.

Fed up, in 2000 the IMF began looking into kicking Liberia out for intransigence—a devastating blow that would have crippled efforts by future Liberian governments to get the country back on its feet, since getting back into the global fund once you've been kicked out is an exercise in bureaucratic hoop-jumping. That is when an unlikely ally stepped in to plead Liberia's case: Madame.

Remember, at the time Madame was furiously undermining Taylor on the international scene in every way she could: giving sound bites to the press about his misdeeds, exhorting her United Nations buddies to sanction him, and generally making his life as difficult as she and her global bureaucratic friends could. But when she heard that the IMF was getting ready to expel Liberia, she quickly changed tactics.

"Don't do that," she told Steve Radelet. The U.S. deputy assistant secretary of the Treasury for Africa was part of the team representing Liberia's biggest creditor, the United States, during these IMF discussions. "Do everything but that."

He asked her why.

"Someday we'll be back," she replied.

"She knew that once you're expelled, it's a whole different story, and much more difficult to get back on track," Radelet recalled. "She understood that back then."

So the IMF didn't expel Liberia.

Still, by the time Madame won the presidency in 2005, the country's foreign debt was $4.7 billion, and no one was going to be loaning it any more money. Worse, it was so far in default that it couldn't qualify for any IMF, World Bank, or Millennium Challenge Corporation assistance reserved for poor countries that have good governance and credit. In order to get the country back on the gravy train of foreign loans and World Bank and IMF goodies, Madame had to first convince the world to write off $4.7 billion in debt.

The day after Thanksgiving 2005, Steve Radelet was relaxing at home and eating leftover turkey when he received three telephone calls. Radelet, who had left the U.S. government and was working for the Center for Global Development, a poverty-reduction think tank, knew everything there was to know about highly indebted poor countries (second cheat sheet item: HIPC, pronounced "hih-pik") from his days in the U.S. Treasury Department. He was the one who engineered the trip that Bono, of U2, took to Africa with President Bush's Treasury secretary, Paul O'Neill, which yielded the hilarious photos of the usually buttoned-up O'Neill standing next to Bono, both of them wearing colorful African clothing, in some village in Ghana looking like they are about to exchange wedding vows.

The first call came from Steve Cashin, Madame's investment bank friend from her Equator Bank days. "She needs some help with the Liberian debt," he said.

Radelet was thrilled. The first democratically elected woman of an African country wanted his help restructuring that country's debt. For a finance and development geek like Radelet, this was ice cream and cake indeed.

The phone rang again a few minutes later. This time it was Eleanor Cooper, Madame's personal assistant, on a very scratchy line that sounded like she was calling from the bottom of a well. "Please hold," Cooper said, "for the president-elect."

Madame got on the phone, not bothering to identify herself or, for that matter, to make small talk. "Steve, I've got a lot of things on my agenda. One of the biggest issues is debt. I know you know a lot about it. Can you help?"

Radelet launched into an explanation of HIPC and the IMF, ending with the prognosis that it would likely take Liberia at least three years, and a lot of blood, sweat, and tears, to get its debt forgiven. There was a long pause. Then, "Well, can you help?"

Radelet knew his boss at the think tank would be wary of his taking on Liberia. "I'd really like to," he told Madame. "It's the end of the year. Maybe I can come to Liberia early in the new year?" That was, after all, only six weeks away and would hopefully give him time to work it out with his boss and clear up other commitments.

Another long pause.

"I was hoping you could come next week."

When he got off the phone with Madame, Radelet was shaking his head over her sheer nerve. She thought she could just call him up and he would drop everything and haul himself to Liberia in a few days? What was he supposed to tell his boss?

The phone rang again. This time it was a deep, distinctive Hungarian accent. "Tell Nancy," said George Soros, referring to Nancy Birdsall, Radelet's boss, "that I'll pay for everything." The Hungarian American billionaire and philanthropist had met Madame years before and had almost immediately become an ally.

A week later, Radelet was on a Brussels Airlines flight to Monrovia.

* * *

In order for a country to get its debt forgiven, it must satisfy three different types of creditors: multilateral institutions (the IMF, the World Bank), big donor countries (the United States, the United Kingdom, Germany), and private creditors (Citibank, Joe Blow's vulture fund). Radelet knew his way around the multilaterals and bilaterals; dealing with them would require dealing with the same global bureaucrats Madame had cut her teeth on. They would present no problem.

But the private creditors were a different story. At that point, no one even knew how many private creditors held any Liberian debt. Over the past three decades, many of the banks had sold off these nonperforming assets to vulture funds and God-knew-who. Now Liberia would have to negotiate with them, and such creditors would not be rolling in philanthropic benevolence.

Radelet put in a call to Lee Buchheit, an attorney in New York who specialized in trying to get poor countries off the hook from vulture funds. His request was straightforward: While neither Radelet nor Liberia had any money right now to pay him—they would find some later—might he be interested in representing Liberia in its quest to sweet-talk the vulture funds into forgiving most of Liberia's debt?

After asking for some time to consider, Buchheit called Radelet back the next day. In the twenty-four hours since the earlier call, he had put out a "conflicts clearance" through the legal system in New York, asking a clerk to ferret out all private debt lawsuits against the government of Liberia. Surprise, surprise. "You know," he told Radelet, "there's a court case tomorrow scheduled on Liberia in New York."

Buchheit got the court case postponed, then headed to Washington. It was March 2006, and Madame was in the middle of her sweep of the U.S. Capitol, including her address to Congress. After meeting with the lawmakers and giving her speech, she would meet at the Four Seasons Hotel in Georgetown with Radelet and Buchheit, who had agreed to represent Liberia in the fight with the private creditors.

Before the meeting began, Radelet stepped out into the hallway to talk with Buchheit. "She's mad about the court cases," Radelet told him. "That's what she wants to talk about."

This was all Buchheit needed to hear about what kind of client he would be dealing with. Many sovereign governments, he had found, didn't want the bad publicity that came with duking it out in court with a private hedge fund over loan money that country hadn't paid back. But Madame didn't care. She knew that in 2006, she could capitalize on the growing public distaste for phantom corporations and hedge funds that fed off distressed entities, sucking them dry, while adding nothing substantial to the greater good. These funds hadn't even been the ones that had given Liberia the original loans; they had bought up the loans for a few cents on the dollar, and now they thought they were going to wring money out of Liberia's poor, huddled masses? Of course Madame was not happy. "Her ire was up," Buchheit recalled later.

Reading his new client perfectly, Buchheit told her, "We would like to mount a very vigorous defense, a counterpunch strategy defense. These funds are expecting us to roll over. But if we collapse like a deck chair, there'll be no end to it."

Moments later, he was walking out of the meeting with a grin on his face. Madame had given him unequivocal instructions: "Be as aggressive as possible."

But before Buchheit could even start smacking the vulture funds around, Madame—joined by Radelet and her finance minister, Antoinette Sayeh, a bureaucratese-spouting Madame protégée minus the political nose—had to get the multilaterals and bilaterals on board.

Debt relief for Liberia had to begin with the IMF and World Bank. For a HIPC country to get debt relief, it must meet criteria set up by the IMF, including clearing all its arrears, getting creditors to write down the vast majority of its debt, and promising not to borrow any more funds for a certain period. Everyone—well, everyone except perhaps a few vulture funds—knew there was no way Liberia would ever be able to repay $4.7 billion in debt. So the trick was to get that debt forgiven.

But before Liberia could even get to the point of gaining access to the one-year IMF program from which all debt relief flowed, it had a giant wall to scale. Back in 1999, amid a flood of goodwill and pressure from anti-IMF and anti–World Bank protestors and Bono, a sea change had occurred at those two financial institutions. It was the end of the millennium, and poverty reduction was the new cause. Out of the mouths of NGOs and advocates for the poor came one seminal argument: the debt of poor countries with good governments should be erased. The world had made bad loans to a generation of African dictators who lined their pockets with the money. Now democracy was taking off in Africa, why saddle newly democratic governments with old debt?

So the IMF and World Bank came up with a plan through which HIPC countries could get their debts forgiven if they demonstrated that they meant business this time and would stop behaving like banana republics and more like Switzerland. The big economies came up with a huge trust fund—$75 billion—to forgive the debts of all the HIPC countries if these countries met certain conditions.

All the HIPC countries, that is, except three basket cases no one ever thought would amount to anything: Somalia, Sudan, and, of course, Liberia. So even before Liberia could negotiate agreements with all these different multilateral, bilateral, and private creditors, it had to first scrounge up $800 million for its portion of the pot of money. That meant going hat in hand to all the shareholders in the IMF—from the big donor countries like the United States to the wee ones like Thailand—and getting them to put in some money on Liberia's behalf so that the IMF would be solvent enough to forgive Liberia's debt when the time came. In the world of international finance, few were actually writing checks of $800 million for the IMF; it was more a case of shareholders coming up with IOUs to recapitalize the IMF for the $800 million. But it was a slow, laborious process that had to be done before Liberia could even get to the starting gate on the debt relief road.

Everywhere else, Madame was getting the traction she needed on debt relief. At the World Bank, Paul Wolfowitz, the director, was a huge supporter, going back to his days at the U.S. Defense Department when the Pentagon parked warships off the coast of Liberia while Taylor was on his way out. During 2006 and early 2007, Wolfowitz pushed the Bank hard to come up with $460 million in internal funds to clear Liberia's arrears.

Following Madame's grand tour of Congress and Washington and her handover of Charles Taylor, U.S. Secretary of State Condoleezza Rice announced to great fanfare that the United States, Liberia's biggest creditor, was forgiving its portion of the country's debt. As predicted, many of the other big donors fell in line behind the Americans.

But the IMF, then headed by a Spaniard named Rodrigo de Rato, was not getting its act together. The easy shareholders—like the United States—were on board, no thanks to him, but he wasn't doing the legwork to get Malaysia, Thailand, and the smaller shareholders to contribute. Whenever Radelet or one of the Liberian officials asked IMF staff members for an update, they were told to hold their horses, Rato was getting around to it.

Madame got fed up and called in Bono.

She had met him earlier that year at the World Economic Forum in Davos, Switzerland, an annual confab in which high-rollers like Bill Gates gather to express their concerns about the state of the world. Bono was immediately charmed by Madame. He told Radelet at the time that if Liberia needed him for something—specifying that he was willing to do one big thing—he was ready.

Madame and Radelet decided they had their one big thing in October 2007. The annual meetings of the IMF were beginning in Washington, and all the global financial architects were coming to talk international finance and how to help poor countries. Unnoticed by most people, Rato, who was nearing the end of his tenure at the IMF anyway, was still not advancing Liberia's debt package.

So Madame struck, through her good friend Bono, who offered an exclusive interview to Britain's *Financial Times*. He told the newspaper it was "an IMF-ing outrage" that Liberia had overcome civil war and met stringent reform standards to qualify for debt relief and was now getting jerked around by those goof-offs at the IMF. Poor Madame, Bono told the *FT*, was having to "waste time fighting with IMF modalities, bureaubabble and unaccountable distant red tape in DC."

He then delivered his coup de grace: "If we cannot back a heroine like her, then who can we support and what is the point of global debt agreements and G8 promises?"

Madame made sure she was available when the *Financial Times* called her for a comment. The issue, she sighed, was "consuming endless amounts of scarce time and energy, and delaying a strong signal to the Liberian people that the world is behind us. We urgently need to move forward and resolve this issue as quickly as possible."

Rodrigo de Rato, when approached for a comment, was left to talk about how he was trying, but that the "effort hinges on securing the resources needed to finance the cost of IMF's debt relief to Liberia." Talk about stating the obvious. The *Financial Times* relegated his response to the bottom of the article, which ran in prominent display just as the annual meetings opened. All anyone could talk about was Bono's "IMF-ing outrage" quote. Reportedly, Rato's staff had to explain the nuances of the word play to the Spanish managing director.

The pressure was growing, but Rato still wouldn't act. His last day at the IMF was shortly after the end of the annual meetings, and he left Liberia's unfinished business on the plate of his successor, France's Dominique Strauss-Kahn. The change was immediate. Strauss-Kahn didn't need anyone to translate "IMF-ing outrage," and as one of his first actions he started making phone calls to shareholders to ante up on Liberia's behalf. Within days, the $800 million—in the form of promissory notes and various banking sleights of hand—had materialized. The IMF shareholders had agreed to compensate the fund sufficiently to clear Liberia's arrears and to make Liberia's debt current. Should Liberia meet all of the other conditions of debt forgiveness, the funds were now—theoretically—there to actually forgive the debt.

The bureaucratic hoop Madame had just jumped through was one no other HIPC country had ever confronted because the IMF and World Bank had raised all the money they needed for other countries in advance. But this successful jump simply got Liberia to the starting gate of debt relief. There was still a long way to go.

Still, by October 2007, the drama with the IMF and the multilateral institutions that held so much of Liberia's debt was largely over. Meanwhile, Madame and her emissaries had been negotiating in tandem with the bilaterals and had reached an agreement with the so-called Paris Club, a group of officials and creditors from rich countries that help poorer countries to restructure their debt, and then set terms going forward; it is called the Paris Club because the first negotiations took place in Paris in 1956, for Argentina's debt. The Paris Club includes the United States, which held a whole lot of Liberian debt. (There is also a "non-Paris Club" of big donor countries.)

The agreement with the Paris Club was so generous that even Lee Buchheit was stunned. The Paris Club agreed to accept 3 cents for every dollar Liberia owed—in essence, to forgive 97 percent of the debt. Buchheit had expected, at most, around 90 percent forgiveness if Madame played every card right, dotted every *i*, and crossed every *t*. But she and her wunderkind finance minister, Antoinette Sayeh, surpassed those nuances, going so far as to write up and present detailed steps describing all the checks and balances they were putting in place to keep Liberia financially solvent in the future.

In Sayeh, Madame had found a clone of herself. She had a PhD in international economic relations from the Fletcher School of Law and Diplomacy at Tufts University. She had worked for the World Bank for seventeen years, as country director for Niger, Togo, and Benin, and as country economist for Pakistan and Afghanistan. With Madame's election, she had agreed to return home to Liberia to work on the debt relief fight.

Sayeh had gotten the big donors to agree to 97 percent forgiveness. But then all of the members voluntarily agreed to go beyond those terms and forgive 100 percent of Liberia's debt. Just like that, $1.3 billion in bilateral debt was gone.

But what made the Paris Club deal even bigger was that it included a "comparable treatment" clause: this meant Liberia could not settle its debt with private creditors for anything more than 3 cents on the dollar. That gave Buchheit, Radelet, Sayeh, and Madame herself a giant shield to hide behind when they went into negotiations with the various hedge funds, banks, and vulture funds that held Liberia's debt. They could simply say, "We can offer you only 3 cents on the dollar because of our Paris Club deal."

Needless to say, the banks and hedge funds and vultures weren't happy about that. Some of the more circumspect banks, like Citibank, accepted the terms immediately. For one thing, Madame used to work there, and having Citibank on the résumé of the first woman elected president of an African country gave the bank some additional street cred in the developing world. And heck, they were getting 3 cents back on loans they had written off during the Liberian Civil War. Call it a victory and go home.

Alas, not everybody was so magnanimous.

From the moment he finally cobbled together the full list of private creditors holding a whopping $1.1 billion of Liberia's debt, Lee Buchheit knew there would be trouble with many of them.

These were the vulture funds, who had bought up Liberia's debt on the secondary market, and for peanuts, on the hope that the country would eventually be stupid enough to put some asset—an oil find, its shipping registry—somewhere, perhaps in a commercial bank, where it could be seized by claimants with court judgments that ruled the country owed them money.

Think of it this way: Liberia borrows $100 from Citibank, doesn't pay the interest on the money, let alone pay back the loan, so Citibank sues Liberia and wins a judgment in court that says Liberia has to pay back the $100 plus interest or Citibank can seize enough Liberian assets to satisfy the loan. But Citibank sees the television images of rebels dressed in wedding gowns and wigs overrunning Liberia and says, "Screw it, we'll never get our money back from this place," and so it writes off the $100 Liberian loan and sells it for 50 cents to Joe's Vulture Fund, based in the Cayman Islands.

Joe's Vulture Fund has now purchased what it considers to be a loaded revolver, ready to fire. A court has already ruled that Liberia owes Citibank—and now Joe's Vulture Fund—$100 plus interest. So Joe's Vulture Fund can now seize Liberian assets worth way more than it paid for the written-off loan. "From the standpoint of the vulture fund, to buy a court judgment saves you the tiresome step of going to court yourself," Buchheit explained. "The revolver is loaded when you buy the judgment, especially since these countries never show up to defend themselves in court."

Except Madame wanted to turn the tables on Joe's Vulture Fund.

First, she told Radelet to hide Liberia's pitiful assets where the vulture funds couldn't get them. That meant shifting the few assets, including income from the shipping registry, to the two places immune to court orders: the New York Federal Reserve and the Bank for International Settlements, in Basel, Switzerland. Both of those banks have privileged exemptions so private creditors can't seize the assets of customers, no matter what kind of court ruling they wave around.

Then she told Buchheit to make sure the vulture funds knew that Liberia's new government would fight them every step of the way. The days of not showing up at court hearings were over, she said. The vulture funds might have the law on their side, but they would have to litigate and relitigate, and that 50 cents they paid for that Liberian debt would end up costing them a hundred times more in legal fees alone.

Finally, Madame's team got the New York Federal Reserve to act as the host for the first meeting between Liberia and its private creditors.

This took place in a gilded room at the New York Fed's fortified and storied building on Liberty Street, in the heart of the financial district. While many of its neighbors were heavily damaged or destroyed in the September 11 attacks on the nearby World Trade Center, the New York Fed's headquarters had been spared. And now that building, of all buildings, was the site of a lunch between Liberian officials, led by Finance Minister Sayeh, and a bunch of vulture funds. Talk about making a statement.

Terrence J. Checki, executive vice president of the New York Fed, hosted the lunch. Around twenty-five people listened as Sayeh laid out Liberia's position: just coming out of two decades of civil war, a dirt-poor country, trying to get out from under the monstrous debt piled up by the lunatics who ran the country into the ground, now Madame and her team just want a chance to get the country back on its feet, and so on.

But the important presentation was not Sayeh's. It was a simple statement by Terrence Checki at the close of the meeting. "This is one I will be watching very carefully," he told the assembled vultures. "I'll be interested in seeing whether each of you wants to be part of the problem or part of the solution."

The pledge "sent a signal to the funds that if you're going to go rogue on this debt restructuring, you're going to offend the New York Federal Reserve," a delighted Buchheit recalled.

Later, a reporter asked Radelet whether George Weah, or any of Madame's other opponents in the 2005 presidential campaign, could have gotten a top official at the New York Federal Reserve to host a lunch on Liberia's behalf to scare a bunch of vulture funds into making nice with the country.

Radelet paused. Then he laughed. "Ahh, no."

On February 22, 2008, *Air Force One* touched down at Robertsfield Airport for only the second time in history. President George W. Bush, in the waning months of his presidency, alighted to signal to the world that America was behind Liberia's debt relief efforts.

In a speech at Barclay Training Center, the same army barracks where Ellen was imprisoned and her colleagues executed by firing squad, Mr. Bush promised cheering dignitaries that the United States would do all it could to lift Liberia's debt burden so that the country "can unleash its potential and the entrepreneurial spirits of its citizens."

Then he danced. Yes, danced.

At a lunch afterward, Liberian crooner Marron Dwah Cassell was singing the hit "Liberia, You're Lifted," the sort of gospelish inspirational patriotic song in which Liberian artists specialize. And of course it comes with a high-life calypso beat, because Liberians don't really believe in music that you can't dance to. Marron Cassell's song certainly got Madame up on the stage dancing—Madame knew how to play to her people. And then, just as Marron Cassell was getting into the hip-swaying jiggly part, who comes bounding around the table to the front of the stage to join Madame but President Bush himself, apparently moved by the music.

It's difficult to describe Bush's moves—some clapping interspersed with what looked like an aborted attempt to bump Madame at the hip, followed by a kind-of sort-of Wop, but he did stay on beat, even getting so into things that he ripped off his jacket and tossed it to a handler behind him, sending the assembled crowd into a roar. Or maybe he just got hot in the sweltering February dry-season temperature and humidity.

Whatever the case, First Lady Laura Bush was having none of it. She smiled and clapped politely from the back, but when her husband gestured to everyone to come join him shaking his hips with Madame onstage, she stayed right where she was.

For Madame, though, it was a political triumph. Thirty years before, when the last American president visited Liberia—for four hours— government officials had been thrilled beyond belief when Jimmy Carter put his water glass on the floor, which the eager-to-be-pleased Liberian officials took as a signal that the American president was relaxed and felt at home. Now this American president had gotten up and danced to "Liberia, You're Lifted." After promising to help with debt relief.

The game wasn't over, though.

While most of the high-risk takers that held Liberia's debt fell in line after Checki's directive and acquiesced to the Paris Club terms, there were two notable holdouts. The first was a shadowy reinsurance fund in London that was not responding to missives or meeting requests and in general not being helpful. So Buchheit and Radelet went to work trying to find out just who owned the fund.

"All roads led to Omaha, Nebraska," Radelet announced. The fund was owned by another company that was owned by another company that was owned by another company owned by Warren Buffett, the billionaire American investment guru who famously told President Obama that the American corporate tax rate should be restructured because his secretary paid more in taxes than he did. Buffett has promised to donate 99 percent of his $60 billion net worth to charity, which, when it happens, would make him the biggest philanthropist in the world.

And this philanthropist, without knowing it, had a fund that was nickel-and-diming poor Liberia just when the country was trying to shed two decades of mismanagement and put children back in schools and food back on tables and all other good things? This would not do.

So the Liberian team got on the phone to some top officials at the Bill and Melinda Gates Foundation, who got their people on the phone with Buffett's people in Omaha, suggesting that perhaps Mr. Buffett might want to tell his London fund to quit trying to shake down poor struggling Liberia.

"One week later, we get a message from the reinsurance fund, saying they'd be delighted to take 3 cents on the dollar," Radelet recalled.

One down, one more to go.

The last holdout was a vulture fund called Hamsah Investments. It had a court judgment against Liberia for the interest on a $6 million debt that Hamsah had purchased for pennies on the dollar. The company was refusing to play ball. The Paris Club argument was going nowhere. Ditto for the "we're so poor" argument, leading Buchheit to remark ruefully, "Some of these creditors—mercy is not part of their DNA."

Liberia had lined up everyone else—the IMF, the World Bank, the United States, Britain, Saudi Arabia, Thailand, Citibank, Warren Buffett— but it couldn't get its debt forgiven until it settled all the court judgments against it, and Hamsah wasn't budging. Things were looking grim for Madame.

Then she talked to Greg Palast, an investigative journalist and self-described "top investigator of corporate fraud," who was working on a documentary for the BBC on vulture funds. In the case of Hamsah and Madame, Palast found the perfect villain and heroine for his morality play.

"Welcome to Liberia in West Africa," Palast intones at the beginning of his documentary, over footage of Liberians looking downtrodden and forlorn, "where 80 percent of the people survive on less than a single dollar a day. Now these people are being told that they have to pay $28 million to a bunch of financial speculators known as vulture funds."

Cut to Nelson Mandela saying, "Sometimes it falls upon a generation to be great" and that it was time to end the debt crisis for poor countries. Then Palast says, "Just as Britain, Europe, and America were about to pay off all of Liberia's debts, down swooped vultures, who put their claws on the money."

Next up is his exclusive interview with Madame.

"Where's their conscience?" she demands, managing to look mournful and outraged at the same time. "What do they say as a conscience? They don't care?"

Palast introduces Eric Hermann, the villain who had sued Liberia and won a $23 million judgment—"And here he is, at a chandelier-lit gala." Then, in true gotcha-journalism style, Palast shows up at Hermann's offices, camera crew in tow. He can't get in, so there is the ubiquitous trip to Hermann's "huge gated estate," and of course Palast can't get in there either. But the video from the trip to Hermann's estate serves its intended purpose, providing a lovely juxtaposition with the village of Demeh, where poor Liberians are shown "rebuilding their homes with mud bricks they made themselves."

Game over.

On June 29, 2010, Liberia formally secured $4.7 billion in irrevocable debt relief from the World Bank, the IMF, the African Development Bank, and bilateral and private creditors. "Today, ladies and gentlemen, is a day for us, as Liberians, to celebrate," Madame told her subjects in her victory speech. In Monrovia, people took to the streets, horns blaring, dancing and singing.

Madame, however, was not in the streets dancing with the crowds. It was 2010, only a year to go until she was up for reelection.

Madame had a campaign to plan.

Chapter 17

MONKEY AND BABOON

Monrovia, 2011

Monkey Still Working, Let Baboon Wait Small.
—Ellen Johnson Sirleaf reelection campaign poster

Election Day 2005 was supposed to be the last time Madame's name was on a presidential ballot. In what appeared to be an attempt to break with the country's long-established practice in which presidents don't leave office until they die of natural causes (William Tubman) or are disemboweled by their own army (William Tolbert), cut to pieces by beer-guzzling rebels (Samuel K. Doe), or run out of town as war criminals (Charles Taylor), Madame had promised back in 2005 that she would serve only one term.

Maybe she was more like her predecessors than even she initially believed. Declaring that too much remained to be done, Madame, now adopting the moniker of the traditionally hardworking Monkey from the Liberian parable "Monkey works, Baboon draws," in 2010 announced that she planned to run for another six-year term come 2011.

Naturally, the Baboons in the opposition groups were not happy. They thought six years was plenty of time for Monkey to have turned Liberia into Sweden and it was now time for them to get their country back. Baboon had a good argument for why it was time for Monkey to step down. Yes, the government buildings and commercial offices and what passed for the Liberian middle class—those who lived in cement houses—had electricity for a few hours a day. But that electricity was expensive and came from generators, since the hydro plant at Mount Cuffee still hadn't been repaired. So most of the people with electricity ran it for only a few hours at night—just long enough to keep their refrigerator cold so their food wouldn't go bad, and perhaps to provide a little lamplight at night and, among the really lucky ones, a few hours of air-conditioning to cool down their house "lil' bit."

But most Liberians didn't have access to electricity in a form they could afford. And hundreds of thousands still didn't have access to clean running water, let alone flush toilets. All across Monrovia there remained huge outdoor holes over which people stood and pissed or squatted and defecated.

The UN Human Development Index still ranked Liberians as among the world's poorest people.

Monkey had started a much-publicized campaign to build roads into the interior so that the cities, towns, and villages outside of Monrovia would be more accessible and so the people living in those cities, towns, and villages would have more access to trade, jobs, and development. But it still took three to four hours on a good day with a very good SUV to get from Monrovia to Gbarnga, a distance of only 120 miles, on the best road the country had to offer. The craters, potholes, and overflowing rivers were winning in the battle to get up country, leaving the defeated carcasses of cars, pickup trucks, and SUVs on the side of the road.

Children were still more likely to be found begging in the street than sitting in a classroom. The streets of Monrovia were still overflowing with people and cars; Monkey had not put much money into public transportation. There were few buses, so Liberians still crammed into overcrowded and more expensive taxis to get around. Or they climbed onto the back of those rapidly proliferating mopeds, called pen-pens, weaving in and out of stalled traffic and, if lucky, got to their destination in one piece.

All that said, Monkey herself had a good argument for why the Liberian people should give her another term in office. For one thing, the peace in Liberia had been maintained. There was no question that the majority of Liberians, at every level of society, were better off than they had been before Monkey was elected. Professionals now had passports again and could travel, since international flights had resumed. Middle-class Liberians could pull into gas stations and fill their tank with gas, just like in a normal country, instead of hailing young boys on the side of the road to buy a plastic gallon of something that looked like gasoline but could be kerosene. Poor Liberians could hawk plastic bags of ice water on the street without having to worry that a grenade might explode in front of them.

Monkey could also point to the fact that the country's economy was actually growing, for the first time in three decades. Foreign investors were coming back to Liberia; Firestone was no longer the only game in town for employment, although Baboon could rightly point out that most of the foreign investment was still in extractive industries. Still, ArcelorMittal was mining iron ore in Greenville; Chevron had shown up to hunt for offshore oil; and Robert L. Johnson, the American entrepreneur, had built a five-star resort called Kendeja just outside Monrovia. Kendeja came complete with villas containing seventy-eight plush rooms on thirteen acres overlooking the Atlantic.

And Monkey had launched public campaigns against rape. Men who raped young girls these days might even face prosecution. She had also appointed more women to positions of power than anyone before her. And she had been harping about female literacy from the moment she took office.

But Monkey had also inflicted unnecessary political damage on herself. The appointment of two of her sons to high-profile jobs opened her up to charges of nepotism that were impossible to ignore. For all of her rock-star status overseas—and, no mistake, she was a rock star overseas, had even shared top billing with Bill Clinton for an address at Yale University—the appointment of her son Rob, in particular, to head NOCAL was the first thing that even her foreign admirers brought up when criticizing her. This was not helped by the fact that another son, Charles, was a governor at the Central Bank of Liberia. But he had been at the Central Bank since 2004, before his mother was elected president, so he did not draw as much talk as his brother did. Rob Sirleaf's appointment to NOCAL was particularly offensive to people and quickly became a tool Baboon would use, very effectively, against Monkey during the campaign.

Baboon assembled the usual cast of characters to run against Monkey in the 2011 elections. Charles Brumskine was resurrected to lead the Liberty Party ticket. Winston Tubman's decision to back George Weah against Madame in the 2005 election finally paid off; Baboon put Tubman at the top of the Congress for Democratic Change ticket, with Weah as his running mate. Baboon put Weah in the number two spot in an effort to mitigate the expected complaints from Monkey's supporters that football players shouldn't be running the country.

Then Baboon set out to rewrite Liberia's history, declaring that it was Monkey, not Baboon, who had been responsible for two decades of civil war.

Tubman, who had once served as Doe's justice minister and was the emissary Doe sent to the United States at the start of the Civil War to plead for Doe's rescue, told reporters that his presidential "credentials" were better than Madame's because she initially supported Taylor. He allowed that if he and Weah won, he would do "many of the things she is doing," but he also said that during the Civil War, Madame had supported "people who were killing, disemboweling pregnant women, cutting off limbs." Tubman made no mention of what Doe did to Thomas Quiwonkpa or any of the thousands of other people Doe murdered.

Brumskine too picked up Baboon's new campaign and ran with it, telling a reporter, "Ellen is part of the problem." Then Brumskine, a key Taylor ally and supporter from 1997 to 1999, added, "Ms. Sirleaf has been involved in just about every war this country has had."

But Monkey had never been squeamish about fighting dirt with even dirtier dirt. First her people went after George Weah.

Somehow, a fourteen-year-old commercial for cologne that Weah made in Italy surfaced in the Liberian media. In the commercial, Weah, at the time a world-famous striker with AC Milan, walks into a restaurant to greet his (white) dinner date after dousing himself with cologne. He's fully clothed at the beginning, but when the woman sees him from across the room, she's so overcome that she imagines him naked. The commercial then cuts to a naked Weah strolling across the restaurant to his date, as other (white) women in the restaurant drool and fan themselves. Finally, Weah arrives at the table, leans over it toward his date, and smiles. When he sits down, he is clothed again, and he says, suavely, "Tutto bene?"

To get an idea of how this commercial played in Liberian politics, you have to understand this country's Bible-spouting Puritanism and deep racial anxieties. Many of the freed American slaves who founded Liberia were the mixed-race children of white slave owners who proceeded to set up the same kind of society from which they had fled, except this time, the lighter-skinned colonists were the upper class, lording it over the native Liberians. So matters of race still struck deep into the heart of the average Liberian. That's why, for many Liberians, it was bad enough that Weah was strutting around naked on Italian TV, but in front of *white* women—that was too much.

"Weah Walks Butt Naked!" screamed the headline in the *New Democrat* newspaper, which provided this hilarious synopsis of the commercial for those without access to YouTube: "The video scene portrays white women, in looks of sexual awe and ecstasy, glancing at the black man with his athletic build and muscular features, exposing his genitals flipping, walking before them."

Weah's political supporters tried to brazen their way out. "Mr. Weah committed no crime by posing butt naked," one party official helpfully told reporters. "Only constitutional deviants should not be elected."

But the body politic quickly dusted off their holier-than-thou cloaks. Adopting the convoluted sentence structure at which Liberian men were particularly adept, Joshua Duncan Freedom, principal of the King Pentecostal High School, told reporters, "If the Congress for Democratic Change through its vocal spokesperson Acarous Gray can justify George Weah's butt naked video on the international information highway on some constitutional right, then Liberians must be prepared, God forbid, under a CDC rule, to give audience to the legality and normalness of murder and even cannibalism."

The truth is this cloak of religious indignation simply covered up what Liberians of both sexes were really mad about: that Weah was flashing his oiled, well-chiseled body, buttocks included, in front of white women. Liberian women saw it as a rejection of black women. Liberian men were jealous. Either way, this was a loser issue for Weah, as the Monkey camp knew it would be.

Having dispensed with Weah, Monkey and her supporters turned their attention to Brumskine. (Monkey didn't waste time with Tubman since everyone knew he was the head of the ticket only to counter claims that the country shouldn't be handed over to a footballer.) Like Weah, Brumskine made himself an easy target. First, he spent a lot of time complaining that the 2005 elections, which the entire world had watched and proclaimed free and fair, were rigged against him. Then he made a public statement at a journalism symposium that could easily be understood as a threat, vowing that "we will take the necessary action to ensure that the elections are free and fair—that we are not cheated."

Monkey's supporters accused Brumskine of promising war if he didn't win. A branch of her Unity Party put out a statement in the *Liberian Journal* in December 2010 that they weren't sure "what Councilor Brumskine is implying when he starts making early threats that will undermine the results of the general election." The Unity Party piously pointed out that Liberians didn't need the "politics of fear" and sniffed that Brumskine's statement marked "the resurgence of itty-bitty political mentality" that caused Liberia's fourteen years of war.

The statement was not as potent as the Weah video, but it did implicitly remind war-weary Liberians of Brumskine's history with Charles Taylor and, indeed, the days of "You killed my ma, you killed my pa, but I'll vote for you anyway."

Baboon did the best he could. All through 2011, Baboon sounded a steady drumbeat of anti-Monkey news. He complained that Monkey had filled the National Elections Commission with supporters who had gerrymandered the country's voting districts to make sure that Monkey won.

Baboon commissioned a song that became a hit on the Liberian airwaves, "Monkey Come Down." It had a festive calypso beat and plenty of steel drums, and Liberians danced to it at parties and clubs. "Monkey come down, you not able; Baboon able," a peppy duo chirped during the refrain.

Baboon boldly went after Monkey's women, telling reporters that, actually, women didn't really even like Monkey. "She hasn't really improved the lot of Liberian women," Tubman told NPR. "She only makes that claim among foreign audiences. All they've done is have seminars."

Baboon even filed a lawsuit attesting that Monkey couldn't be president because the Liberian Constitution had a residency clause requiring its presidents to have lived in the country for ten years prior to their election. Monkey had moved back to Liberia in 2003, after the war ended. So she couldn't be president again in 2011. Brumskine too, though, had moved back in 2003, after Taylor was run out of town; Tubman didn't show up until 2004. As for Weah, he still lived in Florida. But so what? Baboon would deal with the problem of finding a good president who stayed in the country during the war later. Maybe Sekou Conneh, the LURD leader? Or General Butt Naked? (No, not George. The other one.) The Supreme Court threw out the suit, but Baboon kept fighting.

Liberia's 2011 election season was a cacophony of charges and countercharges, a hodgepodge of tomfoolery. The Liberian press, now free for the first time in history to print whatever they liked, swelled with polling reports and pages and pages of special campaign news.

As Election Day approached, it became increasingly clear that the race was, once again, between Monkey and Weah masquerading as Tubman, a replay of 2005: the old lady versus the football player. It would go down to the wire again, complete with a runoff. Journalists started writing stories about the one-term rule of Africa's first woman president.

But Monkey, unbeknownst to the rest of the country, had one more trick up her sleeve.

Chapter 18

NOBEL

Monrovia

October 7, 2011, four days before Election Day. We interrupt this presidential campaign to bring you the following announcement: "Today, three women won the Nobel Peace Prize, sharing $1.5 million. Two of the winners are Liberian—Africa's first democratically elected female president and a peace activist, and the third, a woman from Yemen, who has been a powerful voice in the Arab uprisings."

To understand just how miraculous it was for a Liberian president to win the Nobel Peace Prize, of all things, one must simply look back at the panoply of Liberian presidents since the prize was first awarded, in 1901.

William David Coleman (1898–1900) sent his soldiers into the interior of the country to defeat Gola men who were objecting to the appropriation of their land by the ruling Congo people. When Coleman's military was defeated, the soldiers went on a raping and pillaging tear so depraved that the Congo elite back in Monrovia couldn't stomach it; they called for Coleman's ouster, and he resigned in disgrace. He was succeeded by Garretson W. Gibson (1900–1904), best known for losing Liberian territory to the British in Sierra Leone.

After him came Arthur Barclay (1904–1912), who presided over mounting international debt and an economic depression. Daniel Howard's (1912–1920) term was marked by his inability to pay salaries of government workers and to keep Liberia out of World War I. Charles D. B. King (1920–1930; known throughout Liberia simply as C. D. B. King) sold Liberian men as slaves to Spanish colonists in Equatorial Guinea. Edwin J. Barclay (1930–1944) took the country to the edge of bankruptcy. William V. S. Tubman (1944–1971) modernized Liberia and paved a lot of roads;

he also killed his political opponents. William R. Tolbert (1971–1980) allowed his police to fire on unarmed protesters during the rice riots of 1979, then was disemboweled for his trouble.

Samuel Doe (1986–1990) executed Tolbert's cabinet, chopped up his opponents, and ran the economy so far into the gutter that its currency became worthless, its postal service was extinguished, and its credit was obliterated. Charles Taylor (1997–2003) was convicted of war crimes by the International Criminal Court.

Liberia, in other words, was not a country brimming over with leaders apt to win the Nobel Peace Prize. Which is why, when Monkey received the telephone call in late September, she thought at first it was a joke.

Monkey was on the Gbarnga Road headed back to Monrovia after a day of rallies when her cell phone rang. Elva Richardson, an assistant, was on the line. "I just got a call from the Nobel people," she said.

"What Nobel people?" Monkey asked.

"The Nobel Prize people. They say you being favored."

"Hehn?"

"They say you being favored. For the Nobel Peace Prize."

Monkey hung up the phone. That couldn't be right. Putting it out of her mind, she went back to her campaigning. Team Re-Elect Ellen (TREE) had just launched with a massive rally at Unity Party headquarters, complete with drummers, music, dancing girls, and special "Da Mama Ellen Areas," Monkey's version of the popular Liberian song "Da Ma Area."

"When I say something, y'all ma respond by saying 'da ma area'!" Monkey, full campaign-time Liberian-English-accent on, yelled at the rally, before proceeding into a raucous listing of her accomplishments in the first term.

"We built a two-thousand-known professional army!" Monkey yelled.

"Da ma area oh!" soldiers and their families yelled back.

"We built a coast guard, we give dem boat, they on de water!"

"Da ma area oh!" the whole crowd, apparently feeling especially nautical at the moment, yelled back.

"We brought back de RL in de World Bank!"

"Da ma area!!!" Any effort at parceling out specific areas was now gone;

everybody in the crowd was claiming credit for every area, jubilantly pointing at Monkey.

"We reopen de iron ore mines!"

"We increase the civil service pay!"

"We pay pension to pepo!"

"We pave de road to Buchanan!"

"We paved all de roads in Monrovia!"

"We brought lights back!"

The crowd broke out in spontaneous dancing and singing. The band kicked in, as thousands of people chanted "Hey! Ho!" in unison.

"I not finish!" Monkey yelled, taking back control. "I not finish, oh! De market women were sitting in the sun and the sand, we building new market for them all over de place!"

"Da ma area!" Forgetting all the fuss they put up about being moved, market women were dancing too.

"We went out there, waaaaaay out there to Nimba County, we put de best hospital there!"

Now the dancing crowd had switched to singing "Da ma area, oh-oh," accompanied by steel drums and guitar. At the microphone, the diminutive grandmother—Monkey was sporting very quaint earrings to set off her green and gold *lapa* and head-tie—continued to whip up her followers.

"Dis time, when you get your check, youn't gotta carry your check to Finance Ministry to wait for nothing, you can carry it to de bank!"

"Da ma area!"

Monkey took a brief dancing break. She jiggled a little to the music, then grinned. "I not finish! I not finish! Dey took de pepo money, nooooo, all de interest, interest, dey pack it, pack it, pack it"—her hands hacking the air to indicate Liberia's ballooning debt—"we came, we look at de ting, we say 'Oh! Dat how our small-small children dem will be paying dis ting twenty years from now?' So we call our pepo, we say dis debt gotta go. It gone. Da our area oh."

More dancing to the new "Da Ma Area" song.

More Monkey: "We ain't finish oh! We ain't finish oh! Ma pepo, look all round, wha' we trying to do, clean those beaches, da ma area. Look at all de new schools in the country, da ma area. We ain't finish.

"We ain't finish oh. Every time I think of something else again."

"Today, today, today, you can speak freely. You can say anyting you want. Because we respect de human rights."

"Da ma area!"

Proving that, in fact, freedom of speech was Monkey's area, Baboon was making full use of it. On the airwaves, Tubman and Weah were accusing Monkey's government of corruption. They held their own rallies, the hip young soccer player accompanied by his aging grandfather.

"Fellow CDCians," Tubman, a septuagenarian, said at one rally, "the young people of Liberia have it in them to make the country better!" He went on to heap Liberia's woes at the foot of Madame, concluding that corruption, long the bane of the country's government, could be easily solved: "People say, 'what will you do to fight corruption.' The first thing we will do is get people who are not corrupt! . . . We will break that cycle by employing young people who have not yet been corrupted by corruption. And that is the way we will be able to tackle the problem of corruption."

At least Baboon had a song as good as Monkey's, and Baboon's wasn't co-opted but was made solely for Baboon to use. Cue calypso beat and steel drums: "Monkey you not able to take care, oh, Baboon able. . . . Monkey come down."

Elva Richardson was on the line again when Monkey picked up the phone. "It is *done*," Richardson said.

Monkey didn't say anything.

"You heard me? The announcement coming out."

Still nothing.

"You have been named one of three recipients of the Nobel Peace Prize!" Richardson spelled it out, trying to make sure Monkey understood. "The head of the committee will be calling you tomorrow."

And sure enough, the next day Monkey, back at her office at the Ministry of Foreign Affairs, got a call from Thorbjørn Jagland, the former Norwegian prime minister, who headed the Nobel committee. Jagland told Monkey the Peace Prize, with its $1.5 million purse, would be announced shortly. Still not ready to believe what she was hearing, Monkey kept quiet.

The next morning, October 7, 2011, Monkey was having breakfast with her sister and brother-in-law and the usual passel of friends and family members who showed up at her house every morning to eat cassava and fish gravy, when the news broke on CNN. Ellen Johnson Sirleaf, Leymah Gbowee, a Liberian women's activist, and Tawakkol Karman, a Yemeni journalist and human rights activist, were being awarded the Nobel Peace Prize "for their non-violent struggle for the safety of women and for women's rights to full participation in peace-building work."

The yelling and screaming that erupted around the dining-room table was so loud that Monkey's security detail came running into the house to see what was going on. Jennie and Jeff and the rest of the group were hugging, screaming, and high-fiving, while Monkey sat there grinning. Amid the uproar, the big question from her close advisers was this: Would the upcoming announcement help or hurt Monkey's reelection campaign? What would Baboon make of this news?

The answer came shortly. It was as if the announcers on the radio stations couldn't believe the bulletins they were reading. Two Liberian women had won the Nobel Peace Prize?

"Madame President, Ellen Johnson Sirleaf, our president, has won the Nobel Peace Prize!" one announcer squeaked. "Liberia has been honored with a *peace* prize!"

Baboon went ape-shit. Tubman did an interview with the BBC that afternoon. "Well, I'm glad that Liberia has come to this honor from the Nobel Committee," he began. "As far as the honoring of Mrs. Sirleaf"—he couldn't even call her the president, he was so mad—"we in Liberia don't see any reason why she should be given this honor. It's undeserved; she's done more to bring war to my country than anybody else. And for her to be honored in this way is a big shock, not just to me but to the Liberian people."

The BBC interviewer interrupted at that point, as if unable to believe what he was hearing. Monkey had brought the war to Liberia? Not Baboon? "Surely, Mr. Tubman, what will come as a big shock to people is your view on this? Surely it's a big recognition of your country after all its history?"

Baboon was too angry to take the lifeline he had just been thrown.

"Well, let it come as a shock to them! This is my reaction! She doesn't deserve this honor!"

"Why not?"

"Because she's brought war here! She's a warmonger! She did more to cause war in this country than anybody!"

This appeared to surprise the interviewer, who remarked, "A lot of people will say she stopped the war."

That really sent Baboon into paroxysms. This is what Baboon—Doe's former justice minister—said: "I did more to stop the war than she did! Because she was in for continuing the war! And now that the war has stopped, she wants to stay on top of the country as if she's some liberator; she's not. She doesn't deserve this honor, it shouldn't have been given to her, and if you want to take a poll of Liberian people, you wouldn't find five people who would agree with what the Nobel Committee has done!"

Meanwhile, at the football field in front of Airfield, just off Tubman Boulevard in Monrovia, Monkey was celebrating with hundreds of her women. "She has brought us together as women, she has made us realize that what men can do, women can also do," said Cecelia Danuweli, one of the women's rights organizers. "All of these women here, they know what their rights stand for."

Walking onto the field with Leymah Gbowee, Madame exchanged hugs and handshakes and high-fives with her base. This was, poignantly, the very same spot where the women used to sit in the sand during the LURD bombings of Monrovia in 2003, begging the men to make peace. This was the same spot where the women in the white T-shirts kneeled and fasted and prayed for days, weeks on end, for peace. This was the same spot where Beatrice Freeman and Louise Yarsiah had huddled on their knees, hearts beating, while Charles Taylor's feared security chief, Benjamin Yeaten, and fifty soldiers cocked their machine guns and aimed at them.

This afternoon, there was no kneeling, only dancing and clapping. There were tears and hugs. "This is my hero," the charismatic Gbowee shouted into the crowd, lifting Madame's arm into the air. The two women complimented each other, raised their fists, showed their solidarity.

It was an extraordinary tableau, and one that would not last. Indeed, it would soon shatter, as, months later, Gbowee would fly to Europe and in a series of interviews sharply criticize Madame for not doing enough to combat government corruption in Liberia. In particular, Gbowee criticized Madame for naming three of her four sons to government positions, although one son was later suspended for failing to declare his assets and another, Fumbah, wasn't actually Madame's son but rather the son of her former husband's extramarital affair. Robert Sirleaf, though—he of the oil company NOCAL—surfaced as a key figure in Gbowee's critiques. "This is wrong and I think it is time for her to put him aside," she told the BBC. "He's a senior economic adviser, and that's well and good, but to chair the oil company board—I think it's time he stepped aside."

But all that would come later. On the day of the Nobel announcement, there was only camaraderie and mother-daughter bonhomie between Madame and the forty-year-old Gbowee. Just days before Election Day, Monkey had won the world's most prestigious international honor—for peacemaking.

Baboon couldn't touch that.

Chapter 19

MISS LIBERIA IMPOSTERS

Monrovia, January 2013

It was a push-pull, this relationship with the women.

At times the women of Liberia were Madame's best friends and fiercest defenders. The minute opponents launched political assaults on her, Holy Ghost women flooded the streets to stage marches of solidarity. Market women squatted outside the city jail to demand that rapists be tried. They assembled at prayer meetings across the country to pray for their president.

But then there were other times. Take the case of the dueling Miss Liberias.

"Miss Liberia Imposters under Probe," was the January 11, 2013, headline in *New Liberia*. Two women had gotten into a fight over the results of the Miss Liberia beauty pageant, each insisting she had won, and had both showed up at the Miss ECOWAS (Economic Community of West African States) pageant in Nigeria. "The government of Liberia," the article reported, "has categorically condemned those individuals who misrepresented the country."

Having won the Nobel Peace Prize and not one but two democratic elections, Liberian women had decided not to stick to the profiles-in-courage script assigned to them. The contradictions abounded: the same women who had donned white T-shirts to pray for peace in the field off Tubman Boulevard were refusing to help their female president by moving their stalls from the side of the road to newly constructed markets built to relieve traffic.

Many of the same young women who had fought so hard to get a woman elected president of an African country were now abandoning natural African standards of beauty and self-worth for Western ones. A veritable outbreak of wigs and hair weaves had erupted in Liberia, so widespread that the minister of education had issued a ban on fake hair worn by public elementary and high school students amid concerns that young girls were spending all of their time and money trying to look like Barbie dolls.

If only they could ban skin bleaching as well. It was now enormously difficult to find any moisturizer for sale in Monrovia pharmacies that didn't include bleach, as thousands of women sought to lighten their skin tone. This was a sad legacy of both the Congo people—who prized the lighter skin of their freed slave ancestors—and the overt messages women saw on their television screens and in their magazines. The result was that more and more women were trying to submerge their natural beauty, with their gorgeous hues of black ebony, for the milky variety promoted by Hollywood, colonial history, and deeply skewed Western standards.

But none of this touched the problem of the Poro and Sande, the traditional societies, one for men and one for women, in the bush. The Sande society routinely practiced female genital mutilation in the name of preparing girls for marriage. In much the same way that Liberians clung to traditional burial practices like washing the dead bodies, they were clinging to female genital mutilation. Many of the proponents of the practice were themselves women. In the past the Liberian government had said that such cultural traditions should be respected, despite pressure from international health organizations to make the practice illegal.

Trying to straddle the line, Madame—whom many Liberians considered too Western for her own good—had recently tried to educate women out of the practice, saying the government would come after anyone who pulled girls out of school and sent them to the Sande bush. But she was finding the greatest resistance to her recent edict was coming from the women who ran the Sande bush themselves.

In February 2013, matters came to a head when Madame found the women were cutting girls right on the edge of her family farm in Julejuah. It was the last morning of her weeklong county tour. Her entourage had spent the night at the family farm, a pretty and sprawling place dominated by the three-bedroom bungalow that Madame had built on a hill overlooking pastures, bush, and the village school.

The day before, she had stopped at school after school on the way to Julejuah. Most of the schools were one-room affairs with barely any books.

Or girls.

By the time Madame arrived in Julejuah, she was fuming. "They now send all the girls to the Sande bush?" she exclaimed.

The next morning, after a breakfast of cassava and smoked fish gravy and avocado, which Liberians call butterpear, Madame walked onto the verandah to hold court. A succession of village dignitaries arrived to receive gifts from her—charcoal pots, bags of rice, cooking paraphernalia—and to air their grievances. But Madame was waiting for someone in particular.

Finally, she turned to one of the village elders, an old man with barely any teeth. "Where the women I sent for? Those Sande bush women?"

"De woman, she sick."

"No," Madame insisted. "She must come here. Where de young girls from the village? We told you people the law is clear. School time, you can't put these children in the bush."

"Ma mouth full," the old man replied. "I na able to talk."

The two went back and forth for thirty minutes until three women suddenly showed up on the back of three pen-pen scooters coming up the driveway. Dressed in *lapa*s and head-ties, they strolled onto the verandah, nodded warily at the president, and sat down on plastic chairs.

"Zoe? You the Zoe, right?" Madame began, gesturing at the tallest woman. The Zoe is the name for the traditional head of the Sande Bush. "School is open. Where all the girls from the town?"

The Zoe flicked her hand dismissively, deliberately insolent.

"Y'all got the children in the bush. You know what the government law say?" Madame was approaching full rant. "We told y'all over and over. When it's school time, the girls must go to school."

The Zoe looked at the village elder, who translated for her in Gola, as she appeared not to understand English. Then she shrugged.

Madame was visibly agitated now. Her voice rising, she continued her lecture, turning to the village elder. "Tell her, they want spoil business now. We will make one law and we will carry you to jail! We finish with this bush business, we want school business."

The Zoe stared stone-faced at the president as Madame continued, switching from lecturing to cajoling and back to lecturing. "You want spoil those girls! You want them to grow up and not know book like you? You want your child to be like you?"

After another fifteen minutes, the Zoe and the other two women conferred, then whispered to the village elder in Gola.

"Ma, they say they sorry. Please just give them this month."

"When you say this month, you mean February?"

"Ma, certain things have to be done. What the forefathers have done, they have to pass through it."

At that, Madame erupted, standing up. "Y'all want the government to make some strong law! We will make strong law! You'n't hearing what I say but next month business, if I come here next month and those girls not in school, you and myself will fight!"

Three stubborn stares, oozing attitude.

Madame stormed over to the corner where sat a few remaining charcoal pots, boxed up for gifts, and started pointing to the people she wanted to give them to, all the while talking furiously. "Y'all right outside my own village, wha' kind of shame you bring on me? You want just be bush people? All right! Then we will close down all de roads, everything. Just be bush people, then."

Her entourage assembled into the SUVs in the motorcade, preparing to leave. The Zoe walked up to Madame. She spoke clearly in English. "But you will not give us anything?"

Madame huffed in exasperation. For a minute, she seemed about to relent, and she reached into her purse. Then she noticed the people watching her, including a journalist. Her wallet in her hand, she climbed into the back of the SUV. She turned to the Zoe, who, with her two cohorts, was repeating their pleas for money. This was the most they had spoken—and in perfectly clear Liberian English—since arriving.

"Aye Ma, we beg you, you gotta leave us something."

"Ma, that just woman business we da be doing."

Madame looked at the cash in her hand, then back at the women. Finally, she signaled to her protection service agent. As the SUV began to move, she turned to look at the Zoe and the other women. "Let the bush feed you," she told them, closing her wallet and putting it back into her purse.

Chapter 20

AMAZING GRACE AND MARY THE MENACE

Monrovia, 2013

Madame was in her element one February afternoon in Tunis, sitting at a conference table surrounded by African finance officials and the big donors who funded them. She was attending one of those global bureaucratic sessions at which she excelled, since it was a chance for her to present big, carefully detailed plans for Liberian infrastructure before a crowd with the money to pay for those plans. Just a few months before, she had left a similar meeting with nearly $50 million for the Fish Town–Harper highway in southeastern Liberia.

Just as the discussions were reaching a critical point, an aide slipped Madame a note: "The Liberian legislature has ordered the arrest of Grace Kpaan."

Grace Kpaan's political aspirations had ignited almost three decades before, when, as a teenager, she abandoned the pot of cassava leaf and rice she was supposed to be cooking for her mother to sneak to Unity Party headquarters and watch her idol speak to the faithful after getting out of prison. Starry-eyed, young Grace-tee McGill listened to Madame recite the second stanza of the Liberian national anthem as she stood on top of a table: "In union strong, success is sure, we cannot fail."

Grace had grown into a quiet, studious-looking woman with full cheeks and spectacles, who seemed to blend into the background. Usually clad in Western-style pantsuits, she eschewed the traditional Liberian full-gowned attire in which Madame usually cloaked herself. She was a part-time preacher. She spoke softly.

But all of that studied quiet was deceptive.

Grace Kpaan spoke out against female genital mutilation, annoying both men and women in Liberia's secretive Poro and Sande societies who still believed in the practice of yanking adolescent girls out of school, taking them up into the bush, and cutting out their clitoral hood.

She had worked as the head of the labor union at the Liberian port, organizing workers to demand salary and pension benefits. Her dock workers needed safety gear and access to medical help. Why were they paid in Liberian Liberty dollars when the port itself was generating U.S. dollars? She packed the kind of counterspy equipment that would make James Bond's Q proud: tape recorders, tiny camera-phone–video recorders to take secret surveillance photos, the better to chronicle the goings-on around her. In 2007, after repeated letters never got through, she had shown up at Madame's house near Fish Market on the day of Madame's regular Open House. She told Madame she was trying to organize a collective bargaining agreement that would spell out benefits for workers. Of course management was against that, so Kpaan wanted Madame to intervene.

Madame had quickly seen the potential in Kpaan. When she eventually appointed her superintendent of Montserrado County, which includes Monrovia, Kpaan attacked her job with gusto, cleaning out the headquarters, putting a lid on county scholarship funds so they would go to students instead of members of the House of Representatives, and setting up accounting practices to keep a close eye on county money. That put her on a collision course with the Liberian legislature.

Then she secretly tape-recorded Montserrado County representative Edward Forh trying to get her to agree to steal county funds and share the pot with him. Such corruption is normal among government officials in Liberia; the only thing of note here is that Kpaan, a political ally of Madame's, chose not to keep quiet about it. But since Liberian government officials always deny such accusations, Kpaan made sure she had proof. Meeting Forh at a Chinese restaurant near the ELWA Junction, she recorded him proposing his kickback scheme, which he did right after ordering a pork dish, a seafood dish, mixed fried rice, two orders of plain rice, a shrimp dish, "tha' thing with tha' plenty sauce," and a beef dish.

But she wasn't happy with the quality of the tape, so a few weeks later, she recorded him again, this time during a telephone conversation. "The money in question must be divided amongst us. You eat some, I eat some, the minister eat some," Forh said on the tape.

Kpaan played the tape for Madame. She told Liberian media outlets she had it, and they reported it. Forh countered that it was Kpaan who was crooked, not he. So Kpaan appeared before the press with the recording: "I am pleased to present this copy of the audio CD which contains the actual voice of Representative Forh requesting that I apportion funds intended for the Liberian people to him."

And there he was, clear as a bell. Over and over, radio stations broadcast the audio. "The money in question must be divided amongst us. You eat some, I eat some, the minister eat some."

The recording outraged the House of Representatives. But not because Forh had tried to steal money. The legislators were furious that Kpaan had broadcast a recording of him doing so.

They accused her of disrespecting them. They also accused her of being the crooked one, claiming that she stole $20,000 in county funds that was supposed to go to students for scholarships. She asked them to provide proof; they had none. Then they wanted to know why she had refused to release $15,000 in county funds that they wanted to use to decorate a library in New Kru Town. Kpaan replied that the money was supposed to be used for scholarships for students, not for decorating libraries. Back and forth the two sides went, Kpaan versus the legislature, until finally, furious, the legislature called for a vote to arrest her.

Just before the vote, Miatta Fahnbulleh, the well-known Liberian singer and human rights activist, showed up at the Capitol to speak in defense of Kpaan. But she was quickly surrounded by dozens of angry young men who pushed her to and fro, all the while chanting, booing, and hurling epithets. Eventually, someone pushed the Liberian icon into a taxi and she got away. Laughing, the young men excitedly made calls on their cell phones to tell their friends what they had done. No one in the august body of the House of Representatives made any move to protect Miatta Fahnbulleh from the mob outside. Instead the legislators went ahead with their vote to arrest Kpaan.

In Tunis, Madame read the note, then told her aide to get Justice Minister Christiana Tah on the case, to quickly get a writ that would keep

Kpaan out of Monrovia Central Prison. The House of Representatives had no legal authority to arrest people.

Madame turned her attention back to the African Development Bank. This was serious business she was engaged in, trying to convince the bank to continue funding Liberia and other fragile states. Meanwhile, her country was up in arms over the legislature's trying to jail a county superintendent for disrespecting them. What nonsense, she thought.

From Tunis, Madame flew to Freetown, Sierra Leone, for the inauguration of Ernest Bai Koroma as president. But when her plane landed, an aide handed her the phone to hear the latest report from Monrovia.

Mary Broh and a group of women had massed in front of Monrovia Central Prison to stop the arrest of Grace Kpaan. There was a fight. Someone—Mary Broh? Grace Kpaan? Gender Minister Julia Duncan-Cassell?—pulled the button off the coat of the House sergeant at arms while he was still in it. Was that assault?

Broh and Kpaan were on the run.

The House of Representatives had had another vote. This time, they voted 49–0 to declare Broh and Kpaan "wanted fugitives."

Oh Jesus, now Broh was involved. Remember Mary Broh? She had used her vacation time from her job at Marvel Comics back in 2005 to campaign for Madame with her team of Spider-Man–backpack-carrying women? In return Madame had appointed her acting mayor of the city of Monrovia.

"This is unbelievable," Madame erupted.

Too many people were clustered around her at the airport in Freetown for her to have a proper phone conversation with her vice president, so Madame went into the ladies restroom to make her call.

"I'm calling you from the bathroom," she barked at Vice President Joseph Boakai.

"These people are enraged," he told her.

Worse for Madame was that Broh had now become involved because for all that the name Grace Kpaan could send the men in the legislature's hallowed halls into conniptions, the name Mary Broh sent them into apoplectic fits, the equivalent of waving a red flag in front of a starving, bloodthirsty bull.

The Angela Davis period, at an African Development Bank meeting in Addis Ababa, Ethiopia, 1970s.

4

5

African Development Bank days, 1970s.

6

The assistant finance minister waits in an airport transit lounge, headed to an African Development Bank meeting in Mauritius, 1970s.

Ellen's parents,
Carney Johnson and
Martha Johnson.

"Coming-out ladies":
Ellen, seated on the right,
and friends, Liberia.

Ellen (third from right)
and Clavenda (second
from left), at a party on
Clavenda's porch, 1970s.

With Clarence Parker in 1979, just a year before he was executed by Samuel Doe.

Enjoying life in Alexandria, Virginia, early 1980s.

With Rob, Alexandria, Virginia, 1980s.

Nairobi office of Citibank.

On the way to the
sedition trial,
Temple of Justice, 1986.

Released from jail, Unity
Party headquarters, 1986.

At Lake Malawi for a
United Nations
Development Program
meeting, 1990s.

With Jes, 2000s.

16

George Weah holding his Arthur Ashe Courage award at the 2004 ESPY Awards at the Kodak Theater in Hollywood. The award honors individuals whose contributions transcend sports.

17

Boys for Weah, November 2005.

18

Girls for Ellen, November 2005.

19

No Weah, No Peace. A Weah supporter wears foliage, just as the fighters did during the civil war, November 2005.

Madame President.
Thanking the women who got her there,
during her inaugural address, January 2006.

Condoleezza Rice and Laura Bush, be-hatted of course, at Madame President's inaugural ceremony in January 2006.

21

22

Hillary Clinton comes to visit, August 2009.

23

Air Force One lands at Robertsfield.

The legislature hated her so much that when Madame appointed her mayor of Monrovia, they refused to confirm the appointment. So for three years Broh had been the acting city mayor, riding around in her black SUV with the "Mayor-1" tags that sent everyone who saw it running in the other direction. She was the epitome of the legislature's worse nightmare: a tough-talking woman with absolutely no fear of alienating anyone in her path.

It was Broh who had cleaned up the city of Monrovia—taking on the job abandoned by Beatrice Sieh's police after her ignominious indictment for corruption. There were far fewer open latrines in the city now, far fewer mounds of trash, far fewer illegal market stalls in the middle of the road. Broh and her crews of young women in green T-shirts could be seen on the side of the street early Saturday morning with garbage bags, picking up trash. They descended on one neighborhood after the next, confronting residents for littering.

Broh tore down the illegal houses, stalls, and lean-tos that had taken over the city's landscape and swelled its suburbs. First, she and her teams drew yellow chalk markings around the structures, as a warning that they didn't belong in the middle of what passed for the sidewalk. When that was ignored, as it usually was, the team went in with another warning. When all the warnings were ignored, as they usually were, Broh sent bulldozers, hoes, axes, and heavy equipment, and the structures were destroyed. The result is that now one could walk down some patches of Broad Street without plowing straight into a mass of illegal stalls.

Monrovians were both happy that their city was cleaner and angry that their favorite illegal stalls were no longer available to service their needs. T-shirts sprouted up, sporting the clever caption "Don't Raze Me, Broh." Broh retaliated with her own T-shirts, emblazoned with the words "City Ordinance Number One," a reference to the ordinance passed in 1975 under President Tolbert that set environmental standards for cleanliness and public health in the city.

Cleanliness became Broh's central issue, and she went after it with such a vengeance that she was the first—and only—Liberian official to receive funding from the Bill and Melinda Gates Foundation for her efforts, a $5 million grant to continue cleaning up the city.

Yet people were still angry. She wasn't nice enough. She was too rough. She cussed people out too much. She didn't give out enough waivers to this friend and that cousin, who just wanted to stay in their illegal structure for one more month until their new place was fixed up.

Even Madame's executive branch employees were angry. Some of those charged with enforcing the law had no qualms about using the illegal structures that sprang up all over the city. When a young bureaucrat got on the elevator at the Ministry of Foreign Affairs, the elevator attendant noted that the young man's hair was longer than usual.

"Man, Mary Broh na break down people barber," the young man said, running his hand over his bushy head.

The attendant laughed. "Mary Broh. Tha' one da serious woman, oh."

So the city was cleaner because of Broh, but it was also angrier because of Broh. The market women, especially, hated her; mention the name Mary Broh to the women at Ma Jobar Market—an illegal market due for relocation per Broh's decision to turn it into the city's only park, funded by Chevron—and the women selling their kola nuts started hissing.

The young boys who still believed George Weah was the messiah hated her too. They had begun building an enormous statue of the football hero and twice-unsuccessful presidential candidate right in the middle of downtown Broad Street. It was almost completed, in glorious detail, and cars driving by slowed down to admire it.

It was illegal, of course—imagine putting up a statue of Mitt Romney on Constitution Avenue in Washington, DC, without getting permission from the city first. When the boys showed up one morning to continue working on their statue, it was gone. Overnight, gone. In its place was a coconut tree, just planted, its stump painted a pristine white.

The boys were outraged. Broh was unrepentant. "After all the sweat people put to clean this city, you think I letting those children put that mess up on Broad Street?" she said. Actually, she yelled. Mary Broh was very good at yelling.

One afternoon at City Hall, the only government building where visitors were greeted by understated young women proffering bottles of cold water, Broh seemed torn between cussing out her young aides ("I will make y'all shame, then you will do wha' people tell you to do!") and singing their praises to a visitor ("You see how respectfully you were greeted when you came in?"). She flew from office to office like a whirling dervish, ordering one aide to make sure to put six lumps of sugar in her coffee, then shouting into the telephone, "That's their job! Just get it done!," then turning with a smile to a bureaucrat from Nepal to explain to him, "Monrovia is not Kigali. What we're trying to construct is the Kigali of the future."

But Broh saved her best scenes for her foes in the House of Representatives. Just before Madame went to Tunis for the African Development Bank meeting, there was a huge fracas between Broh and Representative Solomon George, a Weah ally. It is almost impossible to describe the origins of the fight; Broh and George had been at each other's throats for months and had scuffled when she dared to enter the Capitol to attend the president's State of the Nation speech, ignoring a recent decree from George that she was not welcome in the hallowed halls. So enraged was George that the acting mayor was entering his Capitol that he and some of his legislative friends surrounded her and ordered her to leave. She refused at first, but was eventually escorted out.

A few nights later George held a Town Hall meeting at which he threatened to defecate on the acting mayor.

Standing behind a desk in front of dozens of people, he embarked on a long and rambling soliloquy on the nature of corruption. "Corruption," he said, "is breaking down the homes of the poor and leaving those of the rich. . . . That's corruption.

"Corruption is having a city mayor that disrespects her equals and even the poor. . . . She seizes market from the peddlers, then when she seizes the market, you are to pay a minimum of $50 U.S. . . . I am saying to the president, and when I told her, she apologized on behalf of Madame Broh." But the president, he added, "needs to find someone else. As hard-working as Madame Broh is—and look, let me tell you something, I love Madame Broh, she's hard-working—but if you do something that makes people to pick up cutlass? There are some guys in Liberia that still have their guns buried. They still have their guns buried!

"If the president continues to keep Madame Broh where she is—disrespecting the people, disregarding the rights of the people—there will be a fight. There will be a very serious fight. Because we are not afraid!" His voice rose, riding the outrage at these women who tried to clean up the city. "I am not afraid!" he said. The president "needs to take her away from that position because she has become Dennis the Menace! Mary the Menace is who she is!

"Mary Broh was brave enough to enter the premises of the Capitol Building. . . . She entered the Capitol Building, whipped our protocol officer, handcuffed him! . . . The woman is a menace! And the president is in awareness of what she's doing. Because whenever she does wrong, the president will go and apologize on her behalf. I am saying *that* is corruption!

"If she does not take her away from that position, we will fight. I am saying it, we will fight. I'm telling you, look, I will take Mary Broh and carry her to one of the toilets. We will tie her. They will be shitting on her until they come for her."

George sat down as the room erupted into horrified giggling.

The next morning, Mary the Menace was on ELBC radio. "The battle lines," she vowed, "have been drawn."

That night she got a call from Madame, who sounded weary. Yes, she had her back, but could Mary the Menace please take it down a notch?

Two weeks passed in relative quiet. Then Madame went to Tunis, the legislature voted to arrest Grace Kpaan, and Mary the Menace came out swinging.

When Brigadier-General Martin Johnson, the House of Representatives sergeant at arms who was ordered to take Kpaan to jail, arrived at Monrovia Central Prison with his charge, things went downhill quickly. Recounting the events later, when he explained to the House how he managed to lose his prisoner to a bunch of obstreperous women, Johnson struck an aggrieved tone. First, he said, the prison authorities didn't want to let him into the prison compound with Kpaan. "They disallowed my vehicle from entering the prison compound," he complained. After a lot of back and forth, he finally got through the gate with his charge.

"I asked her out of the car. By the time she got off the car, I saw Mary Broh coming with a group of people from the opposite direction."

Mary the Menace approached with a large band of sisters, including Julia Duncan-Cassell, Madame's minister of gender and development;

Counselor Pearl Brown-Bull (gold tooth, sleepy eye, quick to cuss people out); and other "co-horts," as described in one Liberian newspaper account of the ensuing melee. Broh took Kpaan's arm. "Let's go," she said.

General Johnson tried to stop them, grabbing Kpaan and pulling her back toward him. But before he could do anything, he was surrounded by irate women who pushed and shoved him instead. "They started hitting me from the back, to the extent they cut my uniform button," the brigadier general said, as if discussing a war wound. "In that process they overpowered me and they took her and put her on Mary Broh's pickup." And peeled away like gangsters leaving the scene of a crime.

These were the events Madame's aide relayed to her on the airport tarmac in Freetown when her plane landed. Squeezing her eyes shut, Madame took a few deep breaths. Not enough. She took a few more.

"This is the one woman who has done so well at cleaning up Monrovia," she fumed. "This is the only single person who gets money from Bill Gates. Wha' wrong with these people?"

She ordered both Broh and Kpaan suspended. Her instructions to Broh to take it down a notch meant, among other things, that she was not supposed to go to the city jail with a bunch of women, spring Kpaan, and assault the outerwear of the aggrieved House sergeant at arms, a charge Broh later denied. Furious that Broh hadn't given Justice Minister Tah time to free Kpaan in a less inflammatory way, Madame flew back to Liberia, where she found the capital city in an uproar.

WHERE ARE THEY? HUNT CONTINUES FOR MARY BROH, SUPT. KPAAN —*Inquirer.*

LAWMAKERS WANT KPAAN, BROH ALIVE —*All Africa.*

GRACE KPAAN, MARY BROH, IN DOUBLE TROUBLE —Public Agenda News.

Interestingly, none of the press reports delved into the illegality of the House of Representatives' attempt to arrest Kpaan; it was as if the Liberian media just assumed that, as elected representatives, the majority men of the august body were perfectly within their rights to vote to arrest anyone who tape-recorded them soliciting kickbacks and bribes. Instead, the press coverage revolved around the sheer chutzpah of Mary the Menace to stop the legislators from exercising their God-given right to throw Kpaan in jail.

Front Page Africa's top story was representative of the way the Liberian media were reporting the fracas: "An outraged Plenary of the House of Representatives of the 53rd legislature gathered in full Thursday to regain their sanctity which they say was desecrated by suspended Acting Monrovia City Mayor aided by some influential women when she obstructed justice by freeing a prisoner belonging to that august body in person of Montserrado County Superintendent Grace Kpaan."

Broh and Kpaan lay low for a few days while the legislature voted again to arrest (and, in the case of Kpaan, rearrest) them. On February 28, Broh resigned her post; Kpaan followed suit a few days later.

Five days after accepting her resignation, Madame appointed Broh to lead a $30 million project to build large-scale community housing in Monrovia, and then on to head the General Services Agency.

And within a month, mountains of trash were growing around Monrovia again.

Chapter 21

THE ORACLE

Monrovia, 2013

They came from Senegal, from Rwanda, from Ghana.

It started as a trickle, just weeks after Madame first took office in 2006. A group of market women from the Ivory Coast arrived in Liberia wanting to ask her market women supporters who had worked their stalls while they were busy campaigning for Madame. Because the Ivorian marketeers were now wondering whether they might turn to politics.

Soon afterward, a delegation arrived from Senegal, this time real live political aspirants. Then came a group from Rwanda, and then a bunch of clan chief hopefuls from Ghana. That trickle turned into a stream of women from all over the continent, coming to Liberia to talk to Parleh Harris, Vabah Gayflor, Etweda Sugars Cooper, Amazing Grace Kpaan, Mary the Menace Broh, and of course Madame President herself.

By the time Madame was reelected, she was receiving an average of three visiting delegations of African female political hopefuls a week. She saw them all.

On a January morning in 2013, in the middle of negotiations with former soldiers of the Armed Forces of Liberia over back pay from the Taylor and Doe years, Madame found time to talk to her latest delegation of women. Her meeting was supposed to start at 12:30, but the former soldiers kept her late. But the fifteen women waiting to speak to her had been waiting so long that an almost palpable weariness had descended on the room. The silence was oppressive. The women were all done up in their most colorful finery, high heels, bangles jingling down every arm, deep primary-color Fanti cloths. Every single woman wore a wig or a hair weave and bloodred lipstick. Each looked very nervous, eyes darting around the silent room, as they waited for their audience with the woman who had quickly become the Oracle at Delphi for aspiring African female politicians.

Finally, Madame swept in, and the women rose as one. "Welcome! Bienvenue!" Madame said, beaming at them.

It was as if someone flicked an electric switch. The silent conference room exploded into a cacophony of chatter and laughter, as the women strained to reach out toward Madame.

Suddenly Madame—who just minutes ago had been angrily ranting that the former AFL soldiers and their widows had wrung the last cent out of her—looked happy and enthusiastic. It was evident the women recharged her stores of energy.

The ascendance of Madame to power in Liberia, and the immediate bump in the country's fortunes that came with her inauguration, gave the air of possibility to the political aspirations of women across Africa. In the ultimate irony, Liberia, long viewed as one of the most godforsaken countries on a godforsaken continent, was now an example of democratic empowerment. If *Liberian* women could do it, then what of the women of Senegal and Nigeria and Ghana? None of those countries had sunk to the depths Liberia reached during its years of madness; those countries were veritable Norways and Swedens compared to Liberia.

Zahra Iyane Thiam Diop of Senegal was the first to speak. Her voice trembling, she smiled at Madame. "There are 180 political parties in Senegal," she stated. "Three of which are led by women." She looked around the table and pointed to two others. "Here we are."

The Oracle nodded and smiled congenially at the three Senegalese. Before she could say anything, another woman interrupted. "Please excuse my happiness," she gushed. "I am in the presence of the first woman ever elected president of a country in Africa. I am Mariam Ly."

And so it went, on and on.

Just a year before these delegates came to call on Madame, Joyce Banda, only two weeks into her presidency of Malawi, made her first international trip; she chose to go to Liberia, to see Madame. Banda had assumed the role following a two-day political crisis during which supporters of her now-deceased predecessor tried to keep her from becoming Malawi's first female president. For a brief while, Africa had two.

All around the continent, the fever was spreading. In Rwanda, where years of fighting culminating in a horrific genocide had decimated the male population, the Parliament was now dominated by women—women held 56.3 percent of the seats, more than in any other country in the world. In Senegal, women held 42.7 percent of parliamentary seats, in South Africa 42.3 percent, in Mozambique 39.2 percent, and in Tanzania 36 percent.

Now the women politicians had decided they needed an umbrella association to guide them. They had come to see if Madame would agree to be their benefactress and mentor. Sitting next to Mariam Ly, the group's translator jangled her gold Jesus earrings as she flipped her head from side to side.

Zahra Iyane Thiam Diop explained the point behind the umbrella organization. "Before, women had never had the idea of bonding together politically," she said. Not until they saw the Liberian women do it. "When we saw the example of the Liberian women, we knew what we had to do." She slipped in some other do-gooding verbiage about how women view their countries "as their own babies" and how "as a woman you always want your child to have good health," then she got back to the main point of the meeting. "We know that if President Ellen Johnson Sirleaf accepts this alliance group, and picks up the telephone and tells everyone that she accepts this alliance, then all doors will be opened to us!" And, in case the Oracle didn't get her meaning, she added, "More funds."

She sat back and let some of the other women talk. There was the usual fawning: "you give us courage"; "this barrier you've broken"; "this bridge you've built." Then it was time for the Oracle to speak.

At first, Madame seemed to think she was at another one of her international bureaucrat meetings. "Do you plan to form a secretariat to work with the first position?" she asked.

Befuddled, the women looked at each other around the table. The translator hesitantly worked at what the Oracle had just said, then seemed to give up, trailing off uncertainly.

"We have come to you?" Diop said, her voice ending in a question.

The Oracle nodded. "What I will do is consult a bit," she explained. When the women continued to look at her uncertainly, she broke into a grin. Then she dropped a few names designed to elicit cheers from aspiring female politicians. "I will talk to Graça Machel," the Mozambican politician and humanitarian who became Nelson Mandela's third wife. "I'll talk to Dr. Zuma," Nkosazana Dlamini-Zuma, the South African politician (and one of the many wives of South African president Jacob Zuma) who became the first woman to lead the African Union in 2012. "I will get their ideas of how we can get an organization going. We also should be looking in our countries, at who are the women vying for power whom we can help."

Now the women around the table were beaming at each other, perhaps entertaining images of the Oracle coming to their hometown to personally campaign for their election.

The Oracle concluded, "Let me gather the women in politics around the continent." She stood up.

The women rose. "Thank you so much."

"Thank you."

"Thank you."

They pressed a number of gifts on the Oracle—a green cloth for protection, placemats and tablecloths "because, as women, we always take care of family." Then they made sure to get the one other thing they were seeking from this meeting. "May we have a photo, Madame President?"

The Oracle posed with her admirers, then took off. She had a plane to catch; she was flying to Washington for twenty-four hours to get a signature on a joint declaration—the official name was "partnership dialogue." Buried under the usual diplomatic verbiage about sustainable development, food security, and "Feed the Future" initiatives was one critical fact: the United States was promising to commit more money and pay more attention to Liberia.

The agreement had been reached the year before; all that was left was for the Oracle and the U.S. secretary of state to sign it. But the Oracle wanted to make sure that not just any U.S. secretary of state signed the agreement. She wanted a particular signature—one that she could get only if she got to Washington before President Obama's inauguration. It was the height of the Liberian summer—the dry season—when Madame boarded the flight from Robertsfield to Brussels and then to Washington, where it was the depths of winter. But Madame didn't care about the weather.

The signature she wanted on that joint declaration was Hillary Clinton's.

Clinton, still recovering from a blood clot in her leg that had left her incapacitated and away from the State Department for a month, had deeply slashed her public appearances; in fact, she hadn't met with any visiting leaders since before Christmas and had even failed to show up for congressional hearings on the attacks on the American consulate in Benghazi, Libya, much to the ire of Republican legislators.

Now, with only a few days left as secretary of state, Clinton made time for one more public appearance at the State Department. Standing beside Madame in the State Department's ornate Treaty Room, just in front of the painting of George Washington, Clinton stressed her "great personal pleasure" at working with Madame and spoke of their "personal friendship."

Then it was Madame's turn at the microphone.

"Madame Secretary," Madame President began. Then she paused and smiled. "Hillary," she corrected herself, as the audience tittered. "You've been a true friend of Liberia and to me personally." She went on to talk about Clinton's two trips to Liberia as secretary of state, about her support for settling Liberia's external debt, about the "significant dividends" that Clinton's support for Liberia would eventually play. But really, the words spoken that morning did not matter. Madame had the signature she wanted on the document. It was a signature she was convinced would be valuable to her in the years to come.

Less than forty-eight hours earlier, Madame had met with the group of aspiring female politicians from around Africa, nursing their hopes that one day they could lead their country. Now, by insisting on flying in to get Clinton's signature on that joint declaration instead of waiting for the next secretary of state, John Kerry, Madame was all but shouting from the rafters that she believed Hillary Clinton would be the next president of the United States.

America, she was sure, would follow the example of Liberia.

But what Madame didn't count on was that while she had won her elections on the strength of the women's vote in Liberia—on all those women from Martha Nagbe to Parleh Harris to Masawa Jabateh—Hillary Clinton couldn't count on the same thing. Mrs. Clinton had 94 percent of black women and 68 percent of the Latina women vote, yes. But she earned only 47 percent of the white women vote. Perhaps that demographic in the United States hadn't stared into the abyss that their Liberian counterparts had.

They hadn't watched as their sons were kidnapped by drunk soldiers; they hadn't been submitted to gang rape to save their daughters from similar fates or seen their country literally torn apart by wig-wearing madmen fueled on amphetamines and cane juice. And apparently, chaos and devastation is what it takes to upend centuries of male rule and roll the dice for a woman leader.

The women of Liberia had made that leap. But while close to half of their sisters in America were ready to do the same, Hillary Clinton needed more than half. To win as a woman, you need more than half of the female vote. You need all of it.

Chapter 22

CONTAGION

Monrovia, March 2014

There is a saying in Liberia: "When Bad Luck call your name, rotten banana break your teeth." It means exactly what it says: when bad luck comes, even the simplest of efforts will defeat you.

Bad luck came in March, in two telephone calls. Taywah Taylor's cell phone rang first, on March 20, while she was at her home near the Firestone rubber plantation, an hour outside of Monrovia. On the line was a cousin in Foya, Lofa's second biggest city, with disturbing news: Taywah Taylor's sister, who had recently returned from a trip to Guinea for a funeral, was feverish, delirious, and vomiting blood. No one was sure what was wrong.

In Liberia, if you hear "your people' them sick," you go take care of them. The next day, Taywah Taylor sent her older two children to school, grabbed her one-year-old son, Joe, and headed up to Foya, a hard day of travel on broken roads, transferring from taxis to mammy bus—so named because it has long been a go-to travel option for West African women transporting their wares from farm to market. Finally, she arrived to find her sister spitting blood, toggling between hot sweat and bone-cracking chills.

Across Foya, a bustling market town of 20,000 that saw daily border crossings back and forth to nearby Guinean border towns, a handful of people were coming down with sudden onset fever, intense weakness, muscle pain, headaches, and sore throats. These were all symptoms of malaria and Lassa fever, two illnesses that just about every West African who has lived through rainy season has gotten.

Except it was dry season.

What was making Taywah Taylor's sister sick wasn't malaria or Lassa fever. It was something that would make malaria and Lassa fever look like a head cold.

So arrives the second phone call. That phone call came to Madame on Sunday, March 23. She had just returned the night before from Grand Bassa County where she had chaired a meeting of the Liberian Development Alliance. It was just the kind of numbers-driven wonk festival that Madame loved; her boy-wonder finance minister, Amara Konneh, had informed the assembled bureaucrats that the development alliance had invested $130 million in various infrastructure and development projects as part of implementing Madame's "Agenda for Transformation" initiative.

The meeting ended that Saturday afternoon and Madame headed back to Monrovia. The phone call—straight to her personal cell phone—came the next day. On the line was Dr. Walter Gwenigale, the crotchety minister of health, known universally as Dr. G. He had been at the Buchanan meeting the day before, where he had seemed preoccupied. But he had chosen not to say anything then. He wanted to get his facts straight.

"Madame," Dr. G. said, "I think we got trouble."

Ebola arrived in Liberia in March 2014, traveling the same route that numberless generations of market women carved out of the bush over centuries. It crossed the border from Guinea and eventually showed up in Foya. Its hosts were Taywah Taylor's sister and a handful of others.

Medical experts in the region believe that Patient Zero was a two-year-old boy in Gueckedou, which sits at the crossroad of Guinea, Sierra Leone, and Liberia, the intersection of the three countries that would soon become the epicenter of the worst Ebola outbreak in history. The location of the start of this outbreak would play a dispositive role in the spread of the virus; past Ebola flare-ups had occurred in remote largely unpopulated areas and so were snuffed out efficiently.

But Gueckedou was Grand Central Terminal. English, French, Liberian English, Sierra Leonean patois, Guinean creole, Kpelle, Lorma, and Temne all competed to be heard in the frenetic markets where women converged to buy dried meat and mangoes—both of them suspected Ebola transmitters—in the tropical heat. This part of Africa had not seen the disease before, and people thought they were dealing with malaria and Lassa fever, which kill enough people on their own.

No one knows how the Gueckedou toddler contracted the disease; he died after four days. The virus can reside in fruit like the aforementioned mangoes, as well as in chimpanzees, gorillas, fruit bats, monkeys, antelopes, porcupines, rodents, dogs, and pigs. For the Gueckedou toddler, theories ranged from contaminated fruit to contaminated needles. A week later, his mother, three-year-old sister, and then his grandmother were dead. Two mourners at the grandmother's funeral incubated the virus, taking it home with them to their village. Health workers carried it to their villages. And so it spread.

Once people became ill, their bodily fluids infected others. The only protection was not to touch anyone who had Ebola. In a country like Liberia, where people kiss strangers on the cheeks when they first meet, and rush to take care of family members when they get ill, this was cataclysmic.

Madame President didn't know any of this when she got the call from Dr. G. She had heard of Ebola before, to be sure. Wasn't it a disease that people got in the Congo, half a continent away? It was fatal, but not all the time, right?

"Wha' this mean?" she demanded into the phone.

Dr. G., with his medical degree from the University of Puerto Rico and four decades of experience in medicine, knew exactly what Ebola meant. His presentation boiled down to three stark facts—one good and two so bad they canceled out the good.

Good: Ebola was not airborne.

Bad: It was still highly contagious.

Really bad: It had a high fatality rate.

"This disease," he said, "it da' just spread." The government needed to tell the Liberian public. The two agreed that Dr. G. would show up at the next day's press conference that was scheduled at the Ministry of Information.

Madame hung up the phone. She was concerned, but not overly so. Hopefully this Ebola thing would peter out in a few months as it had in previous episodes in Congo and Uganda.

She had bigger fish to fry, the kind of fish she loved frying. Her Agenda for Transformation was a year old. The meeting the day before in Buchanan had gone well; she was on her way to bringing her war-scarred banana republic into the twenty-first century. By 2030, Liberia would rival Ghana, by universal acclaim the most highly functional African country, despite their bland jollof rice. Just wait and see.

Up in Foya, Lofa County, Taywah Taylor—her sister now dead—had a fever. She headed home to Firestone with her son Joe; by the time the two arrived, she was vomiting. Her husband, Joe Fallah Taylor, rushed her to the Firestone hospital. Firestone health workers by now had heard that Ebola was in Foya, but none of them had any experience with the disease. They spent the day scouring the Internet for information. They cleared out a building on the hospital grounds and set up an isolation ward. They donned the hazmat suits meant for chemical spills at the rubber factory and placed Taywah Taylor in isolation.

They isolated her husband, Fallah, and baby Joe, as well. The other two children had been at school when their mother arrived home from Foya sick; they were not allowed to come home.

Within days, Taywah Taylor was dead.

But somehow, neither her Fallah nor Joe—now nicknamed Miracle Joe by the Firestone workers—contracted the disease. On April 23, twenty-two days after Taywah Taylor arrived back in Firestone, Fallah Taylor and Miracle Joe were released from isolation. The company presented Fallah with a new house—the old house was contaminated and possessions there burned. He received an envelope of cash. There was a celebratory ceremony at Firestone to pronounce Fallah Taylor and Miracle Joe Ebola-free.

Ebola had not spread at Firestone; the rubber company had somehow stopped the virus cold. It was a textbook case of how to manage the spread of a deadly communicable disease.

But there is a big difference between a self-contained rubber plantation run by a highly competent foreign company that comes complete with its own hospital and a chaotic country of 4 million obstinate, affectionate, superstitious, emotional people, as Madame was about to find out.

The Ministry of Health confirmed the first six cases of Ebola by the end of March, and Liberia's chief medical officer, Dr. Bernice Dahn, told reporters that she had sent a team to Lofa to investigate, that they were already tracing contacts, collecting blood samples, and instructing local health authorities on the disease.

It all sounded very orderly, unless you actually know Liberia, in which case you realize that the team will be met by peevish and stiff-necked people who will insist their sick relatives have malaria and not Ebola, who will accuse the government of manufacturing the crisis to get more foreign aid, and who will throw the teams out of their homes.

In any event, the Liberian government continued to put out pronouncements that it was on top of things. Two people had died, but the implicit message was "come on, this is West Africa." People dying in stunning numbers, years before their time, was the way things are, what with civil wars, disease, poor sanitation, and dismal health infrastructures. In Liberia in 2014 the life expectancy was fifty-eight years, a huge jump from the thirty-eight years that it was when Madame was elected president in 2005, but still middle age by Western standards. Many people in Liberia still didn't live long enough to die from cancer. Bright and beautiful young children still died from whooping cough.

Dr. G. urged market women to suspend trips to Guinea. "If you are living along the border and you really do not have any reason to go into towns where this disease is reported, you do not have to go there," Dr. G. warned.

To no one's surprise, the market women ignored him and continued to cross into Guinea for their foodstuffs. Telling a market woman she can't go get her wares is like telling her she should die; making market in a marginal postwar economy in a country with no social infrastructure and no government safety net was how families managed to buy enough rice to get through the next day.

By April 23—the day that Fallah Taylor and Miracle Joe were pronounced free of Ebola—six people in Liberia, out of thirty-four cases, were confirmed dead of the disease, most of them in Lofa County, although there were many more suspect cases in which people had died unreported. But the closest it had gotten to Monrovia was Taywah Taylor in Firestone, an hour away.

On the radio airwaves, people questioned whether Ebola really had come to Liberia. The press didn't seem to believe it; newspapers and radio shows continued to accuse the government of making the whole thing up to get more foreign aid.

Even among the people with intimate knowledge of the disease, there were still challenges. A day after he was pronounced Ebola-free, Joe Fallah Taylor told a reporter with the Liberian newspaper *New Dawn* that he wanted to know where the government had buried his wife so he could go clean her grave. Neither he nor Miracle Joe had been allowed near her during her last hours—for that is the curse of Ebola, that to stay virus-free, family members must leave their loved ones to die alone, without the comfort of a stroke on the brow, an embrace, or even a warm hand holding your own.

Then, they must allow a government burial team in full hazmat suits to come and take their loved one's body away, to be burned or dumped in a mass grave.

The death of someone you love is never easy. But most Liberians, after two decades of mass graves, sudden disappearances and executions in the night, had come to value that peace meant that you could at least mark the death of a loved one with ceremony. A wake, to tell stories of remembrance. A funeral, to grieve properly. A burial. A place to go on Decoration Day, when Liberians clean the graves of loved ones.

Ebola would take all that away as well.

Meanwhile, Madame President was still fixated on her Agenda for Transformation. She was setting the building blocks in place to lift Liberians from poverty by 2030. Now seventy-five years old, she was continuing her usual breakneck pace of meetings on economic projects and projections. "The Agenda for Transformation is consistent with the principles of the Paris Declaration, the Accra Agenda for Action and the New Deal for Engagement in Fragile States," she announced, as if the typical Liberian had any idea what the Paris Declaration was and seemingly oblivious to the disaster outside. "The call for a combined effort of government, civil society, private sector, and the Liberian citizenry has never been louder."

Still, after the initial fright of March and early April, the course of Ebola in Liberia appeared to be bending to that lackadaisical response. People kept crossing the border, but there was no sharp increase in Ebola cases. The United Nations, Médecins Sans Frontières, and the Liberian health agencies were all pleased to begin the forty-two-day countdown that the international health authorities dictated must be completed before calling the country Ebola-free. (Twenty-one days for the virus to run its traditional maximum incubation period, followed by another twenty-one days in case some unlucky soul contracted the disease on the twenty-first day.)

By late May, there were no new cases of Ebola in Liberia. Whew. The Agenda for Transformation could continue.

But one month later, after lulling Liberia into believing it was on the retreat, Ebola made a stunning comeback in June, sweeping into the country through Lofa, spreading throughout the border areas, and moving across the Sierra Leone border into Cape Mount County. It was a capricious enemy; instead of laying waste to everyone in its path, Ebola seemed to pick and choose, bypassing whole villages in one place only to turn and strike entire families in another. It didn't carpet-bomb the countryside, it was more like a drone strike. It would skip one village and settle in another, annihilating whole families.

That made it easy for Liberians to pretend it wouldn't happen to them. In the initial months, when they should have been buying Clorox and training themselves not to touch each other, young men sat around on benches and plastic chairs outside shops and bars arguing about how the government—that impotent old lady at the helm—was making up the whole thing as a ruse to get foreign aid money.

"No, I don't believe Ebola is real," one young man told VICE, the Brooklyn-based media company. "Apparently it's a scam to get some money from the international donors," journalist-turned-fixer Emmanuel Nagbe, escorting the VICE crew around, helpfully added.

So Liberians kept on eating dried bush meat—groundhogs, possum, "street deer" (a clever euphemism for dog) which is actually fine. It's the cooking and butchering of fresh meat, with its attendant blood and gore, that many scientists believe can cause the virus to jump from animals to people.

But even during the phase when Liberians were denying the reality of Ebola, the virus was on the move, about to do something it had never done anywhere since it was first identified in 1976: enter an urban area. On June 17, Liberian public health officials reported that seven people in Monrovia had just died of Ebola, including five in one New Kru Town household, just west of downtown. Up country, where hospitals were sparse and doctors—in a country where fifty doctors serviced 4.3 million people— even more so, people began fleeing to the already overcrowded capital as soon as they got sick.

Madame President continued to insist, meanwhile, that Liberia's economy should not be forgotten in all the Ebola noise. "Her number one concern seemed to be the economic repercussions of Ebola," one senior international bureaucrat stationed in Liberia said. "She was adamant in our conversations that this not be described as a humanitarian crisis," lest foreign companies flee.

But they fled anyway, all those foreign investors so carefully wooed by Madame. As the numbers of those infected with Ebola continued to climb over the summer, so too fled the airlines that Madame had proudly welcomed back to Liberia, using the new air routes as proof that the country had finally returned from its two decades in the wilderness. Air France, British Airways, Kenya Airways, Delta Air Lines, all stopped flying to Robertsfield Airport. Only Royal Air Maroc and Brussels Airlines kept coming, its flight attendants donning masks and gloves, but, at least, still flying to Liberia.

"Force majeure," the grona boys—unemployed street boys who survive by their wits—said, pointing to shuttered storefronts. Suddenly, ordinary Liberians were flinging around the obscure phrase usually found in insurance clauses to explain why businesses had shuttered, employers had fled, road construction had ended, and the economy had ground to a halt.

Still Madame continued to operate as if the Ebola outbreak was only going to be the most temporary of setbacks. The country would soon emerge from the grip of the virus, she assured her beloved international community. The Agenda for Transformation was on track.

She was kept busy by the sort of politicians who never saw a crisis they couldn't exploit; a group called the Movement of Liberians Against Corruption announced that there were "high level" discussions taking place among Liberians about whether the country needed an interim government, or a trusteeship, to take the place of Madame's government. In other words, a coup.

"Liberians in barbershops, Liberians in beauty salons, Liberians in churches, Liberians in the community are talking about what is happening in their country," Seyon Nyanwleh, secretary-general of the Movement of Liberians against Corruption, told the Voice of America. "And, everyone has settled on one thing: Madame Sirleaf has failed."

Madame ignored them. "We are up to our chest in alligators, but the sharks are no longer circling," she said in an email to a journalist in the United States. "So we will overcome this."

She was getting ready to attend President Obama's Africa summit in Washington, scheduled for early August. Most of the continent's presidents had been invited to attend a days-long conference where they would meet with American chief executives and politicians, talk about development and good governance, and get their photos taken with Mr. Obama at a White House dinner. Madame would be the star—there was no African head of state with more name recognition—let alone a Nobel Peace Prize. The White House couldn't stand Nigerian president Goodluck Jonathan, and Joyce Banda of Malawi had flamed out a couple of months before, demonstrating that in Africa, it was still easier to assume power by appointment than through democratic elections; she had lost her own presidential elections. President Paul Biya of Cameroon and President Idriss Deby of Chad had "won" way too many elections (thirty-four years in office for Biya, twenty-four for Deby) to be held up as examples of anything. Madame was going to be the headliner of the event.

Then, as the rains peaked in July, Ebola made it known that it was not going to be silenced. How did it do this? It infected white people.

Suddenly, this was no longer a West African problem. With the infection of two white missionaries, Kent Brantley and Nancy Writebol, who would be quickly evacuated to Atlanta, where they survived, Ebola suddenly became the subject of global hyperventilation and panic.

George W. Bush had 9/11; Barack Obama, the global economic collapse. Most presidents face a single epic challenge. For Ellen Johnson Sirleaf, every year presented a new epic challenge. War had destroyed her country, taking not only 200,000 lives but blowing apart the rules that governed society, from respect for old people to protection of women and children. Children were empowered to take up guns and drugs and to turn on each other.

Rebuilding was a consuming task, hobbled by what seemed to be a different challenge every year, from the herculean effort to put her tattered country back together after fourteen years of carnage to giving voice to the Liberian women who have, for decades, carried the country on their backs. In fact, those were easy by comparison.

After she finished all of those, it turned out that the fates had one more, far more difficult challenge left for her: the challenge of Ebola. It was almost as if she were receiving one last directive from the omnipotent chroniclers in the sky: if you care as much as you profess to about leaving a legacy of economic growth and empowerment for women and children after you leave office, then we have one more little hurdle for you to jump.

And it's a hurdle you'd better clear. Because if you trip, it will wipe out everything.

On August 6, 2014, Madame moved to act, declaring a state of emergency.

She canceled her trip to Washington, telling Guinean president Alpha Conde to represent the Ebola Belt—Guinea, Sierra Leone, and Liberia. She closed Liberia's borders with Sierra Leone and Guinea and sent all nonessential government workers home. She shut down the country's schools, rationalizing that children at home may be less prone to touch each other and contract the disease, a dubious conclusion because children not in school would be in the street. But nonetheless, the message came across, echoing the billboards across the country and the public service announcements on the radio. "Ebola is Here and Real! Stop the Denial."

Jumping in her SUV, Madame rode through Monrovia at night, identifying sites for Ebola treatment hospital units to be built. The country didn't have the money. But Madame knew she could get it. If there was one thing she knew she could do, it was extracting money from donor countries.

A realization had finally come to Madame. That moment had come when she suddenly saw that all the while she had been focusing on her development fund, the abyss has crept to just under her feet. Because suddenly now, with the infection of the white people came increasingly dim forecasts from the World Health Organization and the Centers for

Disease Control and all the global health authorities. One thing was now absolutely clear: This virus was not going to vanish. There would have to be a fight.

Madame put out a notice shutting down all markets along Liberia's borders, including Foya and Ganta. She ordered chlorine stations be constructed in front of public buildings and video clubs—where people went to watch movies—then later shut down video clubs altogether. She warned that any increase in the prices of sanitation supplies would be treated as an "offense against the people of Liberia" and duly prosecuted.

Still, she appeared to those watching her closely that she was a woman in shock. In all of the many crises she had navigated in her life, she had never seemed small, despite her diminutive height and slight figure. But now she was looking every one of her seventy-five years, as she lurched from meetings to phone calls to speeches trying to reassure a panicking public that help was coming. "She was coming to grips with the tsunami that was headed her way," said Tom Kenyon, director of the U.S. CDC's Center for Global Health, after visiting Liberia and meeting with Madame in August.

Because what the CDC and the WHO and all the other international organizations that track global pandemics were now saying, in August of 2014, as the Ebola death toll in Guinea, Sierra Leone, and Liberia climbed above one thousand, was that this was only the beginning. Far worse numbers were to come.

Madame had assumed office in 2006, making history as the first woman ever to be elected president of an African country, the woman who came after two and a half decades of war and unrest brought on by the country's male leaders. In taking office, she had vowed to do everything possible to prevent a return to the senseless war that had taken more than 200,000 Liberian lives and left the country a wasteland.

So Madame went to battle. And was immediately handed a defeat so stinging it almost destroyed her presidency.

In August, with the number of cases in Monrovia rising into three digits, the health ministry quietly turned a primary school in the almost impossibly dense downtown slum called West Point into an Ebola isolation center. No one knows exactly how many people live in the one-square-mile crush of tin-roofed, dirt-floored shanties of West Point; the estimates go up to 120,000, all on a small peninsula that juts out to the Atlantic Ocean between the two rivers that meet in downtown Monrovia.

There are few sanitation facilities; people defecate where they can—on the beaches or in tributaries that run into the rivers. There are four public toilets in West Point. The sea has been encroaching into the slum for years, but past efforts to move people out of West Point have all failed, as residents have clung to their neighborhood for its proximity to downtown, to markets, and to the sea for fishing.

The hardheaded quality of West Point's residents became visible in August when Ebola arrived. The government decided to open an Ebola isolation center in the slum as a kind of halfway house for people suspected of being infected. The nearest hospital, Redemption, was already strained. The health ministry did this without informing West Point residents first.

As word spread throughout the slum that the cries of the desperate infected could be heard coming from the center, anger grew. And then, it exploded.

On Saturday, August 23, a group of twenty or so angry young men, chanting "No Ebola in West Point," committed an act so monumentally counterproductive that only raw panic and a profound distrust of government could possibly explain it.

These young club-carrying men broke into the Ebola holding facility and stripped it bare. They "freed" the patients, carrying many of them off into the streets to be "reunited" with their families. They loaded up on the gloves, masks, biohazard suits, and plastic wraps that health workers used to protect themselves from Ebola. Many of the items they took were already dirty and infected with Ebola; they took them anyway. They took bloody sheets. They took vomit-stained towels. And all the while that they were ransacking the place, they were yelling.

"The president says you have Ebola, but you don't have Ebola, you have malaria," the young men yelled to the people in the isolation unit. "Get up and go out!"

At her office at the Ministry of Foreign Affairs, Madame held an emergency cabinet meeting to formulate a response.

The group huddled around a table, panicked by thoughts of children getting hold of Ebola-infected sheets. The health officials talked about community education and awareness. The security men talked about quarantine.

The group split. You can't quarantine 120,000 people, the health officials said.

You have to quarantine them, the security officials shot back, or it will be 4 million people soon with Ebola. Suddenly, all the talk about the difficulties of fighting Ebola in an urban setting were starkly and horrifyingly real.

Sitting around the table listening to her advisers, Madame finally nodded. She was siding with the security and defense officials. The Liberian military, she decreed, would go into West Point and quarantine the whole neighborhood.

The Liberian military. The same military that overthrew and disemboweled President Tolbert in 1980 before launching their campaign of rape and murder that eventually transmogrified into a fourteen-year civil war. Madame had disbanded the old Liberian army and set up a new one. Former combatants were strongly discouraged from enlisting. The army even put posters up of prospective recruits when they applied, in villages around the country, asking if locals knew of any war crimes the recruits may have committed.

The new army had a new chief of staff—the granite-faced General Daniel Dee Ziankahn, who had stayed out of the fray during Liberia's deadly civil wars. But he wasn't at the table, he was studying at Harvard University at precisely the moment his army was tasked with its biggest job since the war: putting in place a quarantine at West Point. His deputies would be the ones to see to it.

The next morning, the residents of West Point woke up to discover that they were now, all of them, under quarantine in their slum. The waterfront was blocked by Coast Guard boats that stopped canoes from setting out, and soldiers formed a cordon around the streets leading from West Point into greater Monrovia.

What happened next is a case study in the inadvertent creation of panic, the sort of stampede that inevitably arises when healthy people are told the government is quarantining them with the fatally infected. West

Point went insane with fear. Young men hurled rocks at soldiers stationed around the slum to enforce the quarantine. They stormed barbed wire barricades, trying to break out.

The panic spread to the soldiers. A few fired live rounds just above the crowd to drive back the young men. They chased young residents down the crowded muddy streets, beating them with batons.

In the melée, a soldier shot a young man, Shakie Kamara, fifteen, in the right leg. The bullet snapped his leg in two; the bottom third was barely hanging on by pieces of bone fragment. He crumbled to the ground, screaming for help. He was eventually taken to the hospital, but too late. He died from blood loss.

During the next ten days, Madame hit the lowest point of her presidency. The quarantine was an utter failure; it obliterated what little trust had started to be reestablished between the Liberian military and the Liberian people—who still referred to the army as "soldiers them," as in "soldiers them came and beat up my son" or "soldiers them whipped my husband at the checkpoint." The quarantine also deeply angered the people trapped inside, who believed they were being consigned to die.

And it wasn't even enforced rigidly. The same soldiers them who shot into the crowd and beat up the West Point residents also accepted bribes from West Point residents to slip through the barbed wire fence and onto the streets of broader Monrovia. "Wha' you got?" they asked West Point residents who approached looking for a way out, before negotiating the bribes.

Madame's political opponents, smelling weakness, called for her resignation, but now they were joined by an increasing number of newspapers. The condemnation became more intense when she announced that she had fired high-ranking government officials who refused to return to Liberia because of the Ebola outbreak.

Sharpening the pain, Madame's beloved international support base started to show signs of weakening. Suddenly, her quarantine was being criticized in the international press. Each story included mention of the shooting of Shakie Kamara.

Madame knew she had a problem.

She arrived in West Point five days into the quarantine, surrounded by a phalanx of guards from her executive protective services, some of them wearing plastic gloves and linking arms. She was dressed simply, in a long-sleeved blue pantsuit, her hair, for once, not wrapped in an elaborate head-tie. Unlike her guards, she wore no gloves. But her agents surrounded her, making sure no one touched her.

A crowd immediately gathered. "We suffering!" one man yelled at the president. "We beg you, Ma!"

So now she was "Ma" again. That always happened: Liberians complained about her on the radio and in the newspaper, but face-to-face she always became "Ma," the mother of the country. When Liberians want something from a woman, they will call her "Ma," whether or not she is older than they. Madame, Ma Ellen, or just plain Ma—she had learned to respond to all of her monikers.

Behind Madame, her aide Toe Wesseh wore gloves as he handed out wads of cash to people, who immediately started fighting over the money.

"We want go out!" another man yelled. "We want be free, Mama, please."

Grimly, Madame made her way about the neighborhood until she found Eva Nah, Shakie Kamara's aunt, who had raised him after his own parents died. She was in tears as the president apologized to her for the shooting of her nephew.

Madame spent forty minutes in West Point and was sweating heavily by the time her entourage left, her guards taking off their gloves as they exited the slum and tossing them on the ground behind them. With the exception of her apology to Eva Nah, she had said little. But there had been one exchange, overheard by reporters. When Toe Wesseh handed two men around 1,000 Liberian dollars—the equivalent of US$12—Madame had admonished the recipients, "Don't spend it on drink."

Four days later, she lifted the quarantine. It had been in effect for only ten days—nowhere near the originally planned twenty-one days to account for Ebola's incubation period. But it had been a failure; it had led people in West Point to believe they were being condemned to die and had eroded their already scant trust in Madame's government. And it had led to the death of Shakie Kamara.

Madame was angry; it seemed as if every option she tried was the wrong one. She put an isolation center in West Point, and young men ransacked it and stole bloody sheets that they took out into the neighborhood. So she quarantined the neighborhood to protect the rest of the city, and her soldiers shot a fifteen-year-old. "Nobody gave me a better solution," she would later say.

Now the number of Ebola deaths in Liberia had reached 754, a third of them in Montserrado County, home to Monrovia, and no end in sight. Under the weight of Ebola, the country's public health infrastructure had collapsed: JFK Hospital no longer accepted patients; Redemption Hospital was overwhelmed; Ebola treatment units turned away the dying; corpses accumulated in the streets. Ordinary citizens, some horrified, some voyeuristic, took photos of the dead and posted them on Facebook.

All the hospitals were turning people away, whether or not they had Ebola. In the Monrovia suburb of Paynesville, thirty-two-year-old Comfort Fayiah was turned away from a private hospital, so she gave birth to her twins in the rain and dirt on the side of Du Port Road. Passersby surrounded her to try to give her what privacy they could while a local woman and man delivered the two girls. Comfort named her daughters Faith and Mercy.

Liberians were crowding into churches and touching each other, against the advice of the Ebola experts, to demonstrate their faith in God's mercy. In early September, that mercy was elusive.

By September 2014, Precious Diggs, a thirty-three-year-old contractor with Firestone, had heard all the warnings from the battalions of public health workers who had descended on Liberia during what now seemed like the country's latest visit to the ninth circle of Hell. She had seen the signs that dotted the road from Harbel, where she worked, to Monrovia: "Ebola is here and real!" they said. "Stop the Denial."

She wasn't in denial; she made sure not to touch anyone when she went to work, and she wore long sleeves to boot. But when her two-year-old daughter, Rebecca, started "toileting" and vomiting, there was no way that Precious Diggs wasn't going to pick her up. "Na mind, baby," she whispered in Rebecca's ear. "I beg you, na mind."

But Rebecca didn't stop vomiting.

Weak and listless after vomiting everything in her to vomit, Rebecca lay prone against her mother's breast, her breath coming in laborious, far-apart hiccups.

Precious prayed as she had never prayed before. "I beg you, God. I hold your foot, plee' don't take my baby."

But God took Rebecca anyway.

And before she went, Rebecca passed Ebola to her mother.

That is the devil in Ebola: it punishes you for taking care of the people you love. It makes pariahs of the sick and condemns its victims to death without a last touch of human skin. And for those who discard caution, those who say they would rather die than not pick up their sick child, Ebola takes them at their word.

In Liberia, there is another saying: "Small Shame better than Big Shame."

In September, as Rebecca lay dying, Madame President chose Small Shame, and called in the cavalry.

First she got on the phone with U.S. Senator Chris Coons, the Democrat from Delaware who was now head of the Senate's African Affairs Subcommittee. She was one of the few African presidents with the private telephone numbers of influential members of the U.S. Congress plugged into her cell phone. "We need help," Madame told Senator Coons. The two had met before; the senator had been impressed and slightly intimidated by the blunt yet reserved Madame, dressed in a long colorful skirt and blouse with matching head-tie, who spoke English with an American accent when it suited her.

She had clearly prepared what she was going to say. There were so many bodies that it had become impossible to stop the spread of infection. Beyond Ebola treatment units and health workers and doctors, the country needed a crematorium so the dead could be burned instead of buried. She painted a picture of Liberia teetering on the edge of an abyss that so moved Coons he asked to pray with her on the phone, something he had never done before with a world leader.

"Of course," Madame replied. So, for several minutes, she and the American senator prayed for Liberia. "Please God," Coons prayed, "give Liberia the strength to get through this."

After the phone call, he went to work on Madame's behalf. He lobbied his colleagues to help Liberia in a forceful and meaningful way.

On September 9, Madame sat at her desk and wrote a letter to the man she had first met in 2006, when he was merely a junior senator from Illinois and she was delivering her address to the Joint Session of Congress. "Dear Mr. President," she wrote. "I bring you greetings from the people of Liberia and in my own name."

She continued, "I am being honest with you when I say that at this rate, we will never break the transmission chain and the virus will overwhelm us." Without help, Liberia was headed back into the chaos that had enveloped the country for two decades. She requested 1,500 additional beds in new hospitals across the country and urged Obama to, in essence, send in the marines. Someone needed to set up an effective Ebola hospital in Liberia, and she surmised that the U.S. military could do so.

She engineered a public campaign as well. She reminded the readers of the *New York Times*, in a pointed way, that America had historic responsibilities to Liberia. The country exists because of American slavery. It was founded by freed American slaves in 1822 who were sponsored by the American Colonization Society. She bluntly suggested that those same ties were hurting Liberia now in the fight against Ebola, because other countries, among them France and Great Britain, were leaving poor Liberia alone in the fight, assuming that its stepmother country would take care of it. She claimed that a health expert with the group Médecins Sans Frontières had told her recently, "We're French. You've got America behind you; why should we have to do this for you?"

It was odd to hear such a colonial suggestion from a postcolonialist, but Madame's goal was to manipulate the United States into providing meaningful help, and she didn't care how she did it.

"Liberian President Pleads with Obama for Assistance in Combating Ebola," the *New York Times* headlined. Other newspapers and television stations dutifully followed, most of them referencing Madame as a Nobel Peace laureate.

Six days after receiving her letter, Obama announced a response so massive it stunned even his own advisers. The United States would deploy more than three thousand troops to build seventeen Ebola treatment units—1,700 beds—across Liberia. The Pentagon would open a joint command operation in Monrovia to coordinate the international effort to combat the disease. The military would also provide engineers to help construct the additional treatment facilities and would send enough people to train up to five hundred health care workers a week to deal with the crisis.

Standing at a podium in front of health care workers at the Centers for Disease Control and Prevention in Atlanta on September 16, Obama challenged world powers to follow the American example and step up to the plate. "We can't dawdle on this one," he said. "We have to move with force."

Madame didn't stop with just asking the United States for help—after imploring Obama, she moved on to the rest of the world. "Dear World," she said, reading aloud on BBC from a letter she wrote to the world. She had her American accent on, and made sure to read slowly and to enunciate clearly, so there was no chance that she would not be understood. "In just over six months, Ebola has managed to bring my country to a standstill. We have lost over two-thousand Liberians."

The response came quickly. A slew of African countries, many of them struggling themselves, sent health workers and volunteers to Liberia. China pledged $82 million and sent 160 health workers to Liberia to help. A Dutch Navy ship docked in the port at Monrovia with vital medical supplies. And Cuba sent 53 doctors, nurses and other medical officers.

In nearby Guinea and Sierra Leone, officials were stunned when they heard what the United States and the rest of the world was doing for Liberia. Neither President Ernest Koroma of Sierra Leone nor Guinea's Alpha Condé had dared make that kind of request. Both men were still in the denial phase; Madame had shot past them, getting to acceptance weeks before they would.

On September 23, the Centers for Disease Control and Prevention released a stunning and ominous projection: If Ebola continued on its current course, Liberia and Sierra Leone would lose 1.4 million people in the next four months.

Looking at the CDC projections that Tuesday night, Madame was furious. How much more could Liberia take? Her country had gone through a catastrophic civil war, one that featured madmen in wedding gowns and blond wigs terrorizing the population and slaughtering 200,000 people. Liberians were terrorized by their own children, who were kidnapped by warlords, filled with drugs, and turned loose on their own villages. Some 70 percent of women in Liberia were raped, a staggering figure. The country that had emerged after this carnage was a shell of itself, a devastated, depleted, hollowed-out wreck of a place. Yet somehow, a decade after the end of the war, Liberians were functioning again. Only to be confronted with a pandemic that threatened to wipe them out.

When Bad Luck call your name . . .

No. No.

There would be no breaking.

Chapter 23

THE LAST BATTLE

Monrovia, 2014

"God is in Control," declared the hand-painted sign on the bus that had pulled over so the presidential motorcade could pass. It was dusk on the evening of October 6, 2014, and Madame was on the move. In the past month, she had surged into a frenzy of Ebola-related activity, visiting isolated clinics in rural areas and hospitals in urban areas, as she tried to do battle with the disease that was tearing Liberia apart.

As a reporter for the *New York Times*, I had flown to Liberia to write about the Ebola epidemic that was rampaging through my home country. The Monrovia I had left only months earlier, before Ebola struck, still looked largely the same, except there were far fewer people in the streets. When I arrived at Robertsfield late at night, having hitched a ride on a U.S. military flight, there was no horde of people crowded together waiting to greet arriving passengers, just a handful of health workers who pointed laser thermometers at our foreheads to check our temperature. Mine read 35.4 degrees Celsius—normal—and I sighed with relief, before giving myself a mental smack in the head. Had I expected to contract Ebola on the flight *to* Liberia?

In the Monrovia that greeted me, people were mostly staying at home. Those who did go out had their body temperature taken six to eight times a day, before entering any building, restaurant, supermarket. I had never been so knowledgeable about my body temperature, which seemed to hover between 35.4 and 36.5 degrees. Once it got up to 36.9, and I became alarmed. Above 38 degrees is when they start asking questions. No one wants to be there.

After I checked into my hotel room, I furiously wiped down every surface using a few of the more than two thousand Clorox Disinfecting

Wipes I had brought with me. Despite all the coverage, I still didn't really understand how Ebola was transmitted, so in those early days I went around Liberia waving Clorox Wipes as if they were some kind of shield, wiping everything that came into my path.

In Monrovia, I could walk down Broad Street without anyone bumping up against me; the teeming humanity that had characterized the city's downtown areas had moderated into a far more manageable bustle of people. Everyone looked warily at strangers, inspecting them for signs of sickness. Did the man selling the newspapers on the sidewalk on Benson Street have particularly red eyes? Was the woman walking out of Sharp Showroom sweating from the heat or from something else?

A few days after arriving, I joined Madame President on an overnight trip to Gbarnga. I sat beside her as her white SUV bumped along the 187-mile, four-hour trip from Monrovia. The drive normally took three hours, but the potholes and rain—the Chinese contractors hired to pave the road had left in August, along with others fleeing Ebola—meant an even longer trip.

But Madame was determined to go and return by the next night. She had a host of Ebola-related meetings to manage.

She eyed the sign on the bus, "God is in Control," then huffed impatiently. "You see that?" she said. "This is one of our problems right there."

It was one of her pet peeves—that Liberians' tendency to say that God will provide for them leeched away their ability to help themselves.

Except that now, in the midst of the worst Ebola epic the world had ever seen, Liberians were turning that adage inside out. By early October, unbeknownst to the global health authorities who were still putting out increasingly dire forecasts of how many people were going to die of Ebola, Liberians, led by their president, had begun a grassroots effort to climb their way out of the Ebola pit themselves.

The debacle of the West Point quarantine, which had led to the death of Shakie Kamara and the lowest point of Madame's presidency, had been a turning point. She had called in the cavalry in the form of the U.S. military, which was busily constructing Ebola treatment units around the country, and had appealed to the United States and the international community for money, doctors, and health professionals.

But at the same time, Madame and her people—in particular, her grassroots base—had rolled up their sleeves and taken on the fight against Ebola themselves.

This was a country that had lived with demons for two decades, through the Doe and Taylor years. Liberians had become accustomed to learning how to live with devils. EVD, the acronym some Liberians were using (for Ebola virus disease), was just the latest in a long list of them. And if there was one thing Liberians had learned in their two decades of hell, it was that they were adaptable.

By late September, single-family huts in local villages had chlorinated water stations outside the front entryway, and every day Liberians washed their hands with bleach so many times they joked about turning into white people. Volunteer watchdog groups—often led by the same women who helped get Madame elected in 2005 and reelected in 2011—popped up in local neighborhoods, monitoring to make sure people were washing with chlorine, taking their temperature, and, above all, not touching each other.

They set up hand-washing stations all over town. They kept records of who had gotten sick and who had died. They put entire households under quarantine. And they made their own protective gear, using plastic shopping bags to cover their arms and flimsy paper masks to cover their mouth, so that they could take care of their sick.

Fatu Kekula, twenty-two years old and a nursing student, invented the garbage-bag method of protective equipment when her mother, father, sister, and cousin all contracted Ebola. With hospitals full, Fatu took care of her entire family at home, feeding them, cleaning them, and giving them medicine.

She wrapped her hair in a pair of stockings, then covered her wrapped head with a trash bag. She put trash bags over her socks and tied them in a knot over her calves. She put on rubber boots and covered those boots with trash bags. She wore a plastic raincoat, four pairs of gloves, and a mask over her nose and mouth.

For two weeks, she nursed her family. Her cousin did not make it. But her father, mother, and sister survived. And Fatu didn't get sick. By October, people in Liberia were talking about Fatu and her garbage-bag method. Her gear became known as Liberian PPEs (personal protective equipment), and all across the country, in villages and isolated communities, Liberians started to cobble together their own garbage-bag PPEs.

As the international community galvanized to help, Liberians were abandoning their age-old "God will provide" adage and trying to help themselves.

Mary Broh, unsurprisingly, was at the center of the action. One of the first things Madame did when the epidemic struck was to appoint her friend to her Ebola response team. Broh had already been named to head the Government Services Agency, after the House of Representatives ran her out of town for helping Grace Kpaan escape their congressional jail sentence. The former controversial "Mayor 1" took her job at GSA and her appointment to Madame's Ebola response team seriously. So seriously, in fact, that she personally went out into the middle of Tubman Boulevard, the busiest street in Monrovia, near Vamona House, clad in bright plastic boots, and pulled over government-registered vehicles, commandeering them for the Ebola response. "People are dropping and dying," she exhorted aggrieved drivers and their passengers. "We need this vehicle to go pick up dead bodies."

In the past, when Mary the Menace had gone after people for various infractions as part of her quest to clean up Monrovia, she had gotten nothing but blowback for her trouble—not to mention Solomon George threatening to lock her in a latrine and defecate on her. Now, in the time of Ebola, things were different. All of her exhortations about cleaning up the city suddenly were starting to make sense.

At the GSA compound, she set up a food court, complete with chlorine stations for people to wash their hands before entering. Well before Ebola, back in her days as Mayor 1, Broh had instituted hand-washing at City Hall, which became known for having the cleanest bathrooms in all Monrovia. "We will be like Kigali, Rwanda," she had said rapturously at the time. "Oh, it's such a clean city!"

After all the years of Sturm und Drang, Mary the Menace was looking prescient. Now she had no trouble from anyone about her water tanks full of chlorine. She turned a room in the GSA compound into a call center, where she monitored young women and girls making and taking calls on an Ebola hotline. During the long days, when her team got hungry, she sent out for cans of sardines and corned beef to cook with rice to feed her crew.

Often, people freeze when a crisis hits, unsure of what to do or which way to turn. When Ebola hit, the women running Liberia froze too. But by October they were moving again.

Madame in particular was moving. She started out in the Monrovia area, showing up at clinics and hospitals to give encouragement to beleaguered and, in many cases, dying health workers. She paid little heed to security guards who tried to stop her from entering the clinics, although she did make sure she didn't go into the "hot zone," the areas where hazmat-suited health workers tended to acutely ill patients. She stuck to the reception rooms, where, she noted darkly, some health workers who didn't have gloves were using plastic garbage bags. Liberia PPEs.

"Make a note," she told an aide. "We need to get them plastic gloves."

Then she started hitting the rural areas. In Bong County, at a tiny clinic up on a hill some distance from the main road, Madame picked her way in the rain by foot through potholes soaked in mud, her security guards surrounding her. They climbed, slowly, up the hill, until finally arriving at a place where the nurses had wrapped plastic bags around their hands as they sought to take care of the sick. They had not been paid in months. Most of them were terrified. But there they were anyway, treating patients in the little clinic in Bong County.

A feeling of acute despair swept through Madame. She knew this scene was replicated throughout the country, where clinic after clinic of forgotten people toiled in obscurity, facing incredible risk. She left behind a box of plastic gloves she had brought with her, feeling angry and inadequate.

She didn't wear gloves herself when she went out to see people, although her guards often did. The risk she was exposing herself to was nothing compared to what the health workers in the clinics were dealing with. The closest Madame came to Ebola exposure was when Sharon Shamoyan Washington, the administrative assistant to the minister of foreign affairs, Augustine Ngafuan, contracted Ebola from her sister and died. Washington's husband, J. Wesley Washington, was one of Madame's press aides. Madame quarantined Wesley and continued about her business.

Three weeks later, Madame and I were in her motorcade on the long drive to Gbarnga. "God's Appointed Time" was stenciled on a second bus that pulled over to let the motorcade pass. Looking at it, Madame inhaled sharply, then exhaled, shaking her head.

The messages on the buses were behind the times. Her people were fighting back. They were still sharply criticizing the government about the slow initial response to Ebola, but they were fighting back.

It had been a monstrous day so far. Madame had begun the morning receiving the resignation of Justice Minister Christina Tah, who used her resignation news conference to accuse Madame of trying to block a corruption investigation into the National Security Agency, which was headed by Fumbah Sirleaf, known throughout Liberia as another of Madame's sons even though he was actually Doc Sirleaf's son, not Madame's. But no matter, for purposes of charging the president with nepotism, everyone called Fumbah her son. This same "son" had helped American agents pull off West Africa's largest drug bust, in 2010, when he wired himself to get key evidence. Madame denied the corruption charge.

Just two days before resigning, Tah had sat silently at an Ebola meeting with international donors. Everyone argued around a massive table at the Foreign Ministry, with Madame at the head looking like a stern teacher trying to rein in a bunch of unruly children. Health Minister Walter Gwenigale, whom everyone called Dr. G., harrumphed about international "free agents" doing as they pleased without so much as a by-your-leave from the Liberian government. The American ambassador, Madame's friend Deborah Malac, shot back that there were plenty of mechanisms to keep aid groups in their proper place. For almost an hour, people around the table sniped at each other.

I was sitting—inconspicuously, I hoped—along the wall trying to stifle a snort as the minister of defense, Brownie Samukai, found himself heckled for fifteen minutes by the executive director of a Liberian women's empowerment organization. She was not complaining about the Defense Ministry's efforts in the fight against Ebola; she was trying to provoke him into sharing some of the platters of Spam and cheese sitting on the table. He ignored her, trying to pay attention to the meeting, but his heckler, Yvette

Chesson-Wureh, raised her voice louder. "I say, Brownie, you will not pass people de food?" she demanded. "This how you treat women?"

Finally, an exasperated Madame had had enough and called a timeout. "Very well. Y'all can take a break to have some chips."

After informing her family of Tah's resignation—a bombshell she dropped offhandedly over a late lunch of corned beef and rice crust— Madame hopped in her SUV for the trip up country. Earlier in the day, Edward Forh had been on the radio, saying that Madame's government should take responsibility for the death of his asthmatic daughter, who died after nurses refused to admit her into the hospital until Ebola tests were run. Distraught, Forh took to the airwaves to denounce Madame's government, saying the president was "surrounded by two groups of people: one group completely ignorant and the other group completely deceitful."

Forh was the legislator Grace Kpaan had recorded suggesting a kick-back scheme: "You eat some, I eat some." Clearly, Ebola had turned a lot of things on their head.

But would the wholesale lobotomy the country seemed to be going through be enough? In her motorcade en route to Gbarnga that night, Madame insisted that Liberia was fighting its way out of the Ebola horror. The world couldn't see it yet, she said, but the numbers were turning. We came to a small market along the road, with women selling fruits and vegetables.

"Aye man, I need to buy those women them bananas," Madame said, as her security aides sighed in resignation and slowed down. "Becky, buy those women's red potatoes and bananas. And some of those guavas them." The motorcade stopped, and Madame's aides jumped out with wads of cash and cleaned out the market.

The cash was exchanged, but no one touched anyone. Madame herself had not felt the warmth of human skin in weeks.

It is easy, though, to make the decision not to touch a stranger in order to save your own life. Far more gut-wrenching was not to touch a friend, a sister, a daughter. That was where almost every Liberian seemed to draw the line. It was as if the country collectively had decided that it would follow the world health guidelines on protecting itself from Ebola, but only up to a point. If a few people had to be sacrificed along the way, so be it. It was a sacrifice born of love. Close family ties had exposed the fragility of the belief that you can completely protect yourself from Ebola by keeping your hands to yourself.

So by that October night of our drive to Gbarnga, just about the only people in Liberia who were still coming down with Ebola were friends and family and loved ones of those who had contracted the disease. Because at the end of the day, after listening to all the public health warnings and radio messages and signs on the road, the question still remained: Can you really not touch an ailing mother?

Gaye Dumbai couldn't. When Dumbai got a phone call that his mother had taken ill, he rushed to her house in Dolos Town, the enclave near Harbel where dozens of people had already succumbed to Ebola. He found her in bed, vomiting blood.

His mind went immediately to the precautions against the virus, and he did his best not to touch her. But as she grew worse, unable to keep anything down, he gave her milk and tried to soothe her. His skin touched hers.

His mother died the next day.

Just after her funeral, Dumbai's own forehead got hot with fever. For fifteen days he stayed at JFK Hospital in Monrovia fighting the disease. In the end, he lived. But when he got out of the hospital, he learned that two of his sisters, his brother, his father, his aunt, his uncle, and four nieces and nephews had died. His entire family, wiped out in days.

And yet, he said that in hindsight, he would do nothing different. "That's my ma. That she the one born me."

Call it a line of humanity. Liberians were doing everything to protect themselves against Ebola, but they refused to cross that one last line of defense against the disease. They were still taking care of their loved ones.

The motorcade finally arrived in Gbarnga, at the government rest house, a little before nine that night. I had been interviewing Madame in the car, but the bumpy road had made note-taking difficult. She agreed to give me three more hours late that night, in a small parlor off her bedroom, over two bottles of room-temperature water.

She had been going for sixteen hours straight and showed no sign of flagging; I, on the other hand, was exhausted. But it was during that interview, after all of the questions about the Ebola response so far, that she told me about the time, more than fifty years earlier, that Doc Sirleaf had beat her in the car after catching her at Chris Maxwell's house. I had been interviewing her intermittently for this book for almost two years, and this had never come up before.

Shaken, I stared at her, as she laughed through her recital of the story. "He kept reaching over and hitting me," she said. A chuckle. "All the way back to the house."

In that moment, Madame seemed like any woman who had come out of an abusive relationship, using humor to distance herself from what had been done to her. Yet out of the ashes of that abuse, the president of a nation had risen.

I had to return to Monrovia at four the next morning. A member of Madame's security detail, Varsay Sirleaf, whom I had gotten to know during the two years now that I had been shadowing Madame, on and off, for the book, hopped into the car with me. "She doesn't want you to go alone," he said.

I was happy for the company. The road was part dirt, potholed and dark; one flat tire and you are finished.

About thirty minutes after setting out, on the blackest stretch of the road, the headlights picked up a form on the side. "Stop!" Varsay yelled. "That's a body!" He jumped out of the car, grabbing a flashlight and a pistol. "Lock the doors," he ordered, and took off.

My mind immediately went to the Civil War, to magic soldiers jumping out of the bush. It was quiet except for my heart beating.

Finally Varsay returned. "He wasn't dead," he said. "He was drunk. I woke him up, and he went into the bush."

I couldn't believe he had just gone up to a body on the side of the road. "It could have been an ambush," I yelled. "He could have had Ebola!"

Varsay looked at me. "That what y'all do in America?" he asked. He turned back toward the front, looking ahead. Then he spoke again. "You can't just leave somebody on the side of the road to die."

By the end of October, Liberians were winning the fight against Ebola. The country was still in crisis mode, and the Ebola treatment units were still being constructed. But dead bodies were no longer piling up on the side of the road. Beds in treatment centers were left empty. The numbers of the dying were down, sharply down, even as they kept going up in neighboring Sierra Leone and Guinea.

Because unlike Guinea and Sierra Leone, in Liberia the woman in charge of running the country, slammed by the deluge of criticism that hit the airwaves after her failed West Point quarantine, had quickly admitted that her initial response had been wrong and had moved to change it. The very freedom and democratic process that had flourished in Liberia under her presidency kicked her into action.

What's more, unlike Guinea and Sierra Leone, where Ebola had spread in mostly rural areas, Ebola hit Liberia in Monrovia, the capital city. Ironically, that geography helped Liberia.

In the years since the end of the Civil War, Monrovia had become an overcrowded mecca for the entire country, as well as neighboring countries. Rural villagers traveled there for work, and back home again when work in the city dried up. Market women strapped their babies on their back and their sacks of oranges on their head and walked for miles from village stall to village stall. Packed buses—stenciled with the message "God is on the job"—bounced down the potholed roads, bringing people to the city and back again.

For all of the charges leveled against Madame's government, even her harshest critics agreed on one thing: civil liberty, the right to move freely, and to speak openly even when criticizing the government, belonged to every Liberian.

When Ebola hit in the rural areas of Liberia and Sierra Leone and Guinea, villagers quickly traveled to Liberia's capital for care. And once it hit Monrovia, the infection rates shot up. The silver lining was that because the disease hit the city so hard, it was far more difficult for the government to hide. And because there was freedom to criticize, the Liberian airwaves were full of outraged citizens demanding help. The government couldn't dismiss the disease as the affliction of a handful of rural villagers living in isolation. Because the daughters of legislators and the winner of the country's Miss Liberia pageant and the administrative assistant to the foreign minister were all infected with Ebola, it was not cast off as a disease of only the poor and rural.

Everyone in Liberia became afraid of Ebola. And so everyone in the country, from Madame down, banded together to fight it.

The result: Liberia got hit the hardest. But Liberians hit back the hardest.

And they were the first to get to the finish line.

By the end of October, fewer than half of the country's 649 treatment beds were occupied, a dramatic turnaround considering that patients had been turned away from Ebola units because of lack of space. In late November, the director of the Centers for Disease Control and Prevention announced that Liberia had stopped the exponential spread of the disease and that a previous worst-case projection of 1.4 million cases by late January was no longer accurate. From that moment on, global health officials would hold Liberia up as the example for Guinea and Sierra Leone—both of them months behind in grappling with the epidemic—to follow.

On March 5, 2015, Beatrice Yardolo, a fifty-eight-year-old English teacher who had lost three children to Ebola, was discharged from an Ebola treatment center in Monrovia, bringing to zero the number of known cases in the country and marking a huge milestone. There were celebrations in Monrovia that day, and the country began the forty-two-day countdown of zero cases necessary to declare Liberia Ebola-free.

Finally able to leave the country, Madame flew to the United States and thanked President Obama for his help. She went to the Pentagon and stood on the steps next to Defense Secretary Ashton Carter while a full military honor guard and band played the Liberian national anthem and unfurled the Liberian flag. She met with newspaper editorial boards in New York and Washington, acknowledging her mistakes and vowing to continue the fight against Ebola and anything else that might be thrown at Liberia. And she had one other message: her country, she said again and again, was back in business.

On March 20, Liberia was fifteen days into the forty-two-day countdown. Back home again, Madame was sending messages to Chinese contractors, telling them it was safe to return and get back to work building the country's roads.

One of her aides approached her with a telephone. On the line was Tolbert Nyenswah, the head of the country's Ebola Incident Management System, who told her, "I have to let you know we have a new case."

Ruth Tugbah, a forty-four-year-old street vendor who lived in a one-bathroom house she shared with fifty-two others in a Monrovia suburb, had contracted the disease from her boyfriend, an Ebola survivor. But there was a catch: her boyfriend had contracted Ebola six months before, and had been treated and pronounced Ebola-free. Yet a semen sample he provided after Tugbah got ill found traces of Ebola seventy-four days longer than ever before found in a survivor.

Madame felt a hole in the pit of her stomach. She had been bracing for this, feeling that fear and dread every morning when she woke up. Now all of that hope was wiped out.

Talking later that night about the new case with her sister, Madame started crying. Jennie was shocked. Madame never cried.

Ruth Tugbah's case highlighted how much scientists still didn't know about the disease. Doctors and public health advocates had been warning that even after a man is cured of Ebola, the virus can stay in his semen for three months. But this was six months. Madame's government issued a new recommendation, telling survivors of Ebola to use condoms indefinitely, until more information could be gathered on the length of time the virus might remain in body fluids, including semen.

On March 26, 2015, Ruth Tugbah died.

But she had infected no one. The health protocols and quick treatment decisions that Liberia had put in place were working.

Two days later, the countdown began again.

On May 9, the World Health Organization declared Liberia free of Ebola, making it the first of the three hardest-hit West African countries to bring a formal end to the epidemic.

"The outbreak of Ebola virus disease in Liberia is over," announced Dr. Alex Gasasira, WHO's representative to Liberia, at the Ebola command center in Monrovia. The conference room was full of reporters; a fight over space even broke out between the press and security.

Organizers displayed a map of Liberia, in green, with the number 42 superimposed on it.

There was jubilation in the crowded room, and applause, and tears.

All morning, Madame, wearing a baseball hat and sneakers, met with Ebola survivors and orphans and widows. She visited hospitals and clinics, where workers danced and clapped and sang "No more Ebola."

She knew, as most Liberians knew, that the battle against Ebola was not really over. Now that the virus had surfaced, it would likely show up again. The counting would never really stop. For the rest of her presidency, Madame would wake up every morning and count how many days her country had been Ebola-free. At some point, with any luck, the count would get up to months, and then years, and maybe even decades. But she would always be counting.

Still, she felt strongly that Liberians could deal with Ebola when it came back. They knew what to do now. They had figured out a way to defeat the disease, and they had survived, the same way they had survived the Civil War, the Samuel Doe purges, the aftermath of the Tolbert military coup, the 150 years of political and social instability.

And so, on May 9, as the WHO doctor pronounced Liberia free of Ebola, as Ambassador Deborah Malac cried as she spoke of what it was like to watch Liberians come together, as Health Minister Dr. G. made a formal presentation describing the country's defeat of Ebola, Madame sat regally and silently watching the proceedings.

It was quite a life she had had. Beaten by her husband, jailed by Doe, tasked with trying to pull her country out of the abyss of civil war and the potential catastrophe of a pandemic disease, over a decade of unlikely leadership. There was no question that Liberia, one of the poorest countries on the planet, would face adversity again, and looking into the twilight of her second term as president, Madame knew that she wouldn't always be there to help bail it out.

Who would come after her? Back to the men?

It was Madame's turn to speak. She asked for a moment of silence for all those who had died. For the first to die: Taywah Taylor, who contracted the disease from her sister. For the last: Ruth Tugbah, who contracted the disease from her boyfriend. For all of the 4,700 lives in between. For Precious Diggs's two-year-old daughter, Rebecca. For Gaye Dumbai's entire family.

Madame thanked the international community who showed up to help. She thanked her own countrymen and women. She said, "Let us celebrate, but stay mindful and vigilant."

And then she went around the room, shaking hands.

The warmth of human skin again, at last.

Acknowledgments

First of all, thanks to President Ellen Johnson Sirleaf for the hours of her time that she gave me, even as she went from crisis to crisis. I think it must be inordinately difficult to have someone following you around who is writing a book about you and who refuses to show you anything she's written. Madame President was gracious and patient during the four years it took me to complete this book.

For two books now, Marysue Rucci and Dorian Karchmar have pushed, tugged, prodded, and yelled at me (for my own good, they claim). Without them, I'm not sure I would have finished those books, of which I am proud. At Simon & Schuster, Marysue is my friend, editor, adviser and emergency retail-therapist. Perhaps most important, she is the one who dials back the flip tone that has always peppered—some say plagued—the way I write. At William Morris Endeavor, Dorian is, bar none, the best agent in the business. She is a fierce fighter on my behalf, a close friend, and a visionary thinker all wrapped in one. I can never say enough how glad I am to have her in my corner.

This is the second book that I've done with both Simon & Schuster and William Morris Endeavor, and I remain happy with the incredible people at both of these companies. Jonathan Karp was instrumental in helping me shape this book when I came into his office mumbling of wanting to do something about women in Liberia. Megan Hogan was one of my first readers, and her insight and suggestions were invaluable. A big thank-you also to Lisa Healy, Judith Hoover, Amanda Lang, and Ebony LaDelle. At William Morris Endeavor, Ari Emanuel called me right after the merger just to touch basewhile I was, surprise surprise, shopping at the Prada outlet in Italy. When I think of all the similar calls he would have had to make, that's pretty impressive. Meanwhile, Theresa Brown, Jeff Lesh, and Anna DeRoy have all promoted me in ways that I never thought possible.

And finally, back at Simon & Schuster, Zachary Knoll did heroic work getting me up to speed on how to use a computer. I wish that preceding sentence was a joke, but it's not.

As they did with my first book, the good people at the Woodrow Wilson International Center for Scholars once again gave me a place to work and research: Jane Harman, Robert Litwak, and Michael Van Dusen. Thanks also to Arlyn Charles for her quiet competence.

On a trip to Saudi Arabia, Jeffrey Goldberg offered to read my working draft because he had spent time in Liberia. I didn't give it to him then because my precious baby wasn't ready to be edited yet. But then I ran into him at Costco on a Sunday afternoon two years later, and he repeated his request. And, boy, am I glad I took him up on it. Jeff gave me an intense, four-month edit, eliminating all my Yiddish (said Yiddish didn't belong in a book about Liberia), sprinkling the copy with some gravitas, giving it a full magazine edit, and being an all-round mensch.

David Rothkopf—at one of our many lunches at the Palm, the only restaurant he would eat at between 2006 and 2013—first suggested I write a book that looked at how all the countries that treated women shabbily were the ones that were in the worst shape. I told him that was too depressing, but it gave me a germ of an idea.

And then Philip Parker, just after the Liberian elections in 2005, told me stories about some of the shenanigans staged by the Liberian women seeking to get Ellen Johnson Sirleaf elected. And somehow, between David Rothkopf and Philip Parker, my germ of an idea started to form.

At the *New York Times*, Dean Baquet and Jill Abramson graciously gave me a year's leave to go to Liberia and follow Ellen Johnson Sirleaf. After I returned to work and Liberia was hit by Ebola, Dean threw the weight of the *New York Times* behind me when I asked to go back to cover it. And once I was in Liberia during the Ebola crisis, the embrace of that great institution really came to bear, as everyone from Arthur Sulzberger to my colleagues in the Washington bureau checked on me daily. On the foreign desk in New York Greg Winter was a fantastic and always calm, editor, while in Washington Rebecca Corbett, Elisabeth Bumiller, and Carolyn Ryan helped me to think through my stories while at the same time making sure that I wasn't doing anything stupid. "What's your temperature today?"

they asked, again and again. "Thirty-five point four," I answered. "What's that in real numbers?" they said. "Ninety-five point seven," I said. "Isn't that low?" they said. "Yeah," I said, "but if I drop dead, it won't be from Ebola."

At the Pentagon, Rear Admiral John Kirby got me on an American military flight to Liberia in the middle of the crisis. It was the first time I had ever flown from Washington straight to Robertsfield Airport, and let me just say, the direct Andrews Air Force Base–Robertsfield flight shortens the normal travel time considerably. On East Luray Avenue, my friend and neighbor Wendy Becker Moniz gave me a sharp galley edit, pointing me to missing commas, quotation marks, and redundancies.

My *Times* colleagues Mark Landler, Scott Shane, Eric Schmitt, Carl Hulse, Jennifer Steinhauer, Michael Schmidt, Thom Shanker, Jackie Calmes, David Sanger, Matt Rosenberg, Jeff Zeleny, and Maureen Dowd gave me a ton of book advice. Mark Mazzetti gave me an emergency Chapter 1 crash reading during one of the many deadlines that I blew. And Michael Shear installed Dropbox on my new laptop after my old one crashed and incinerated all of my files.

In Torgiano, Italy, Vittoria Iraci Borgia gave me a place to write for two and a half beautiful months at her La Montagnola agriturismo and olive oil estate, while Carmela Guzzo kept my stomach full of pasta and porchetta and taught me how to make limoncello when I had writer's block.

Shailagh Murray gave me a deep early edit and an early warning about losing the flip tone. Steve Cashin and Steve Radelet answered countless questions about global financing, debt relief, and the black economy, and gave me all the color I greedily requested and some that I didn't, including the color of the BlackBerry that Ellen Johnson Sirleaf used in 2006.

During the London writing phase of my book leave, I was helped by Daniel Levy, Tony Faiola, Bilgin Kurtoglu, Suki Yamamoto, Jim Courtovich, Sarah Herzog, and Isabella Lisk, while Barnaby Phillips told me to get a British Library membership. My landlady, Melissa Berman, allowed me to use her British Museum pass. So I had two fantastic edifices in which to bury myself when writing.

I had so much help in Liberia. Estrada "Jeff" Bernard and Jennie Bernard were generous with anecdotes about life in Liberia in the 1950s. Ethel Holt-Toles, Phemie Brewer, and Shirley Brownell scheduled me time with President Sirleaf. Veda Simpson pointed me to a naked George Weah. Wilmot Dennis and Francis Dunbar were both enormously helpful during my reporting. And Danai Pateli flew all the way from Athens to Monrovia to furiously help me conduct many interviews with the Liberian women in this book—interviews that the two of us emerged from, hours later, in awe over the strength of these incredible women.

I talked to more than a hundred Liberian women in reporting this book, including Parleh Harris, Grace Kpaan, Vabah Gayflor, Masawa Jabateh, Bernice Freeman, Rosie Hungerpillar Sehaack, Etweda Sugars Cooper, and Lusu Sloan. They, and dozens more, were honest and raw with me as I picked through unbelievably painful parts of their lives. To revisit the most traumatic points of your own history is no easy thing. Without them, this book would not exist.

Finally, I am enormously indebted to my family. My brother-in-law Aleksandar Vasilic challenges everything that comes out of my mouth before I can put it to paper, which is helpful in separating reality from delusion. My other brother-in-law, John Walker, walked me through Liberian governmental bureaucratese. My beautiful nephew Cooper welcomed me back home with a running, jumping hug each time I returned from my long reporting and writing trips. My equally beautiful nephew Logosou gave me encouragement when I needed it, as did my brother, John Bull, and my sister-in-law, Pieta.

My mother, Calista Dennis Cooper, came home to Liberia with me when I first went to start work on the book and helped keep me sane during the initial bruising weeks, especially the day when the security guard at the Ministry of Foreign Affairs told me I couldn't enter the building in a short-sleeved blouse. My sister Marlene Cooper Vasilic read draft after draft, telling me when to expand and when to, yes, cut the flip tone. My sister Janice Cooper pointed me to sources, relevant issues, and stories. My sister Eunice Bull Walker told me how to find Taywah Taylor's husband. There was also a point when all three of my sisters, Janice, Eunice, and Marlene, were all home in Liberia with me at the same time. With my mom. It was a rare and incredibly emotional experience to find myself surrounded by the strongest women I will ever know, while beginning work on the story of the strongest women Liberia will ever know.

Notes

Chapter 1

1 "red like one pumpkin": Ellen Johnson Sirleaf, *This Child Will Be Great: Memoir of a Remarkable Life by Africa's First Woman President* (New York: HarperCollins, 2009).

2 In 1820 the first of many shiploads: Records of the American Colonization Society, 1792–1964, Reel 302, Library of Congress, Washington, DC.

3 The Society did this at gunpoint: Archibald Alexander, *A History of Colonization on the Western Coast of Africa* (Philadelphia: William S. Martien, 1846).

4 Liberians seized on the robust Christianity: *Journal of Daniel Coker, a descendant of Africa, from the time of leaving New York, in the ship Elizabeth, Capt. Sebor, on a voyage for Sherbro, in Africa, in company with three agents, and about 90 persons of colour, Daniel Coker, Edward Johnson Coale, John D. Toy* (Baltimore: Maryland Colonization Society, 1820).

4 Her father's father was a Gola chief: Author interview with Jennie Bernard.

5 The first Congo family Martha lived with: Sirleaf, *This Child Will Be Great*, 12.

5 "Oh. I like you": Ibid., 12.

6 During vacations: Author interview with Ellen Johnson Sirleaf.

7 when Ellen made her first public speech: Sirleaf, *This Child Will Be Great*, 12.

7 "I have been witched": Ibid., 26.

8 the Liberian press dubbed the affair a "Tom Thumb wedding": Ibid., 29.

8 Korlu Besyah, who lived upstairs: Author interview with Ellen Johnson Sirleaf.

9 "You better go bring my car": Ibid.

11 "But Mom, you can't remember": Ibid.

11 "I gwen to America," she thought to herself: Ibid.

12 Doc had always had a jealous streak: Ibid.

13 A furious husband waited for her: Ibid.

13 "Adamah is walking": Ibid.

14 Over the months, the abuse escalated: Ibid.

15 But Doc had already threatened to kill Jeff: Author interview with Estrada Bernard.

15 Ellen met Chris Maxwell: Author interview with Ellen Johnson Sirleaf.

16 Maxwell went outside: Ibid.

16 "He hit me again and again": Ibid.

16 "Move, and I'll blow your head off": Ibid.

16 waiting for her with his gun out: Sirleaf, *This Child Will Be Great*, 41.

18 Doc never did show up to contest the divorce: Author interview with Ellen Johnson Sirleaf.

18 "Here's your son": Ibid.

18 "Adamah has never been baptized": Ibid.

CHAPTER 2

19 The name kept her connected to her boys: Author interview with Ellen Johnson Sirleaf.

19 She prayed for her daughter morning and night: Ibid.

20 Enter Gustav Papanek: Author interview with Gustav Papanek.

21 a chronic and familiar narrative: J. Gus Liebenow, *Liberia: The Quest for Democracy* (Bloomington: Indiana University Press, 1987).

22 "austerity measures": "Radio Broadcast to the Nation on Austerity Measures," Monrovia, April 15, 1963, *Official Papers of William V. S. Tubman* (London: Longman, 1968).

22 so light-skinned they looked white: Author interview with Gustav Papanek.

23 The country was standing on the wrong foot: Author interview with Ellen Johnson Sirleaf.

23 Ellen opened with a technocratic dissertation: Sirleaf, *This Child Will Be Great*, 54.

24 "I wonder if it would not be a good idea": Ibid., 55.

25 She wrote a paper seeking to come to grips: Ibid., 60.

26 For reasons completely bewildering to Ellen: Author interview with Ellen Johnson Sirleaf.

26 "You need to stop!": Author interview with Jennie Bernard.

26 "Your president has died in London": Ibid.

28 "I identify myself with you": "William Richard Tolbert, Man in the News," *New York Times,* January 5, 1972, p. 4.

30 "It's time": Author interview with Ellen Johnson Sirleaf.

31 A Monrovia newspaper printed it anyway: Sirleaf, *This Child Will Be Great*, 71.

31 "You don't say things: Sirleaf, *This Child Will Be Great*. Ibid.

32 she felt she was living on sufferance: Author interview with Ellen Johnson Sirleaf.

32 "I think I'm in trouble here": Sirleaf, *This Child Will Be Great*, 74.

33 "What's this 'bout you leaving the ministry?": Ibid., 75.

34 "Give her a break": Ibid.

CHAPTER 3

38   when his cook burned the rice: Author interview with Ellen Johnson Sirleaf.

40   "Bullshit": Sirleaf, *This Child Will Be Great*, 84.

40   "Our eyes are open": Ibid., 87.

41   "ungrateful," "agitants": Author interview with Amos Sawyer.

41   "When they did not check the demonstration": Sirleaf, *This Child Will Be Great*, 88.

41   "wicked, evil and satanic": Carey Winfrey, "After Liberia's Costly Rioting, Great Soul-Searching," *New York Times*, May 30, 1979.

42   Tolbert "extended the hand of forgiveness": Helene Cooper, *The House at Sugar Beach* (New York: Simon & Schuster, 2008), 145.

43   "The president say you ma' come to the Mansion": Author interview with Ellen Johnson Sirleaf.

44   "Mother, Mother open the door": Victoria Anna David Tolbert, *Lifted Up: The Victoria Tolbert Story* (Austin, MN: Macalester Park, 1996).

44   "They're shooting": Sirleaf, *This Child Will Be Great*, 93.

45   "The People's Redemption Council na take over the government": Cooper, *The House at Sugar Beach,* 167.

45   "I not going": Author interview with Ellen Johnson Sirleaf.

46   "Who born soldier?": Cooper, *The House at Sugar Beach*, 184.

46   She telephoned Charles Green: Sirleaf, *This Child Will Be Great*, 95.

47   She never looked behind her: Author interview with Ellen Johnson Sirleaf.

48   Doe went on ELTV to address the nation: Sirleaf, *This Child Will Be Great*, 100.

49   "How they treating you?": Author interview with Ellen Johnson Sirleaf.

50   If ever she looked like Judas: Ibid.

50   "Why you got my brother on that line?": Ibid.

51   accused of treason, "rampant corruption": "Liberia Firing Squad Kills 13 Top Officials," Associated Press, April 22, 1980.

51   "Gentlemen of the press": Author interview with Leon Dash.

52   the thirteen men huddled and watched the execution poles go up: Ibid.

CHAPTER 4

55   "You will be my next president of the Liberian Bank": Author interview with Ellen Johnson Sirleaf.

56   Ellen certainly knew she was being used: Ibid.

57   Walking in flanked by Tipoteh: Ibid.

58   "unrevolutionary" behavior: "We're Soldiers, Not Politicians, Says Gen. Quiwonkpa," *Redeemer*, July 25, 1980.

58   the Mercedes of the former first lady: James Ciment, *Another America: The Story of Liberia and the Former Slaves Who Ruled It* (New York: Hill and Wang, 2013).

Once upon a time, there wa' one farmer: Author interview with Ellen Johnson Sirleaf.

59   he had told the national football team that if they lost to Gambia: Author interview with Joseph Guannu.

60   "I need you to recall me": Author interview with Ellen Johnson Sirleaf.

60   But she was scared: Ibid.

62   complaining that Liberia was assuming an "errand boy" status: Leon Dash, "Liberia Executes 5 Members of Ruling Council," *Washington Post*, August 15, 1981.

62   the plotters, led by "my dear friend": Ibid.

63   "the man to see in Liberia": Charles T. Powers, "24-Year-Old General Is the Man to See In Liberia," *Los Angeles Times*, July 14, 1980.

65   she went to the Executive Mansion to pay the requisite respect: Sirleaf, *This Child Will Be Great*, 117.

66   When asked, she said she doesn't remember: Author interview with Ellen Johnson Sirleaf.

67   Ellen rattled off a list: Author interview with Steve Cashin.

68   "I look at this cross-section of Liberians": Sirleaf, *This Child Will Be Great*, 122.

68   The summons to appear at the Mansion: Author interview with Ellen Johnson Sirleaf.

70   "I feel personally disappointed and surprised": Sirleaf, *This Child Will Be Great*, 126.

70   She wasn't scared; she was bored: Author interview with Ellen Johnson Sirleaf.

70   "To the people," the message began: Sirleaf, *This Child Will Be Great*, 126.

CHAPTER 5

71   charged her with sedition: Sirleaf, *This Child Will Be Great*, 129.

72   temporarily suspended approximately $25 million: Martin Meredith, *The Fate of Africa: A History of Fifty Years of Independence* (New York: Public Affairs, 2005).

74   At the trial, which lasted a week: Sirleaf, *This Child Will Be Great*, 126.

74   a death sentence disguised as a hard labor camp: Gabriel I. H. Williams, *Liberia: The Heart of Darkness. Accounts of Liberia's Civil War* (Victoria, Canada: Trafford, 2002).

75   "Ya'll gotta expel her": Author interview with Ellen Johnson Sirleaf.

76   "I want you to leave the country": Sirleaf, *This Child Will Be Great*, 134.

78   the few tally sheets the Special Elections Commission allowed the opposition to study: John-Peter Pham, *Liberia: Portrait of a Failed State* (New York: Reed Press, 2004).

78   One American journalist reported on the BBC: BBC World Service "Focus on Africa," London, October 25, 1985.

79   Chester Crocker, the assistant secretary of state: Reed Kramer, "Liberia: A Casualty of the Cold War's End?," *CSIS Africa Notes*, July 1995, https://csis-prod.s3 .amazonaws.com/s3fs-public/legacy_files/files/publication/anotes_0795.pdf.

79 "The United States felt that my taking a seat": Sirleaf, *This Child Will Be Great*, 138.
79 "I gwen free her": Author interview with Ellen Johnson Sirleaf.
80 "We decided to take the ultimate gamble": Charles T. Powers, "Doe Says Loyal Troops Crush Liberian Coup," *Los Angeles Times*, November 13, 1985.
80 "They see us on the road, they wi' kill us": Author interview with Ellen Johnson Sirleaf.
80 Looking at her frail mother: Ibid. The story of Ellen's imprisonment at the Schiefflin barracks is based on this interview.

CHAPTER 6

87 "I wanted to be a schoolteacher": Author interview with Ellen Johnson Sirleaf.
89 He obliterated it: Pham, *Liberia*, 86.
90 one's ethnic background was a matter of life and death: Based on interviews with more than seventy-five Liberians, including former members of the Armed Forces of Liberia, former rebel fighters, and ordinary citizens who lived in Liberia between 1985 and 2003.
91 One girl paying attention to the radio broadcasts was Grace-tee McGill: Author interview with Grace Kpaan.

CHAPTER 7

95 he hid out in the underground parking lot: Mark Huband, *The Liberian Civil War* (New York: Frank Cass, 1998).
96 The CIA helped him escape: Marlise Simons, "Ex-leader of Liberia Cites CIA in Jailbreak," *New York Times*, July 17, 2009, http://www.nytimes.com/2009/07/18/world/africa/18taylor.html.
97 begged him not to try to kill him: Huband, *The Liberian Civil War*, 50.
97 He was promptly caught, tortured, and executed: Ibid., 50.
97 The Americans were eventually freed: James Brooke, "Liberia's Leader Orders Release of 2 Americans in Good-Will Step," *New York Times*, November 16, 1988.
97 He sent messengers over the Ivorian-Liberian border: Huband, *The Liberian Civil War*, 52.
97 Ellen received a phone call from Woewiyu: Author interview with Ellen Johnson Sirleaf.
98 Taylor said that during that meeting: Testimony by Charles Taylor, July 15, 2009, at his war crimes trial: The Prosecutor of the Special Court vs. Charles Ghankay Taylor, Case # SCSL-2003-01-T, The Hague.
99 "He has to go": Author interview with Ellen Johnson Sirleaf.
99 Ellen argued in favor of violence: Sirleaf, *This Child Will Be Great*, 171.
100 "They thought we had a multitude": Denis Johnson, *Seek: Reports from the Edges of America and Beyond* (New York: HarperCollins, 2009).

101 learned about the incursion from BBC Africa: Colin M. Waugh, *Charles Taylor and Liberia: Ambition and Atrocity in Africa's Lone Star State* (London: Zed Books, 2009).

101 Doe's soldiers wrapped her mother in a gasoline-soaked mattress: Human Rights Watch, "Liberia: Flight from Terror. Testimony of Abuses in Nimba County," May 1990, https://www.hrw.org/reports/1990/liberia2/.

102 Parleh Harris, a young office worker: Author interview with Parleh Harris.

103 Masawa Jabateh screamed in horror: Author interview with Masawa Jabateh.

103 The fate of Famatta Sherman Nah: Author interview with Bernice Freeman.

104 Elmer Johnson, was going to Liberia to join Taylor: Sirleaf, *This Child Will Be Great*, 174.

105 "This Charles Taylor," the voice said: Author interview with Ellen Johnson Sirleaf.

105 one of his deputies, Prince Johnson: Abiodun Alao, John MacKinlay, and Funmi Olonisakin, *Peacekeepers, Politicians and Warlords: The Liberian Peace Process* (Tokyo: United Nations University Press, 1999).

105 Johnson's parents were quickly found and murdered: Festus B. Aboagye, Ecomog: *A Subregional Experience in Conflict Resolution, Management and Peacekeeping in Liberia* (Accra: Sedco Publishing, 1999).

105 "He say you can come": Author interview with Ellen Johnson Sirleaf.

107 The replacement minister of information lasted a few weeks: Huband, *The Liberian Civil War*, 129.

107 The McGill family was living on Benson Street: Author interview with Grace Kpaan.

108 "Come, you coming cook for us": Author interview with Josephine.

108 Katoumba, seven years old: Author interview with Katoumba.

109 "If they burn the Mansion down": Sirleaf, *This Child Will Be Great*, 179.

110 "There was a great commotion outside": Elizabeth Blunt, "The Death of Samuel Doe," BBC World Service, September 23, 2011.

110 Johnson had run up into the force commander's office: Ibid.

110 Pennue was shot in the head: Alberta Davies, *Raw Edge of Purgatory: I Survived the Liberian Pogrom* (Bloomington, IN: Xlibris, 2011).

114 Taylor became worried that he would become a rival: Stephen Ellis, *The Mask of Anarchy Updated Edition: The Destruction of Liberia and the Religious Dimension of an African Civil War* (New York: NYU Press, 2006).

114 Jackson Doe had crossed over to Taylor's side: Ibid.

115 When Ellen heard of Jackson Doe's death: Author interview with Ellen Johnson Sirleaf.

116 Thirty-year-old Rosanna Hungerpiller Sehaack: Author interview with Rosanna Hungerpiller Sehaack.

117 Howard French, the *New York Times* reporter: Howard W. French, "Liberia's Teen-Age Soldiers Find Civil War Is Over But So Is Hope," *New York Times*, September 11, 1995.

118 raped to death: Testimony of Dorothy Mulbah before the Liberia Truth and Reconciliation Comission, www.TRCOFLIBERIA.ORG/press_releases/186.

CHAPTER 8

120 "Wha you brought your pa here for?": Author interview with Ellen Johnson Sirleaf.

121 Ellen hated every minute of it: Author interview with Jennie Bernard.

123 Jennie wasn't feeling too charitable either: Ibid.

124 "Under our questioning": Sirleaf, *This Child Will Be Great*.

125 "He spoil Liberia—so let him fix it": Waugh, *Charles Taylor and Liberia*, 228.

125 "In the final analysis, when the people had the opportunity": Ibid., 233

125 "He wants me to take care of the people": Sirleaf, *This Child Will Be Great*, 221.

126 his lobbying effort to help Taylor's new administration: Waugh, *Charles Taylor and Liberia*, 247.

127 giving himself the option of diverting revenues: Ibid.

127 Global Witness accused Oriental Timber: "Taylor-Made: The Pivotal Role of Liberia's Forests and Flag of Convenience in Regional Conflict," Global Witness, September 2001, London.

127 Ellen walked in late: Author interview with Steve Cashin.

128 Samuel Dokie, a former Taylor ally: John Lee Anderson, "The Devil They Know," *New Yorker*, July 27, 1998.

128 the case of Norwai Flomo: Sirleaf, *This Child Will Be Great*, 224.

129 There would be "severe consequences": "U.S. Threatens Action Against Monrovia," IRIN, July 18, 2000.

129 "Taylor is Milosevic in Africa with diamonds": Blaine Harden, "2 African Nations Said to Break U.N. Diamond Embargo," *New York Times*, August 1, 2000.

130 "I defy him to expose details": Sirleaf, *This Child Will Be Great*, 227.

131 "You're moving your country forward": Author interview with Ellen Johnson Sirleaf.

131 "I have God and I have guns": Sirleaf, *This Child Will Be Great*, 230.

132 Some, like Lusu Sloan: Author interview with Lusu Sloan.

133 Louise Yarsiah was leading the prayers: Author interview with Louise Yarsiah and Bernice Freeman.

CHAPTER 9

135 combined "warfare, banditry, disease": Robert Young Pelton, *The World's Most Dangerous Places* (New York: HarperResource, 2003).

135 "a chaotic backwater": Ibid.

135 One woman squatted on the side of the road: Author interview with Maisie Togban.

136 She even got an editorial published in the *New York Times*: Ellen Johnson Sirleaf, "What the U.S. Owes Liberia," *New York Times*, August 11, 2003.

136 "I dare you": Footage of the scene between Abubakar and Wylie is on the documentary *Pray the Devil Back to Hell*, produced by Abigail Disney, 2008.

136 "Anywhere we go, they say 'place full'": Somini Sengupta, "Rebels Push toward the Heart of the Capital in Liberia," *New York Times*, July 20, 2003.

137 "History will be kind to me": Tim Butcher, 'I am a sacrificial lamb,' says Taylor, as Liberians cheers his departure," *Telegraph*, August 12, 2003.

139 she gave him $10,000 in cash: Author interview with Ellen Johnson Sirleaf.

139 "Delegates at the Liberian peace talks": "Monrovian Businessman to Head Transitional Government," IRIN, August 21, 2003.

139 "I'm sorry we did not select you": Author interview with Ellen Johnson Sirleaf.

139 "Beyond your reach": Sirleaf, *This Child Will Be Great*, 242.

140 Gayflor had studied economics: Author interview with Vabah Gayflor.

141 a mature man of means and former government minister bragged: Author interview with source.

CHAPTER 10

145 a "real contender:" Jonathan Ernst, "The Man Who Would Be President," *Washington Post*, June 5, 2005.

146 he claimed a bachelor of arts degree: David Goldenberg, "George Weah in Diploma-Mill Scandal," *Gelf Magazine*, April 22, 2005.

147 "You will take our country": Author interview with Vabah Gayflor.

147 But Gayflor did not view her job that way: Ibid.

148 "We will put our country devil there": Author interview with Etweda Sugars Cooper.

148 "Those men want put some grona boy in the chair": Author interview with Masawa Jabateh.

152 a hundred Spider-Man backpacks: Author interview with Mary Broh.

153 "I do believe in God": Sirleaf, *This Child Will Be Great*, 258.

154 "I have to *be* the show": Ibid., 253.

154 The boys had taken women's panties: Author interview with Bernice Freeman.

156 "I'm running on my merits": Author interview with Ellen Johnson Sirleaf.

156 A whopping 100,000 people: "Generations of War-Scarred Youths Yearn to Turn the Page with Polls," IRIN, October 10, 2005.

157 "This is like a roller coaster": Author inteview with Jennie Bernard.

CHAPTER 11

159 "I knew that I could have more influence with George Weah": Author interview with Winston Tubman.

159 "You know book, you not know book": John Morlue, "Liberia: Handicapping the Liberian Elections. A Post-Election Analysis," *Front Page Africa*, November 9, 2005.

160 wouldn't "accept anything less than victory": Jimmey C. Fahngon, "Liberia: We'll Accept Victory Only, CDC Declares," *AllAfrica*, November 7, 2005.

161 "You want beer?": Details on techniques used to convince young men not to vote for Weah come from a series of interviews with two dozen women who campaigned on behalf of Ellen Johnson Sirleaf, conducted in January and February 2013.

162 "Liberia," she said, "is ready": Author interview with Vabah Gayflor.

163 Gayflor arrived at work to find reporters camped out: Ibid.

164 Lusu Sloan got up at 5 a.m.: Author interview with Lusu Sloan.

166 "You want borrow de baby?": Author interview with Bernice Freeman.

167 "U-P Up": Author interview with Lusu Sloan.

168 "I felt a chill that day": Author interview with Parleh Harris.

169 "The White House just called": Author interview with Steve Cashin.

CHAPTER 12

173 Abena P. A. Busia, an English professor from Ghana: Lydia Polgreen, "Africa's First Elected Female Head of State Takes Office," *New York Times*, January 16, 2006.

174 "Fellow Liberians," she began: Text of the inaugural address of H.E. Ellen Johnson Sirleaf, January 16, 2006. www.emansion.gov.lr/doc/inaugural_add_1.pdf.

CHAPTER 13

178 Police Chief Sieh showed up with a bullhorn: Description of the clash between the market woman and the administration of Ellen Johnson Sirleaf comes from the documentary *Iron Ladies of Liberia*, directed by Daniel Junge and Siatta Scott Johnson and produced by Henry Ansbacher and Micah Schaffer, September 7, 2007.

182 Malaysia quickly outstripped Ghana: Tim Carrington, "Ray of Hope amid Africa's Agony, One Nation, Ghana, Shows Modest Gains," *Wall Street Journal*, January 26, 1994.

183 Ghana in thirty years: Author interview with Ellen Johnson Sirleaf.

184 Information Minister Lawrence Bropleh quickly began siphoning: U.S. Department of State, 2010 Human Rights Report.

184 Internal Affairs Minister A. B. Johnson allegedly went to work: Rodney D. Sieh, "Liberia's Internal Affairs Minister Resigns—Upon Ellen's Request," *FrontPage Africa*, February 14, 2010.

184 Police Chief Sieh was indicted for stealing $199,800: "Ex-Liberian Police Chief Munah Sieh-Brown Indicted," Africa TV1, February 24, 2012.

184 "It became too much of a headache": Author interview with Ellen Johnson Sirleaf.

185 "We must make collective restitution": "War-Battered Nation Launches Truth Commission," IRIN, February 21, 2006.

186 a way "to have all those young people who caused so much pain": Sirleaf, *This Child Will Be Great*, 281.

186 he boasted that he and his forces killed more than twenty thousand people: The testimony of General Butt Naked, Arab Devil, and others, Truth and Reconciliation Commission. January 15, 2008, Monrovia, http://trcofliberia.org/transcripts/7.

188 "Strewn through the camp": "After Liberia Massacre, a Neglected Mass Grave," Associated Press, January 5, 2013.

CHAPTER 14

190 This was the dollar amount of Liberia's foreign debt: "IMF to Back Liberia with Debt Relief, New Financing," IMF Survey, March 18, 2008.

191 "Mr. Speaker, Mr. Vice President": Liberian President Address, C-SPAN, March 15, 2006.

191 "do-nothing Congress": Albert R. Hunt, "The 108th Congress: A Failure on Every Count," *Wall Street Journal*, June 24, 2004.

191 a "democracy dividend": "State, Foreign Operations and Related Programs," March 28, 2006.

191 "Those head wraps physically increase her stature": Robin Givhan, "A New Leader's True Colors," *Washington Post*, March 24, 2006.

192 "If you want your government to succeed": Sirleaf, *This Child Will Be Great*, 276.

193 But "the president made very clear": Author interview with senior Bush administration official.

194 Taylor was "not a prisoner": Lydia Polgreen, "Liberian Seized to Stand Trial in War Crimes," *New York Times*, March 30, 2006.

195 he said he was never "imprisoned" in Nigeria: Testimony of Charles Taylor during his war crimes trial at the Special Court for Sierra Leone, The Hague. Archives: http://www.rscsl.org/archives.html.

196 "Use the Irish troops": Author interview with Ellen Johnson Sirleaf.

196 "We will exhaust every avenue": *Iron Ladies of Liberia*, directed by Daniel Junge and Siatta Scott Johnson, produced by Henry Ansbacher and Micah Schaffer, September 7, 2007.

CHAPTER 15

200 "One good thing about her": Author interview with Bernice Freeman.

200 "You see how they coming for us?": Ibid.

201 "I want the people who did this arrested": Author interview with Ellen Johnson Sirleaf.

202 the body of Ponawennie Folokula: Author interview with seven members of Wipnet Women Peace Building Network.

202 the body of Annie Kpakilah: Ibid.

202 "The sentence is a first of its kind": Namope Kollie, "Man Sentenced to Death by Hanging," *New Dawn*, July 20, 2012.

203 "We will reach a point where we will have to intervene": *Iron Ladies of Liberia*, directed by Daniel Junge and Siatta Scott Johnson, produced by Henry Ansbacher and Micah Schaffer, September 7, 2007.

205 "I must listen to them": Ibid.

206 "You take the whole army and deactivate them?": Ibid.

CHAPTER 16

207 Fed up, in 2000: Author interview with Steve Radelet.

208 "Don't do that": Ibid.

210 "She's mad about the court cases": Author interview with Lee Buchheit.

213 a Spaniard named Rodrigo de Rato: This description comes from interviews with several former U.S. government officials, two former World Bank officials, and a Liberian government official, all of whom were frustrated about the pace of Liberia's debt relief under Rodrigo de Rato.

213 "IMF-ing outrage": Eoin Callan, "Bono Takes IMF to Task on Liberia," *Financial Times*, October 19, 2007.

216 "From the standpoint of the vulture fund": Author interview with Lee Buccheit.

216 she told Radelet to hide Liberia's pitiful assets: Author interview with Steve Radelet.

217 "This is one I will be watching very carefully": Author interview with Lee Buchheit.

219 "Welcome to Liberia in West Africa": "Vultures Prey on Liberia's Debt," BBC, March 2010.

220 "Today, ladies and gentlemen": Statement by H.E. Ellen Johnson Sirleaf, June 30, 2010, Monrovia.

CHAPTER 17

224 he would do "many of the things": Joshua Keating, "Is Liberia's Future in Her Hands?," *Foreign Policy*, August 2011.

224 "Ellen is part of the problem": Ibid.

224 a fourteen-year-old commercial for cologne: "George Weah Spot Roberts Noir: 'Tutto Bene?,'" YouTube, November 3, 2009, https://youtu.be./dHw3vJYmHvI.

225 "Weah Walks Butt Naked!": *New Democrat*, August 19, 2010.

225 "Mr. Weah committed no crime": "Liberia: Weah Walks Butt Naked," *TLC Africa*, August 2010.

225 "If the Congress for Democratic Change through its vocal spokesperson": The Analyst, "Liberia: Awful Defense—CDC's Justification of Weah's Nude Exhibits Speaks Volumes," *AllAfrica*, August 2010.

226 "we will take the necessary action": CUBE Takes Issue with Party-Delaware Chapter Misinformation, December 2010. www.citizensforbrumskin.org/?m=201012.

226 they weren't sure "what Councilor Brumskine is implying": Focus on Liberia: December 11, 2018. https:focusonliberia.wordpress.com/2010/12/page/2/.

226 "She hasn't really improved the lot": Keating: "Is Liberia's Future in Her Hand?" *Foreign Policy*, August 2011.

CHAPTER 18

229 "Today, three women won the Nobel Peace Prize": *All Things Considered*, NPR, Washington, DC, October 7, 2011.

230 "I just got a call from the Nobel people": Author interview with Ellen Johnson Sirleaf.

230 "When I say something": The video of Ellen Johnson Sirleaf's "Da Ma Area" campaign speech is on YouTube.

232 "Fellow CDCians": The video of Winston Tubman's rally is on YouTube.

232 "It is *done*": Author interview with Ellen Johnson Sirleaf.

233 "for their non-violent struggle": "The Nobel Peace Prize 2011," Nobel Media AB 2014. October 27, 2016, http://www.nobelprize.org/nobel_prizes/peace/laureates/2011.

233 "Well, I'm glad that Liberia has come to this honor": BBC, "Focus on Africa," October 7, 2011.

234 "She has brought us together as women": Bonnie Allen, "Reaction from Liberia on Nobel Prize," *The World*, PRI, October 7, 2011, http://www.pri.org/stories/2011 -10-07/reaction-liberia-nobel-prize.

235 "This is wrong and I think it is time for her to put him aside": "Liberia Laureate Gbowee Chides Sirleaf on Corruption," BBC News, October 8, 2012.

CHAPTER 19

237 "Miss Liberia Imposters under Probe": Darlington Porkpa, "Miss Liberia Imposters under Probe," *New Liberia*, January 11, 2013.

239 "They now send all the girls": This scene took place in the presence of the author.

239 "Where the women I sent for?": Ibid.

CHAPTER 20

241 "The Liberian legislature has ordered the arrest": Author interview with Ellen Johnson Sirleaf.

242 Then she secretly tape-recorded: Author interview with Grace Kpaan.

243 "You eat some, I eat some": Audio provided by Grace Kpaan of conversation with Edward Forh; the audio was also broadcast on Liberian radio and television stations.

243 "I am pleased to present this copy": Audio was broadcast on Liberian radio stations.

244 "This is unbelievable": Author interview with Ellen Johnson Sirleaf.

246 "After all the sweat": Author interview with Mary Broh.

246 "I will make y'all shame": This scene took place in the presence of the author.

247 he threatened to defecate on the acting mayor: "CDC Rep. Solomon George Plans to Shit on Monrovia Mayor (Mary Broh)," YouTube, January 30, 2013, https://www .youtube.com/watch?v=VyhMbrp0UvI.

248 "They disallowed my vehicle": "Where Are They? . . . Hunt Continues for Mary Broh, Supt. Kpaan," *Inquirer*, February 25, 2013.

249 "This is the one woman": Author interview with Ellen Johnson Sirleaf.

250 "An outraged Plenary": "Ellen 'Slaps' Broh, Kpaan with Suspension," *Front Page Africa*, February 23, 2013.

CHAPTER 21

252 "There are 180 political parties in Senegal": This scene took place in the presence of the author.

253 women held 56.3 percent of the seats: World Bank, "Proportion of Seats Held by Women in National Parliaments," 2014.

255 "great personal pleasure": "Remarks at the U.S.-Liberia Partnership Dialogue Signing," January 15, 2013, www.state.gov/secretary/20092013clinton/rm/2013/202201.htm.

CHAPTER 22

257 Taywah Taylor's cellphone rang: Author interview with Firestone workers.

258 That phone call came to Madame: Author interview with Dr. Walter Gwenigale.

258 Patient Zero was a two-year-old boy: Denise Grady and Sheri Fink, "Tracing Ebola's Outbreak to an African 2-Year-Old," *New York Times*, August 9, 2014.

259 "Wha' this mean?": Author interview with Dr. Walter Gwenigale.

264 Fifty doctors serviced 4.3 million people: University of Liberia president Emmet Dennis, interview with Indiana Public Media, August 6, 2014, http://indianapublic media.org/news/liberia-ebola-outbreak-elevates-iu-collaboration-70313/.

268 Chanting "No Ebola in West Point": "Armed men attack Liberia Ebola clinic, freeing patients," CBS News, August 17, 2014, http://www.cbsnews.com/news/report -armed-men-attack-liberia-ebola-clinic-freeing-patients/.

268 "The president says you have Ebola": Jina Moore, "Mob Destroys Ebola Center in Liberia Two Days after It Opens," *Buzzfeed News*, August 16, 2014, https://www .buzzfeed.com/jinamoore/two-days-after-it-opens-mob-destroys-ebola-center-in -liberia.

268 panicked by thoughts of children getting hold of Ebola-infected sheets: Author interview with Ellen Johnson Sirleaf.

270 A few fired live rounds: Norimitsu Onishi, "As Ebola Grips City, Quarantine Adds to Chaos," *New York Times*, August 28, 2014.

270 Suddenly her quarantine was being criticized in the international press: Ibid.

271 "We suffering!": Norimitsu Onishi, "As Ebola Grips Liberia's Capital, a Quarantine Sows Social Chaos," *New York Times*, August 28, 2014.

271 her guards taking off their gloves: Author interview with Ellen Johnson Sirleaf.

272 "Nobody gave me a better solution": Ibid.

272 Comfort named her daughters Faith and Mercy: Lenny Bernstein, "With Ebola Crippling the Health System, Liberians Die of Routine Medical Problems," *Washington Post*, September 20, 2014.

272 Precious Diggs, a thirty-three-year-old contractor: Helene Cooper, "Ebola's Cultural Casualty: Hugs in Hands-on Liberia," *New York Times*, October 4, 2014.

273 "We need help": Author interview with Chris Coons.

274 "Dear Mr. President," she wrote: Helene Cooper, "Liberian President Pleads with Obama for Assistance in Combating Ebola," *New York Times*, September 12, 2014.

274 She reminded the readers of the *New York Times*: Ibid.

274 Obama announced a response so massive: Helene Cooper and Sheri Fink, "Obama Presses Leaders to Speed Ebola Response," *New York Times*, September 16, 2014.

275 the Centers for Disease Control and Prevention released a stunning and ominous projection: Denise Grady, "Ebola Cases Could Reach 1.4 Million Within Four Months, C.D.C. Estimates," *New York Times*, September 23, 2014.

CHAPTER 23

279 Fatu Kekula, twenty-two years old: "Woman Saves Three Relatives from Death," CNN, September 26, 2014.

280 she personally went out into the middle of Tubman Boulevard: Finlay Young, "Love in the Time of Ebola: Meeting the Locals Struggling to Cope with an Epidemic," *Newsweek*, August 20, 2014.

281 "Make a note": Author interview with Ellen Johnson Sirleaf.

283 the president was "surrounded by two groups of people": Helene Cooper, "Liberia's Ebola Crisis Puts President in Harsh Light," *New York Times*, October 30, 2014.

284 Gaye Dumbai couldn't: Helene Cooper, "Ebola, Ruthless to Families, Leaves Liberian Man Alive and Alone," *New York Times*, March 25, 2016.

285 "Stop!" Varsay yelled: Helene Cooper, "In Homeland, Liberian Native Finds Resilience amid Horror," *New York Times*, October 19, 2014.

287 On March 5, 2015, Beatrice Yardolo: Norimitsu Onishi, "Last Known Ebola Patient Is Discharged," *New York Times*, March 5, 2015.

288 "I have to let you know we have a new case": Author interview with Ellen Johnson Sirleaf.

288 Madame started crying: Author interview with Jennie Bernard.

288 Ruth Tugbah died: Sheri Fink, "Liberia Recommends Ebola Survivors Practice Safe Sex Indefinitely," *New York Times*, March 28, 2015.

288 the World Health Organization declared Liberia free of Ebola: "The Ebola Outbreak in Liberia Is Over," WHO statement, May 9, 2015, www.WHO.int/mediacentre /news/statements/2015/liberia_ends_ebola/en/.

Index

ABOUT THE AUTHOR

Helene Calista Cooper is a Pulitzer Prize–winning national security correspondent for the *New York Times*, having previously served as White House correspondent, diplomatic correspondent, and assistant editorial page editor. Prior to joining the *Times*, she spent twelve years at the *Wall Street Journal* as a reporter and foreign correspondent. In 2015 she won the Pulitzer Prize for International Reporting, an Overseas Press Club Award for International Reporting, and a George Polk Award for Health Reporting, all three for her coverage of the Ebola crisis. Born in Monrovia, Liberia, Helene is the author of *The House at Sugar Beach: In Search of a Lost African Childhood* (Simon & Schuster), a *New York Times* bestseller and a National Book Critics Circle finalist in autobiography in 2009. She lives in the Washington, DC area.